STAND UP!

Creating a Classroom Community that Empowers Students to Learn

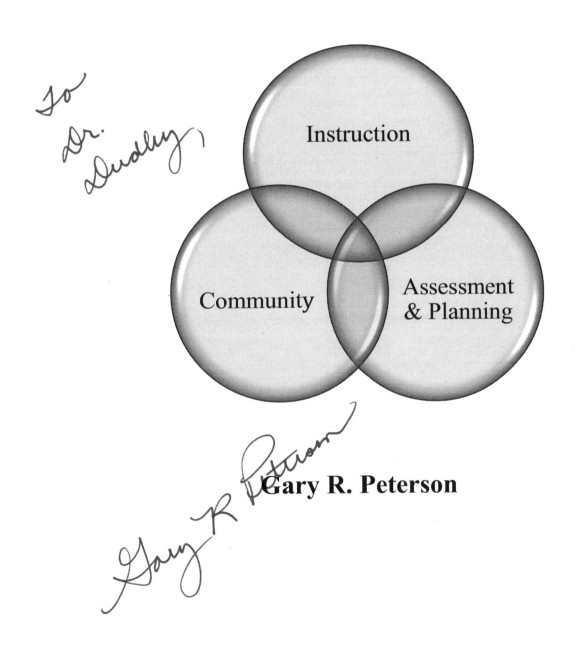

Gary R. Peterson

Moment by moment—every interaction you have, every word you speak—can lay the groundwork for a community of learners, and gently, but steadily support its growth.

—Gary Peterson

When you try something new, always try again and again, because it's a brand-new thing!

—Noelle, 6-year-old.

Why is the title **STAND UP?** *Imagine classroom discussions where students stand to speak, and the teacher remains seated. The feeling tone of the room is notably different, because in this scenario, the spotlight is on students, and what they say matters to the classroom community, not just to the teacher.*

While I was writing this book and refining my thoughts, I was also teaching the strategies to other educators, and helping them solve problems that arose in their classrooms. Inevitably, more ideas, more ways to help kids learn would spring to mind, and I'd want to add just one more thing to the book. At some point, however, I had to stop writing. It was time to hand the reins over to you, the reader. I hope the ideas presented here are a springboard for your own thinking, that you build on them and find yet more ways to empower kids to learn. After all these years in education, I still get excited about teaching, and I hope you do, too.

Acknowledgements

This book would not have been possible without my wife, Barbara. She read every word and suggested innumerable improvements for more coherence and cohesion. Her recurring question, "What did you want to say here?" challenged me to clarify my ideas and present them in ways that I hope are useful and accessible.

Many teachers and administrators read drafts of the book, and their suggestions were invaluable and influenced the final version. Special thanks to:

Jessica Augden	John Beight	Frazer Boergadine
Joan Flora	Tim Hays	Denis Hickey
Bridget Miller	Kristen Paschall	

Although many colleagues, fellow educators, and other sources informed my thinking, any errors that occur in this book are solely my own.

Table of Contents

Section III: Plan for and Assess a Community of Learners

Appendices   272

Preface

I've been in the business of education for a long time—long enough to witness countless reforms, textbook adoptions, curriculum changes, new technologies, and so on. All of them purport to elevate our education system to the ranks of best in the world. Nothing I've seen, however, makes much of a difference unless it acknowledges this one reality: education is about people. There is no program or technology that can take the place of truly effective educators. There is no program or technology that can make students want to learn like a teacher who cares about them, and who has the skills to create a warm classroom community.

Research backs me up on this, and years of experience do, too. I was a classroom teacher for more than 30 years. After that, I developed a program for new teachers to help them become skilled educators early in their careers. As part of my job, I observed hundreds of classrooms and thousands of lessons, and I know firsthand what a difference great teaching makes.

But along the way I learned something else, something even more important. Great teachers weren't just presenting interesting lessons; they were showing kids *how to learn.* They were showing them how to persevere and how to be patient with disequilibrium when concepts were not yet clear. Best of all, they were inviting kids to take charge of their own learning. Instead of just assigning work, these teachers showed kids how that work could help them get smarter. They knew the power of getting students on board, and consequently, their students excelled.

This book will help you make that happen in your own classroom, too. It is organized around a three-part instructional framework. Part one shows how to create a **classroom community** where kids feel supported, where they care about and support others, and where they know the benefits of procedures that allow the classroom to run smoothly, saving time for the important business of learning.

Part two looks at **instruction**—research based practices that actively engage students and dramatically increase their opportunities to learn and deepen the feeling of community.

Part three focuses on **formative assessments**—ongoing checks for understanding that inform instruction, show students where they are on the continuum of understanding, and allow the whole community to celebrate.

Working in concert, these three elements create a kind of synergy of learning. It's wonderful to have a warm, inviting classroom, but without good instruction and assessment, optimal learning will not occur. Giving students opportunities to actively participate in a lesson keeps them focused—but it will be more effective if the routines of participation are clear and inclusive. Knowing what your students understand allows you to develop lessons to meet their needs, but without a learning community and best practice instructional strategies, those lessons will fall short. If community, instruction, and ongoing assessments are isolated from each other, the learning community falters, and only episodic bursts of energized, focused learning occur.

Each element—community, instruction, and assessment, is an essential part of the whole. Together, these three elements transform the classroom experience, optimizing learning, guiding students toward greater independence, and fostering an understanding of their role in the community. I invite you to read on and see how empowered students become an integral part of each of these elements.

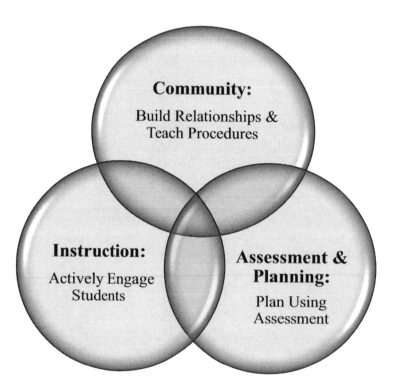

Community:
Build Relationships &
Teach Procedures

Instruction:
Actively Engage
Students

**Assessment &
Planning:**
Plan Using
Assessment

INSTRUCTIONAL FRAMEWORK

Chapter 1: STAND UP!

Empower Students

If you are hesitant to let students take more control, keep in mind that you don't lose power by giving it away; there's no power pie with only so many slices. In fact, the more you share power in the classroom, the bigger the pie gets—and the happier and more empowered your students will be.[1] —Eric Jensen

Imagine a classroom community where student language such as the following is the norm, not the exception:

- *I need some time to process that information.*
- *Could I clarify my thinking with a partner?*
- *I cannot hear what Noelle is saying.*
- *I'm in disequilibrium.*
- *I am not sure, but I'd like to share my solution anyway.*
- *Can I have some more think time?*
- *Could Jacob repeat that?*
- *What is the target for the lesson?* or *I don't understand the target.*
- *How will I know if I meet the target?*
- *I need some more practice.*

Clearly, this is not typical student talk. The language here is telling us something important—these students are empowered. They know what they are learning, how they are doing, and understand the benefits of being in a community of learners where they feel safe to verbalize their thinking or make mistakes. They are comfortable with not knowing and unafraid to ask for more help or time.

Next, imagine that students in this classroom talk to each other using words like:

- *I noticed you didn't give up.*
- *I noticed you worked the whole time.*
- *I need to share my thinking with you.*
- *Congratulations on meeting the target.*

Again, not typical student talk, but comments such as these build community, reinforce work ethic, and show students that others care.

Is it possible to create a community of learners where these kinds of comments and questions occur daily? Yes. But it doesn't get that way using the conventional classroom model. It takes intentional words and actions, and teaching and learning decisions, based on research, that work for all students.

For decades (perhaps centuries?) the archetype of classrooms has been the teacher at the front of a classroom writing on the board or talking, and students sitting quietly or raising their hands in hopes of being called upon. It's a teacher-centered model, and decisions are made based on what works for **teachers**. When lessons don't go well, all too often it's the students who take the blame: they didn't pay attention, try hard enough, come to school with a decent work ethic, etc.

There is another way—a student-empowering approach to teaching. In this model, decisions are based on what works for **students**, and teachers adjust lessons based on formative assessment. If a lesson doesn't achieve the desired result, students are not blamed and teachers don't blame themselves. Instead, they see these situations as opportunities to problem solve and help kids get past whatever roadblocks are holding them back. Don't misunderstand—student-empowerment doesn't mean kids are making all the decisions, and it doesn't mean they are taking over. It means students are involved in and on board with their own education. They are active participants in their own learning. The good news is that none of this requires a pile of money, and it doesn't heap more work on overburdened teachers. But it does involve a paradigm shift in the minds of teachers and students.

This paradigm shift will be outlined in greater detail in upcoming chapters, but here's a sneak peek at a few key changes you can implement right now to empower kids. These changes don't require expensive technology or costly outlays for equipment, but they do require that you change the way you do business, and they set the stage for students to be real participants in their own education.

Start empowering your students today by teaching them to:

1. **STAND** when speaking to the whole group.

Imagine classroom discussions where students stand to speak, and the teacher remains seated. The feeling tone of the room is notably different, because in this scenario, the spotlight is on students, and what they say matters to the classroom community.

2. Turn their **KNEES** toward speakers.

When students turn toward the speaker, it physically reminds them of their job—to listen and process the thinking of their peer. And the student speaking feels empowered because he has the attention of his classmates.

3. **PUT** their **ERASERS AWAY.**

Are mistakes really okay? We say they are, and we claim mistakes are part of the learning process. So why are we so quick to erase them? Mistakes are evidence of thinking and how thinking evolves. Leaving those errors and subsequent attempts in place allows students to see their learning progression. If you are truly okay with mistakes, have your students do some of their work using pencils without erasers!

4. **THINK** about ideas and answers without looking toward the teacher for confirmation of an answer.

What do most kids do after someone else answers a question? They look to you, the teacher, because they expect your body language or your words to tell them whether or not the answer was correct. But if you do that for them, they no longer have to think. Try something different: keep your body language and facial expressions neutral, and let **them** figure out if the answer offered was on the mark. I remember once leaving an incorrect solution to a math problem on the board, a decision I made intentionally to see if anyone would notice. Sure enough, twenty minutes later (!), a student remarked he didn't agree with the answer. He explained his thinking, and it led the whole class to reconsider the problem, thereby deepening everyone's understanding. As a teacher, my goal was always: how can I maximize the time my *students* grapple with ideas? You might be wondering if teachers should ever give answers—but there is no hard and fast rule on whether to do so or not. As the teacher, you decide whether an immediate correction is warranted, or if you want students to keep thinking.

5. <u>BE AWARE OF THE PURPOSE</u> of the work they do.

It's so important students understand that classroom lessons and classwork are not just something to keep them busy, but work intentionally designed to benefit **THEM**. When kids understand that, they'll be able to tell others, *I'm trying to learn……, so I am practicing.*

6. <u>NOTICE</u> and recognize things their classmates are doing that support the community and learning.

You can teach students to give specific feedback to their peers:

- *I noticed you kept working until you solved that problem.*
- *I saw you sitting by our new student during lunch.*
- *You were taking notes about what Amanda was saying.*

This kind of peer feedback builds community and greatly increases the positive energy in the classroom.

Can changes like these really make a difference? The answer is unequivocally yes, and it can happen very quickly. In the ensuing chapters, these strategies and more will be presented in depth, and you will find out not only why they work, but how to implement them. There are many things affecting student learning that we can't control. Let's instead focus on the things we can, and make instructional choices that empower students and build a supportive classroom community where kids can do their best.

Chapter 1 Key Points

Students' Roles

- ☐ Stand to share with the whole group.
- ☐ Turn toward speakers.
- ☐ Think about how your behavior affects the community.
- ☐ Know the purpose for an activity—or ask.

Teachers' Roles

- ☐ Try one of the suggestions and notice its effect on students and the community.
- ☐ Ask yourself *why* before implementing a strategy or routine. Am I doing something because it has always been done that way—or because it works for students?
- ☐ Consider how a strategy or routine will affect the learning of all students.
- ☐ Look for evidence of a new classroom community being built—what are students saying and how are they acting toward one another?

NOTES
Use these note spaces to jot down ideas about specific students or situations and how you could apply these strategies.

Chapter 2: Students' Roles

A fourth/fifth grade teacher asks his students to share with partners: "Given a perimeter of 24, how would you find the rectangle with the largest area? Go." The room erupts with an explosion of chatter because students are excitedly sharing their ideas with each other. Now that's engagement! But how did it happen?

Kids don't come into a classroom knowing how to engage in a community of learners. Many start the school year with assumptions that are counterproductive, based on past experiences:

- *Teachers usually call on kids who raise their hands first. I'll keep my head down, and she won't call on me.*

- *If I'm not into the lesson, there are other ways I can stay entertained.*

- *The teacher listens to everyone in a class discussion; I don't have to listen.*

- *No one is interested in what I say, and besides, what if I make a mistake?*

So, how do we change these habits and assumptions that short circuit learning, and how do we move students in a more positive direction? **By specifically teaching them the behaviors, language, and attitudes that lead to success** we show them they are not just passive placeholders, but learners with real power to shape their school experience. We can do this by building and empowering a Community of Learners.

What Is Community?

OK, true confession—I was one of those students who managed to navigate my K-12 education without saying a word in class. I did well academically, but at the same time worked hard not to be noticed. For most of my college classes, I was also able to remain silent, and the primary form of instruction, lecture, allowed me to do that. I graduated magna cum laude and Phi Beta Kappa with a degree in political science—a "big success." In only **one** undergraduate class did I have a professor who challenged my modus operandi—he required all students to be actively engaged with one another in robust discussions. It was a class that energized me and caused me to start analyzing and exchanging ideas. I could share, challenge, re-examine…for me it was groundbreaking. What if all my classes had been like that?

As a teacher, I began to realize that student involvement could be started earlier in the educational experience. Even the youngest students could learn to take an active role in their own education and to care about their classmates' success. They could transcend simple compliance and be part of a real community of learners. So that led to my quest to find classroom structures and strategies where this type of community developed over time, one where students' questions and comments like the ones listed in chapter one occurred daily.

A Student-Centered Community of Learners

We all do well when we all do well.[2]

How exactly do we create and empower a community of learners? First, we immerse students in a community that expects <u>all</u> students to learn, and all students to support everyone's learning. We teach them that learning happens through effort, and we make clear the connection between hard work and success. Using targets, we show explicitly what should be learned—and let students know what success looks like. We use formative assessment frequently so we know, and students know, how they are progressing. We show them how to be a student, and how to be successful. Most of all, we help them discover the power they possess to learn and to engage, and that everyone has something unique to contribute to the community.

Students' Roles and Expectations

Student motivation counts for a strong 0.48 effect size toward student achievement. Students want to participate, will engage, and choose to learn.[3] —Eric Jensen

When I first started developing a Community of Learners in my own classroom, I realized that students needed to adopt new roles, and they needed to see the benefits of expectations such as:

- Using all opportunities to engage
- Minimizing passivity
- Maximizing active cognition

Not everything went smoothly at first, but I learned a lot in the process. Here are some examples of my expectations for students, which will be explained more fully in subsequent chapters. In each case, the burden was on me to teach the behaviors and attitudes I wanted to see, and help kids realize the benefits for the class and especially for them.

After my teacher asks a question, I use think time to come up with an answer.

As a teacher, I trained myself to give students think (or wait) time after I posed a question. There were always kids whose hands shot up immediately, but I wanted to give the rest of the students time to think, too. And it worked—there were more students able to share their thinking when they had sufficient time first to reflect.

But I noticed there were still a few kids who rarely had an answer ready, even after wait time. What was going on? I began to see that these students just didn't feel accountable for that time, and they were sitting back, quietly unengaged. It was obvious to me, but not to them that think time was to be used for thinking! These students either didn't know how to do it or didn't think it applied to them. That's when I realized we had to discuss the benefits of using think time—benefits for them and for the community. Then I had to show students how to do it, and give them time to <u>practice</u>. I would demonstrate by asking a question and thinking aloud possible responses. Some kids had not had the opportunity to think deeply, nor interested people ready to listen to them. Maybe this would be their first experience.

If I am called on, I share my answer.

After I taught *why* and *how* to use think time, things were improving, and kids were becoming more comfortable with sharing. But I still had a few students whose standard answer was the default, *I don't know*. Obviously, I needed to continue preaching how important everyone's thinking was to the community. They were each capable of unique thinking and not sharing meant our class conversations would be that much poorer. True, some students really didn't have an answer, and that was OK. In that case, I taught them to add *yet* to the end of their *I don't know*. Adding this tiny word sent the message that the thinking would continue.

When the teacher or a student shares with the whole group, I capture the thinking.

After students got used to using think time to formulate a response, I wanted them to listen to each other and process other points of view. In too many classrooms, the speaker just talks to the teacher while the other students are unengaged, waiting for him or her to finish! I wanted my students to do more, listening to each other and reacting to what was being said by asking questions or commenting. This is what I called "capturing thinking." For most, this was a new skill. I had to teach them what to do when another student was talking—and give them opportunities to respond, not just wait for me to do it.[4]

I share my answer with a partner.

Another strategy I used was partner sharing. It gave kids a chance to express their thinking and to actively participate in the lesson. Through partner sharing, my students could determine their level of understanding, get valuable feedback, and verbally rehearse their responses before sharing with the whole group. Initially, I assumed that when I directed students to share with a partner, they would all do it. Wrong! I soon discovered that some were sharing on topic, others were off topic, and a few said nothing at all. Once again, the class needed to discuss the benefits of partner sharing, learn how to do it, and practice. Then it was up to me to monitor the routine. Sometimes it looked like all the students were engaged in a lively on-topic discussion, but I needed to check for evidence!

I capture my partner's thinking.

I wanted my students to process each other's thinking, but did they? Were they trying to understand what their partner said, and if they didn't, were they asking questions to clarify? Did they agree or disagree? Were they able to add on to what was said? I couldn't assume they knew how to do these things. It was time to teach them.

In a small group, I share my thinking when it is my turn. I capture the thinking of the speaker.

Small groups presented new challenges. There were kids who monopolized the conversation, and kids who rarely shared at all. How could I make things equitable so students could mine the thinking of everyone in the group? I needed to teach my students how to share equitably (e.g., with protocols), and what to do with each other's thinking.

I use non-verbal responses to stay actively engaged.

To keep students engaged throughout the day, I found opportunities for them to communicate non-verbally, too. Without speaking a word, they could indicate a need, respond to a student sharing, or give me information. My class had a signal for agreeing or disagreeing with other students' comments, and sometimes kids put up fingers to show answers to multiple choice questions or math problems. It kept kids actively engaged, and I could quickly see their answers.

When asked to share chorally (whole group), I verbalize out loud.

In my classroom, I often asked students to read chorally or to verbalize a response all together. This was another opportunity for them to think and respond—but only if they chose to do it. Most kids were participating, but when I looked carefully at the class, I discovered that a few students were not interacting with the group at all. They could have had good reasons—but I suspected a few students were slipping back into learned passivity. It was time to step back and discuss the importance of this learning opportunity. When my students started seeing their participation as another chance to activate their brains, they were much more likely to join in.

Evidence of a Classroom Community

Imagine you and your students are in a boat, rowing toward a destination. You are at the front, leading the pace, and most students are following along in sync. But there are a few kids sitting passively, oars resting on their laps, a couple are dragging their oars in the water, and one is even rowing the wrong way. As you can imagine, forward progress would not be speedy. When everyone is not "on board," progress slows, just like it does in our classrooms. The aim of a community of learners is to get everyone rowing together, reaching the class's collective potential, and helping everyone succeed. In a genuine community of learners, students learn the benefits of participating and activating their brains, and they are taught what to do and how to do it. They are given time to practice—and are expected to be active members of that community of learners. When this occurs, students begin using language that shows they are engaged and want to learn. They are not reluctant to admit they are confused or can't hear another student's response, and they value the contributions others make to the development of a classroom community. Best of all, they become stakeholders in their own learning and that of everyone in the class.

NOTES

Chapter 3: Teachers' Roles
<u>Why Aren't Schools Getting Better?</u>

We all know that schools could be more effective places for learning. This is not news. In my forty or so years in education, dissatisfaction and calls for change have been the rule rather than the exception. In recent years, solutions have focused on standards and testing. The rationale is that student achievement will improve if we raise standards or change the assessment—by making it harder, teachers and students will work harder and learn more. The results have been less than stellar.

If raising standards and more testing isn't bringing the results we want, clearly something else is going on. There is nothing wrong with high expectations and standardized testing per se, but they ignore a key element of learning—human interaction. There is no substitute for good teaching and motivated students, and if those things are not in place, nothing else makes much of a difference. The rubber meets the road in the **classroom**, in those vital moments of interaction between teachers and students. In fact, there is a great deal of research showing that **teachers**, not higher standards, tougher tests, or the latest technology, are the most important factor in raising student achievement:

- *Research shows that effective teachers are the most important factor contributing to student achievement.*[5]

- *More than two decades of research findings are unequivocal about the connection between teacher quality and student learning.*[6]

- *Research suggests that, among school-related factors, teachers matter most.*[7]

- *It is good teaching, rather than testing, that leads to higher levels of academic performance.*[8]

So why aren't we focusing on this, and why aren't we directing more of our resources toward raising the level of instruction in our schools? True, there are great books out there on effective teaching and learning strategies. And yes, school districts and colleges provide teachers with hundreds of professional development opportunities each year. But these resources have not resulted in increased effectiveness. Why not? Let's look at some reasons.

The Strongest Influence on Our Teaching Practices Is Often Our Own School Experience

Unfortunately, it's very common for rookie teachers to leave behind the "best practices" they learned during their training and regress to the traditional, teacher-centered instructional practices they see being used by their new colleagues.[9] —J. Thompson et.al.

Consider this—as students in our own K-12 education, we *watched* at least 8,000 hours of teachers instructing.[a] We were "imprinted", you might say, with a particular style of teaching. If we were lucky, we watched hours of engaging lessons with plenty of opportunities for student participation. But most of us weren't that lucky. Most of us watched a lot of pretty average teaching. And that's the model we fall back on when things get challenging. It's comfortable, and it's familiar.

Consider the example of Leslie Mead (not her real name). She had completed a bachelor's program, education classes, and student teaching. She qualified for a license and survived a gauntlet of interviews just to be able to stand in front of a classroom of students. Yet despite all that preparation, she created an atmosphere of learning reminiscent of classroom experiences from the 1950s and 60s where student passivity was the norm. In other words, students were expected to stay in their seat, listen to the teacher, raise their hands to answer questions, and otherwise stay quiet. That is what Leslie learned from her teacher preparation program, her colleagues, and her supervisors. In reality, students were talking to neighbors, blurting out comments, restlessly moving about the room, and not engaging in learning. And it was easy for students (particularly those who struggled) to hide in her classroom. What happened to all the strategies she learned in her teacher education classes? Jane Pollock, in *Improving Student Learning One Teacher at a Time*, writes:

> *"Recently, in a professional development seminar, I asked a novice teacher how she had learned to teach. Her immediate answer: "I learned from my teachers."*
> *Teasingly, the author responded, "Certainly you mean you learned from your college professors?"*
> *"No," she replied confidently, "I mean from my school teachers."*

---

[a] 4 hours a day x 160 days a year x 13 years = 8,320 hours.

Jane Pollock concludes that if each teacher learned from their teachers, the type of pedagogy used in their classrooms could be traced back to the 1950s when classrooms were less diverse.[10]

Dan Lortie, in *Schoolteacher: A Sociological Study*, backs up this finding:

> *Prospective teachers have a preconceived idea of what teaching is by watching others do it. The potential problem with this apprenticeship is that though students form impressions of what teachers do, they are not privy to why they do it. As a result, their conceptualization of teaching is underdeveloped and can lead to imitation rather than intentionality.*[11]

Ineffective Practices

Going from class to class and school to school, I see some common practices—practices that research shows aren't all that effective in providing an equitable education:

- Hand raising, followed by the teacher calling on one student.
- The same lesson or assignment given to all students, regardless of individual challenges. (The exception is small group reading—but independent activities are often the same for all the other students.)
- Teachers teaching from their desks.
- Students being disciplined in front of other students.
- Teachers sitting at their desks looking at their computers while students are working independently (versus walking around the room, collecting formative assessment data.)
- Assignment- or activity-based instruction versus learning target-based—where the goal of the lesson is completing an activity instead of learning from it.

These practices have been passed from teacher to teacher over generations, ignoring reams of research that challenge their effectiveness. After countless hours of exposure to outdated instruction, it's only human that we internalize the ineffective methods we experienced. However, it is also possible to counter this influence via awareness, effective planning, and better practices.

Unrealistic Images of Teaching

When I first considered becoming a teacher, I had an image, like most people, of what it should look, sound, and feel like. Here was my image:

- Desks in a row, eyes facing front, silence.
- Students following directions and completing assignments due to the clear explanation I provided.
- Neat stacks of papers with grades and comments.

When I finally became a teacher, the reality wasn't at all what I imagined. Pretty quickly I became disillusioned and disappointed, a common experience for beginning teachers.

That first year of my teaching career, I often found myself staring at glazed students' eyes and heads resting on desks. I became a teacher so I could teach young students—show them how to solve math problems, understand a text, and learn about history. I had visions of grading papers, providing meaningful feedback that would motivate students and change lives. If I asked kids to do something, they would do it just because I *was* the teacher. I bet a lot of people come into the profession with these same expectations.

It turned out students didn't necessarily learn something because I talked a lot. They didn't always do something just because I asked them to. And actually, grading papers wasn't all that fun. Clearly, this was a learning opportunity for me. But how easy it would have been to cling to my initial expectations, and start blaming students when things went awry.

Professional Development That Under-delivers

Countering the influences of our own experience as students, ineffective strategies, and unrealistic expectations calls for some powerful professional development. But professional development for teachers has often failed to measure up. It is typically haphazard, inconsistent, and variable from year to year. Here's what teachers have told me:

- *There is always some great new idea. We receive a brief training and then are expected to implement a new strategy or program.*

- *Rarely is there follow up to see how things are going with a new program or to help navigate the inevitable issues that pop up.*

- *Every year there are new initiatives, not connected to what we did the year before. And we seldom find out whether the previous ones were actually effective.*

- *We have attended many workshops, but I do not know how to apply these ideas to my classroom. Is there a book out there that outlines step-by-step what I can do?*

Consider this: when a new curriculum is adopted, teachers usually receive some training. Teachers hired the next year do not. Thus, over time a "layered teaching force" develops with teachers' professional training dependent on the year they were hired. If you are hired the year after a math adoption—good luck figuring it out. How are we going to improve our practice with such a haphazard support system?

Welcome to the Comfort Zone

The main reason there's been so little achievement gain over the past few decades arising from the reforms that so many of us have been pressing for is precisely because neither curriculum nor instruction much changed – hence the students' actual classroom experience didn't much change, and hence the students didn't learn much more.[12] —M. Petrilli

Many teachers use age-old teaching strategies—probably the same ones used during the 8,000 hours when they were students. These methods worked for them because most teachers were successful students and they bring positive memories and emotions from their own learning experiences into their classrooms.[b] Additionally these tried, but no longer true methods, are still being used and therefore reinforced by other educators (even mentors) in the school. It is essentially teaching in what I call the "comfort zone."

With so much to do, it is easy to fall back into that zone—there is a certain level of comfort that comes from replicating our own experiences. Even in pre-service programs and student teaching, teachers use a comfort zone lens while learning teaching strategies. It takes an astute teacher candidate to see this and have conversations about moving out of this zone. Let's take a look at a scenario that illustrates a common comfort zone strategy used in classrooms.

---

[b] Depends on the definition of 'worked.' I contend that other strategies (based on research) would have pushed students to deeper levels of understanding and learning.

Learning Target[c]: I can reduce fractions to lowest terms. *(Or is it "complete the worksheet"?)*

Teacher: *5-4-3-2-1, voices off.*

Teacher: *We will work on reducing fractions to simplest terms so that you will be able to complete the worksheet.*

Teacher: *Let's start with 4/16. Who knows what to do first? Sophia.*

Sophia: *You divide the 16 by 4.*

Teacher: *Good answer. But that is not what you do first. Someone else. Mark.*

Mark: *You divide the 4 by 4.*

Teacher: *You are not wrong. But there is a general first step that we always use. Let me give you a hint: Factors. Greg.*

Gregg: *You should first figure out what the factors are of each number.*

Teacher: *Right. So, what are the factors of 4?*

Student shouts out: *1 and 4.*

Teacher: *Please raise your hand. Everyone, please keep looking up here. Put away everything but a pencil. Mike.*

Mike: *1 and 4.*

Teacher: *That is correct. Now, what are the factors of 16?*

Shout out: *4.*

Teacher: *Remember to raise your hand. Tim.*

Sophia: *1, 4, 8, and 16.*

A few more problems are completed as a group using the same teaching strategy. Then students are then given a worksheet to complete independently. The worksheet is turned in and corrected by the teacher. Some students seemed to understand, while others appeared confused. The work is returned to students the next day and stuffed into backpacks.

---

[c] A learning target lets students know exactly what they will learn. Agendas or to do lists can masquerade as learning targets.

I would wager this teacher is teaching exactly how he was taught. It "worked" great for him because he was a "good student."[d] But chances are, there are students in his class that aren't as engaged as he was, and who know he'll call on the "smart kids" first and leave them alone. These are the students that too easily fall through the cracks. If this teacher were willing to move out of his comfort zone, he could start using strategies to ensure all students learn. In section two we will examine some of these strategies.

Resorting to the Control Zone.

When teachers become uncomfortable in the classroom because things start happening that don't match their image of what should be going on, some move into what I call the control zone. They become irritated with students, blaming them for their misbehavior and periodically threatening to clamp down. The classroom climate turns negative, and students start bracing for the inevitable lecture on respect. Some teachers try using a carrot—if students behave, they will be rewarded. Or maybe a stick—if students misbehave, there will be consequences (punishment). The focus is now less on learning and more on a kind of game—students see how far they can go, and the teacher vacillates between carrots and sticks. As students get older, the fear they will get out of control increases, and the consequences for negative behavior increase: detention, in-school and out of school suspension, and on and on. Here is an example of a teacher working in the control zone:

Target: I can reduce fractions to lowest terms. (Or is it, "*the faster the activity moves to silent, independent work, the better*"?)

Teacher: *5-4-3-2-1 quiet please.*

Students do not quiet down.

Teacher (a little louder): *5-4-3-2-1!*

Most students do quiet down. The teacher begins to talk, even while some students still converse.

Teacher: *I am going to show you how to reduce a fraction to simplest terms so you can practice by yourself.*

---

[d] Although, many teachers have told me they really did not understand fractions.

> Teacher: *Let's start with 4/16. I can see that both numbers are divisible by 4. Stop talking in the back. Martin, move up here to the front. 4 divided by 4 is 1. 16 divided by 4 is 4. The answer is 1/4.*
>
> The teacher demonstrates the solutions to a few more problems, and then passes out a worksheet.
>
> Teacher: *Any questions?*
>
> Isaac: *How many problems do we have to do?*
>
> Teacher: *All of them. Stay in your seat and do the 20 problems by yourself without talking.*
>
> When the work time begins, some students begin to talk.
>
> Teacher: *I did not give you permission to talk! When you get your worksheet, start working! Put it in the basket when you are done.*
>
> Most students start to work. The teacher sits at her desk and observes, telling any student who begins talking to stop!

It is obvious this teacher is a lot more concerned with behavior than with learning. Her fear of losing control is apparent even in her thinking—*the faster this activity moves to silent, independent work, the better*—and it is likely the students are motivated more by fear of her frustration and wrath, than by the opportunity to learn. It's a big step for a teacher in this situation to move away from the control zone, but there are huge benefits for doing so. Building a classroom community based on respect, self-discipline, and a desire to learn can transform her class to one where students behave, not because they fear punishment, but because they want to succeed. That's the promise of this book.

Empowering the Community of Learners

Leaving behind the **comfort** and **fear** zones frees us to look at our role with fresh eyes. Instead of expecting **compliance** from students, we can start expecting more:

- understanding of the benefits of classroom procedures,
- contributions by all students to the success of the community,
- active participation,
- cognitive engagement,
- persistence through disequilibrium, and
- collaboration and cooperation.

So how do we forge a new direction, where we move beyond the practices of the past and make our classrooms the effective communities of learning they need to be? And what would those communities look like? My experience as a classroom teacher and later as a professional development coordinator led me to re-examine my beliefs about learning and ask some tough questions:

- What conditions could teachers set up in the classroom so that students would **choose** to behave and to engage cognitively—for their own benefit?
- Could students move beyond external controls and learn to self–regulate their behavior?
- How could teachers make kids realize that what was going on in the classroom was **for them**, and how could teachers and students harness the power of a learning community to foster success for everyone?
- Could they set aside their preconceived images of the classroom and of teacher and student roles to create something different—something far more dynamic and engaging?
- Despite all the obstacles that teachers say prevent students from learning, could classrooms be transformed into communities where students are actively engaged in their own learning?

Grappling with these questions led me to search for answers, reading hundreds of books and articles, engaging in probing conversations with colleagues, observing hundreds of classrooms, and, building on what I learned, to develop the ideas in this book. I'll begin by addressing the teacher's role, delineating step-by-step some key behaviors and strategies teachers can use to create a real community of learners. I will show how to sustain that community throughout the year, even with recalcitrant learners. But I will also address a crucial component that is too often ignored in books about instruction—the role of the student. I will show how to get kids on board, guiding them to re-envision the classroom and their role in it, helping them see that school is something *for them,* not just something that is done *to them.*

The Student-Centered Zone

Schools need teachers who are open to whatever strategies meet the needs of their students and who are carefully prepared to avoid slipping back into comfort or control zones. Schools need teachers who will be reflective and analytical and ready to create a different kind of zone in their classrooms, one that I call a **student-centered zone**. The purpose of this book is to lay out steps for building a community of learners, and in the process to help build better teachers. Perhaps even more important, it shows how to "build better students."

NOTES

Chapter 2 & 3 Key Points

Students' Roles

☐ Think about all the ways you benefit from what happens in school.

☐ Use all the opportunities you are given to think and participate in lessons.

Teachers' Roles

☐ Instead of just expecting compliance from students, empower them.

☐ Teach and expect students to participate actively in lessons.

☐ Encourage students to share their disequilibrium, realizing that confusion is a normal feeling when learning new material.

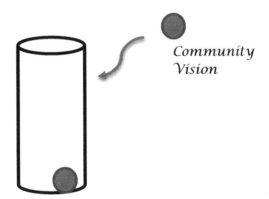

Community Vision

The marbles in this jar symbolize actions that develop community.

Section I: Begin the Process of Empowering Students

What can I do to empower students?

Chapter 4: Develop a Community of Learners

Community: a place in which students feel cared about and are encouraged to care about each other. They experience a sense of being valued and respected; the children matter to one another and to the teacher. They have come to think in the plural: they feel connected to each other; they are part of an "us."[13]   —A. Kohn

1. Carefully Plan the First Day's Words and Actions

Building community starts with the words and actions you employ the very first day of school. You want students to immediately think, *this year will be different,* and to *feel* what it is like to be an active learner. This is crucial because you are setting the stage for the whole year. What will your first words be to this new group of students? What will your first actions be? As students form their first impressions, will they see a business as usual year ahead or the launch of something far more rewarding? Consider these first-day scenarios:

The teacher	Students' perceptions:
Spends an hour talking about rules.	There will be a lot of teacher talk this year. I can just sit back.
Asks a question and calls on the first raised hand.	This year will be another showcase for the smart kids.
Calls on a student who answers in a barely audible voice.	I don't need to listen to other students. What they say is important only to the teacher.

Can you see how these teacher words and actions set students up for passivity? They are pretty common scenarios and most of us recognize them from our own school experiences. Contrast those scenarios with the following:

The teacher	Students' perceptions
Smiles in the first five minutes and talks about her goals for the year. Guides students to draw or write about their goals, also.	The teacher cares about me and is interested in my goals, too.
Asks a question and then pauses. After 7 or 8 seconds, she asks students to share their response with a partner.	I have time to think and will have chances to share with other kids.
After calling on a student, asks him to stand and face the "audience." After the comment, other students are asked to partner share their thoughts about his statement.	The class listens to me. What I say matters.

Our first words and actions are critical. It's just as important to think about them as you do about the content of your lessons. You can open the door to an inclusive and collaborative learning environment the moment students enter your classroom.

2. Start with a Vision, Discussion, and Examples

At the beginning of the year, it's important to spend a few days or weeks (depending on your students' ages and needs) discussing the idea of community and pointing out evidence of community that you and they see during the day.

Give and elicit examples of situations where groups of people work together and support each other to complete a task. For example:

- Construction workers: a group works together on different tasks to build a house.
- Firefighters: firefighters work together to put out a fire.
- Fun Runs: people jog to raise money for a cause.
- Neighborhood, nature area, or school clean up: people get together to renovate homes, river areas, or playgrounds.
- Soccer team: players work together to score goals.

Eventually students will start pointing out evidence of community that they notice, too. It's especially powerful when their examples come from things they see in their own classroom. Capture their students from other classrooms have shared:

- *Zach pair-shared his responses with me.*
- *I noticed Allison inviting kids to play in the soccer game at recess.*
- *Zoey invited Karissa to sit with her at lunch.*
- *Each member of our table contributed three times.*

3. Foster the Students' Vision of Community

A community is a place where everyone is included (*I am part of the group*) and influential (*my thinking counts*)[14]. Let students think about that idea, and become aware that **everything that happens or is spoken in class affects the development and feeling of their community.** As time goes on, generate together a list of ideas and specific actions that should be a part of a classroom community. Personalize it with kids' drawings or pictures they find.

Here are some examples students might suggest:

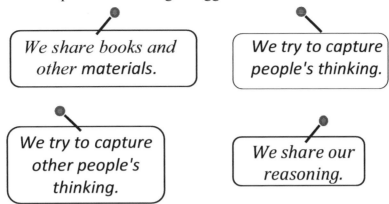

Students, particularly older students, are developing a *new* vision of community and the actions that are evidence of such a community. For many, this new vision of community will be a departure from past experiences. Your beliefs and daily words will be the catalyst for their revisions in thinking, but be patient—it will take time. So, how can you nurture change? By weaving discussions, activities, and expectations throughout the day and across the curriculum, allowing each child to feel they are an important part of the community—that their thinking is valuable and worth sharing. We'll explore specifics in a minute.

As you plan these activities, here is an important point to keep in mind: they must be designed for **100% participation**. Students must know from the very first day, that when everyone participates, there are more ideas for all to "capture." Some students come to school with the habit of passivity, and they need to realize right away that hiding their thinking means fewer ideas that might benefit the community. They need to realize that each of them has potential, and the classroom, or community, has a cumulative potential. This potential can only be reached if every class member achieves—and if everyone feels safe, respects themselves, respects others, actively participates, seeks to understand other students' thinking, reflects and comments, and grapples with ideas in order to make sense of them. This is a tall order, but one to begin putting in place on day one. Let's look at how to do it.

4. Use Purposeful Community Building Activities

One of the best ways to start off the year is to use community-building activities—they help kids get to know one another and to develop teamwork skills. But if you want them to be more than fun diversions, it is crucial to let students know **why** they are doing them and **how** these activities build community. Let kids know the **purpose** for each activity you introduce. Here are a few examples of common activities and how you can highlight the community-building target of the lesson.

Activity #1: Teamwork/Collaboration, Groups of 3 or 4

Task: Use the materials in the bag (raw spaghetti, string, tape, marshmallow) to build a structure that will elevate the marshmallow as far above the table as possible. Teams have 15 minutes.

This sounds like a fun activity, but it is more than that. Before you begin, decide what your community building targets are and share them with the class. If you don't, they'll miss the point and focus only on which team gets the highest marshmallow. Let students know ahead of time what they should be thinking about, and what you will be looking for.
For example,

- All members will participate.
- Team members are resources, not competitors.
- Learn from mistakes.

This activity *does not* have a winner. It's the process and the interactions that are important. Observe and take notes—you will be looking for supportive behaviors to discuss in a post-activity debriefing.

In one session that I conducted, there were several interesting situations that occurred. One of the groups finished early. They could easily have stopped working and started chatting, but instead they decided to try to make their structure taller. At the conclusion of the activity, the new structure would not stand up, and the marshmallow was sitting on the table. I helped students see this not as a failure, but as something positive—they took a risk and challenged themselves!

Another group did not start building for 6 or 7 minutes. They took turns talking about how the structure might be built. When they did begin building, the structure kept falling over. One member said, *I think we are using too much tape and the joints are too heavy.* The group started removing some of the tape, and they were able to elevate the marshmallow one-foot above the table. I wanted the other students to see how this group's process and collaborative skills helped them.

In the post-activity discussion, I told the class what I had noticed and asked a few questions. For example, regarding the targets:

- *I noticed 5 groups had all members participating.*
  - *How did that benefit those groups?*
- *I heard many encouraging words such as*
  - *That's a good idea.*
  - *That worked.*
  - *Nice try.*

  How did these comments help you?

I also asked, *did anyone learn from mistakes?* A key to transforming a learning community is helping kids see everything as a learning opportunity, even when things go awry. I wanted students to think of mistakes, and even failures, as part of the learning process.

Regarding group behaviors, these were my questions and comments:

- *I noticed one group completed the task, but continued to try to make their structure higher. It didn't work out, but what did they gain from this activity? Remember, the brain loves challenge.*
- *Remember the group that waited to begin building because they were engrossed in a discussion about how to construct it? Are there different strategies for completing this task that seemed to work—or not work?*

As you can see, this debriefing period is rich in possible discussion topics.

Another strategy to use with any activity is to stop the groups briefly halfway through. Ask them about the strategies they are using and what is working. This reinforces the positive and keeps the community building target front and center. Consider having students complete the same task on another day so they can use what they have learned from the first experience and feel even more successful.

Activity #2: Ice Breaker: Getting to Know Each Other.

In this activity, students make an outer circle and an inner circle so that everyone is facing someone. The protocol is for each student to share their name and shake hands with their new partner. Then they share about a topic posed by the teacher. For example,

- *Talk about a favorite animal.*
- *Share a skill about which you have confidence.*
- *Converse with your partner about a recent success.*

After sharing, kids exchange high fives, one of the circles rotates one partner left (or right), and the sharing resumes with a new partner.

Again, it's important to make the target of the activity clear from the outset. Here are some examples that you might use, depending on the needs your group:

- I will learn the names of each partner.
- I will learn something new about each partner.
- I will listen to my partner.
- I can share something about my partner.
- I will be engaged in this activity.

5. Use Morning Meetings or Community Circles

A morning meeting or community circle is another good way for students to get to know each other. *The Morning Meeting Book* by Roxann Kriete is an excellent resource for this. Greetings and activities such as the one in the previous activity are part of this daily get together. The class meeting is not a place to "whine" about other students, but a time for them (and you) to get to know each other. When students know a bit about each other, they are more likely to be able to work together in the classroom. As students develop relationships with each other, partner and group work in the classroom becomes more positive and there is often less conflict in outdoor play as well. Other great resources for community building activities include *Tribes* by Jeanne Gibbs and *The Second Cooperative Sports and Game Book* by Terry Orlick.

6. Build Community Year Round

Community building activities are a natural part of September. But use them throughout the year. When a new student arrives, revisit the activities. When groups/partnerships change, revisit them again. It's easy to assume your students all know each other and feel comfortable, but in fact, some never speak to anyone outside their small group of friends. The activities you provide help bridge that gap. For everyone to truly feel safe, to take risks, to know that mistakes are opportunities for learning, each student must feel included and influential in partnerships, small groups, and in whole class situations. Community building makes this possible in September, and revisiting the activities keeps the momentum going throughout the year.

Community building activities year-round

Working with Primary Students

Children entering kindergarten bring with them a desire to do things on their own and an increased awareness of their peers. At the same time, according to Katherine Lee in *Your 5-year Old's Emotional Development,* "many 5-year-olds will point out things that they see as different or wrong in other's behavior and appearance. They can also be very critical of themselves and hard on themselves if they think they made a mistake or didn't do a good job with something."[15] This is then a critical time to start teaching them about community. Students' beginning school experiences will affect them for the rest of their lives, and you want those experiences to be positive. Here are some specific steps to create a positive classroom community in kindergarten and the early grades:

1. Begin using community language the first day of school. Your children will learn important words when they are continually used in context:

   - Community
   - Collaboration
   - Partner Share
   - Goal

   - Agreement
   - Participation
   - Active & Passive
   - Learning Target

2. Spend time observing the students. Point out specific evidence of community that you notice.

3. Celebrate successes with special applause routines. Dozens can be found on the internet. Examples include:

    - Half a clap (*a silent clap made with one hand.*)

    - Round of applause (*move hands in circle.*)

    - Fireworks (*move hands upward, clapping above head.*)

4. Use a positive or at least neutral tone. Keep corrective behavioral comments private.

5. Introduce basic information about the brain and learning.

6. Use simple community building activities.[16]

7. Schedule daily morning meetings where students greet each other and learn about each other.

8. Choose a daily or weekly ritual that will be unique for your class. For example,

    - Sing a song at the beginning or end of the day.

    - Start each day with a morning meeting and/or a special greeting.

    - Use a movement game that is played as a transition.

    - Have students share a specific success they had that day or share about progress they are making on a goal.

    - Play music as a transition between subjects.

    - Brew hot chocolate on Friday.

    - Borrow bread makers and make bread on the last school day of the month.

    - Use fun, inspirational or curriculum-based chants.[17]

    - Greet students at the door with a handshake and a "*Good morning!*"

Working with Intermediate Students

My class has a noticeable breakdown if we don't start our day with at least a greeting.
—Jessica, 5th grade teacher

Intermediate students will be starting the year with lots of preconceptions and habits based on past experience. For example,

- *School is a place where I succeed (...or fail).*
- *My goal is to "not get in trouble."*
- *I want to finish my work so I can go to recess.*

If students have not experienced a student-centered learning community, it will take persistence and a consistent message on the part of the teacher to help them develop different perceptions and habits. Here are some things you can do to start moving kids in the right direction:

1. Use the language of community frequently. Before long, your students will begin using that same language, too.

2. Develop with students a vision of a learning community. Make it come to life by noticing evidence of that community throughout the day. Notice that the following statements focus on students' actions, not how much they are pleasing you.

    a. *I saw 12 students use a non-verbal sign to show they were listening to understand.*[e]

    b. *A student got up to shut the door because it was noisy in the hall.*

    c. *Two students helped another pick up dropped papers.*

    d. *Three kids sat with a new student at lunch.*

3. Model positive language and encourage students to do so also. Take care of any behavioral issues privately. Unless a student action is unsafe, do not use a negative tone or loud voice with a student that all class members can hear. Think of it as a wave of negativity, washing over the whole class and undermining the community you are trying to foster.

---

[e] I recommend not using student names in these statements. Too often, using names contributes to the development of a class popularity hierarchy.

4. Older students are often able to establish group norms by listing what they do and do not like when working in a group.

5. Teach students about the brain and optimum conditions for learning. Say to them: *Think about it—each morning when you enter the classroom, your brain is different than the day before due to all the effort you put in.* (See Chapter 5)

6. Celebrate success frequently. Students will begin to point out celebration opportunities.

7. Use community-building activities in September and all through the year.

8. Set aside time for community circles.

9. Choose a daily or weekly ritual that will be unique for your class. Many of the suggestions for primary kids work well for older students, too.

10. Greet students at the door with a handshake and *Good morning!*

An intermediate teacher I know told me he started every school day by greeting each student at the door. One day, however, his door was closed when the bell rang, and although it was unlocked, none of the students subsequently came in to class. Opening the door, he saw them there, standing in a long line in the hallway. *We were waiting for our handshake!* they told him. That handshake had become an important ritual, a positive way to start their day. Intermediate students have had many years to develop school habits, but be patient. The new rituals you put in place will soon replace the old and become important building blocks in the classroom community you are creating.

Addressing Competition vs. Community

Classrooms are full of diverse students who can easily become caught up in competition and hierarchical rankings. Their self-esteem can be eroded (*I'm not as smart as her, you're dumb, that's a dumb answer, etc.*), leading to replacement behaviors (*Since I can't understand, I am going to get attention another way*)—AND less learning. That kind of negativity makes it imperative that students develop a new vision of classroom community and the important role they play. Listen to the language your students use and see if they view daily classroom life as full of competition or a place where they feel supported.

Do you hear comments like these?

- *I'm* first!
- He took *my* place in line.
- *I* won the game!
- *I'm* done!

Kids with a competitive mindset often voice these kinds of statements, and sometimes classroom activities reinforce that mindset. Unfortunately, even community building activities can turn into competitive games with negative language if we are not careful. What makes the difference is *how* you structure those activities. Consider these two scenarios involving a math activity:

Scenario one: Students are playing a math game with a partner. If a player answers a math question on a card correctly, he moves his marker along the game board. (Answers are on the back of the cards). After 20 minutes, the teacher asks, *Who won?*

Scenario two: Students are playing a math game with a partner. The target of the game is: *I can add and subtract numbers.* If a player answers a math question on a card correctly, he puts it in one pile. If an answer is incorrect, the card is put in another pile. Incorrect answers require discussion between partners. After 5 minutes, the teacher asks partnerships, *How many math problems have you solved?* He then adds up all the problems solved. *As a class, we have solved 56 problems in 5 minutes!*

In scenario one, the target is for students to win the game or beat their opponent. As a beginning teacher, I always wondered why there were so many arguments and complaints about cheating during these math games. From the students' perspective, the goal was to win the game—and losing meant failure. I thought about abandoning math games until I came up with a better way.

In scenario two, the target is to solve math problems. There is discussion and cooperation between partners, and mistakes are not viewed as failures. Over time students begin seeing incorrect answers as *opportunities to talk and learn.* It is a different experience for students and it has the *feeling* of community. On the surface, the game is exactly the same in both scenarios. But the goal of the game and the way we define success are completely different.

When you apply this paradigm shift to all your students' learning activities, it changes the classroom from a place of competition where there are winners and losers, to a place of collaboration where learning and risk taking are reinforced.

The Student-Centered Zone

Lessons in classrooms with transformed communities really do look different. The students are able to examine ideas in depth and learn from each other. Here is an example of a lesson that was conducted in such a classroom. The teacher wanted students to be able to define a circle. She could simply have supplied a definition and moved on: *A circle is the set of all points in a plane that are at a given distance from a given point (the center).* But she knew it would be more meaningful for them to struggle and develop their own definition. She did this by asking questions and providing students with multiple opportunities to think, share, and capture each other's ideas.

Circle Lesson

Teacher: *Today's learning target is: I am able to define a circle in my own words. On your half sheet of paper, please write down your definition of a circle.* (All students write)

Teacher: *When I say go, partner A will share with partner B. Just listen without comment. Go.* (All partnerships participate.)

Teacher: *When I say go this time, partner B will share with partner A. Go.* (All partnerships participate.)

Teacher: *You will now draw a circle based on one of your definitions.* (Each student has a dry erase board). *Mateo, what is your definition?*

Mateo: *A circle is round.*

Teacher: *Use Mateo's definition to draw a circle.*

Now share your circle with your partner and see what you notice. (All partnerships participate.)

The teacher shows what she has drawn:

Teacher: My figure looks round. Is it a circle? Give a sign.

Students: All sign "No."

Teacher: *What did you notice? Partner A share with your partner.*

Teacher*: Partner B: Agree or Disagree and why?*

Teacher: *Barbara, what did you and your partner think?*

(The norm in the classroom: students do not raise hands after questions.)

Barbara: *Circles do not have squiggly lines.*

Teacher: *Agree or Disagree?*

Students use the signal for agree or disagree.

Teacher: *Let's draw another circle. Rita, what is your definition?*

Rita: *A circle is like an oval.*

Teacher: *Use Rita's definition to draw a circle. Then share your circle with your partner and see what you notice.* (All partnerships participate.)

After 3 minutes:

Teacher: *What do you notice? Ian?*

Ian: *Spencer and I both drew similar shapes. But I don't think they are circles.*

After additional sharing, the students drew circles using a pencil and a string. They noticed that the pencil was placed in the center of the circle, and that the distance from the center always remained the same. Discussion resumed for 10 more minutes, the teacher guiding students to conclude a more specific definition was needed. She knew that when they were eventually shown the official definition, it would have real meaning to them. Other activities, such as measuring the distance across the circle (diameter) built on this lesson's understandings.

As you saw, students in this class had many opportunities to listen to and share with partners. They could show their thinking to the whole class by indicating if they agreed or disagreed, and they could expect their thinking would be met with respect. In a community of learners, students learn that this type of interactive lesson is the norm. They develop confidence that through collaborative thinking, they will all reach the target. In a subsequent chapter, we'll take a closer look at student roles and expectations in a community of learners. The class can use the following chart to help gauge progress toward creating that student-centered zone.

EVIDENCE OF COMMUNITY	
Level 1 Celebrate	I regulate my own behavior without reminders.
	I follow procedures, knowing the benefits.
	I work hard and practice skills to reach targets and personal goals.
	My actions help everyone feel included and influential.
	I am able to work with any peer in partnerships or small groups.
	I use positive language most of the time.
Level 2 Practice	I regulate my decisions with some reminders.
	I follow procedures with some reminders.
	I work hard and practice skills with reminders.
	My actions help most peers feel included and influential.
	I am able to work with most peers in partnerships or small groups.
	I use positive language some of the time.
Level 3 More Teaching	I am learning to regulate behavioral choices with reminders and private conversations or lessons.
	I follow procedures to avoid negative consequences.
	I complete work to avoid negative consequences.
	My actions help some peers feel included and influential.
	I able to work with some peers in partnerships or small groups.
	I am learning to use positive language.

Chapter 4 Key Points

Students' Roles

☐ Think about examples of groups of people working together to accomplish a goal.

☐ Use community building activities to get to know your classmates and to learn behaviors to use when working in a group.

☐ Notice and share evidence of community (words and actions).

☐ Think about how your actions impact the rest of the community.

Teachers' Roles

☐ Plan the first day's words and actions carefully.

☐ Create a vision of community with your students.

☐ Use targeted community building activities.

☐ Immerse your students in the positive language of community.

☐ Notice and celebrate evidence of community.

NOTES

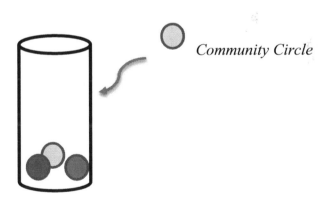

Community Circle

In Tim Hays's classroom, sixth graders brainstormed a list of "Ways we add to our Community."

- Sharing our thinking
- Helping others
- Sign language feedback
- Growth mindset
- Supporting another person
- Listening respectfully
- Wait your turn to speak
- Honoring private reasoning time
- Disagree respectfully
- Asking questions
- Following expectations
- Practicing using self-control
- Showing integrity
- Persevering through challenges

The Iceberg Effect: Hidden Steps

Occasionally, teachers talk to me about strategies they tried and the frustration they felt when things didn't work out. They may have admired a procedure working well in a colleague's classroom, but their own attempts to recreate that success fell flat. *These strategies just don't work with my students*, is a common conclusion. Invariably, the issue is what I call **the iceberg effect**. As we all know, only a small fraction of an iceberg is visible—more than 90% is hidden under water. In the same way, many classroom strategies appear, on the surface, to be easily implemented fixes to common problems. However, nothing could be further from the truth. The appearance of success belies months of teaching, modeling, practicing, and debriefing on the part of the teacher. All that investment of time——the 90% that is never seen by the casual observer—is what results in student ownership of the procedure and its successful implementation in the classroom. In subsequent chapters, look for the iceberg graphic. In each case, we'll examine the hidden underpinnings of classroom procedures and community building, so that you'll know what it actually takes to insure success.

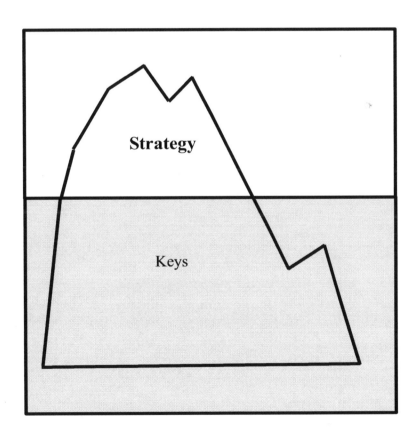

Hidden Steps: Community of Learners

<u>The issue:</u> *There are so many standards to cover. I don't have time for community circles or activities. I have tried some activities, but the students still do not get along.*

—Second Grade Teacher

Community is not built in a day—let alone in the month of September. It is the result of a daily immersion in language and actions that support everyone's emotional, social, and academic growth. It is nurtured by community building activities throughout the year and discussions that take place afterward. In fact, those discussions, where the language and actions that meet the activity's targets are noticed, recognized, and celebrated, are arguably the most important part of the experience. So, start in September and launch a school year where you:

- use **targeted** community building activities every week.
- include ice-breaker activities, so that students get to know each other, find commonalities, and appreciate differences.
- incorporate collaborative activities that teach group social norms and behaviors.
- intentionally use words that inspire community.
- debrief after every activity.
- notice and recognize language and behaviors that help build community.

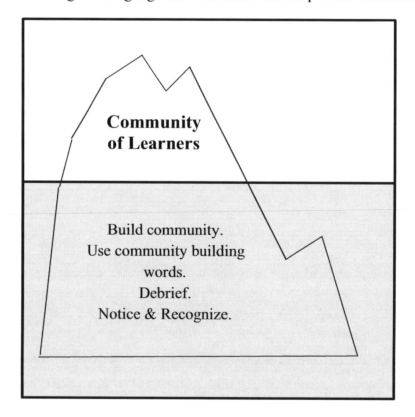

Chapter 5: Teach Students About Their Brains

Doug, a third-grade teacher, has a sign in his classroom: GROW MORE DENDRITES. Emma, one of his students, tells me that they are now working on strengthening the connections in their brains.[f]

What is going to motivate students to work hard and learn? Let them know how amazing their brains are! Research is uncovering new information everyday about how the brain works and how we can "grow a better brain." When we let kids in on these new findings, they begin to see cause and effect: their actions and level of engagement affect the way their brains develop. They have the power to make their brains smarter, and they start to see that school is there to help them do just that. **School is not just something we do to them; school is for them!** Talk about it often and post a sign to keep the idea at the forefront of their thinking.

> *GROW MORE DENDRITES*

The brain is a complex organ made up of some 86 billion neurons, or nerve cells.[18] Each one is connected to thousands of other neurons and other cells in the body, and these neurons are ready, 24/7, to send or receive messages, using tiny electrical impulses. Dendrites are signal receivers. A synapse is a gap between two nerve cells. As we learn, *specific dendrites grow so that neurons **can connect** at specific synapses and form more complex networks. Learning is essentially dendrite growth.*[19]

Neurons can be relatively passive, or we can activate them, causing them to grow new connections and create new learning. How can we do that? By actively engaging and optimizing our opportunities to learn. Amazingly, when we learn, our brains change in structure and chemistry in a process known as plasticity.[20]

---

[f] Check out Dr. Daniel Siegel's hand model of the brain.
http://www.drdansiegel.com/resources/

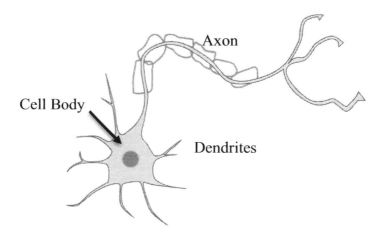

Throughout the day, point out to students what is happening in their brains, as they work hard and challenge themselves. Your words will reinforce their effort and give them a "brain vocabulary" they can use all year. Neurologist and former teacher, Judy Willis, quotes what a seventh grader had to say after learning how the brain works: *Imagine neurons making connections to your brain when you study. You will feel like you're changing your brain when you learn something, understand it, and review it.*[21]

Actions to Grow a Better Brain

As students learn about their brains, they begin to see why taking care of their brains is so important. And when they realize the power they possess to grow a smarter brain, they want to know how to optimize that power. Here is what I tell them:

- <u>Take care of yourself</u>. When you get enough sleep, eat healthy foods, and exercise, you prime your brain to learn.

- <u>Engage your brain</u>. By engaging actively in learning, taking every chance you can to participate, you get those neurons firing up and making new connections.

- <u>Practice</u> using concepts and strategies you are learning. That will make your brain sharper and cement your understanding.

- <u>Space out</u> your practice time. Research says that *distributed learning can in certain situations, double the amount we remember later on.*[22]

- Persist. Don't give up when you experience disequilibrium. That's when a lot of learning happens! It's an uncomfortable feeling, but if you keep working, you will figure things out!

- Share what you are learning. The brain loves feedback. When you share with others what you are learning, you get feedback on your ideas and see how deep your understanding really is.

- Self-test: *Self-examination improves retention and comprehension far more than an equal amount of review time.*[23] Try explaining out loud what you have just learned to yourself or to someone else.

- Capture other's thinking: When others are sharing their thoughts, try to capture their ideas—and make them a part of your brain, too.

- Visualize your brain learning and working. Imagine those neurons making new connections and making you smarter every day!

Simplifying Information for Primary Students

What neurologists are learning about the function of the human brain should have a strong impact on what happens in our schools.[24]   —R. Bucko

Even young children can learn about the brain and get excited about "growing more dendrites." The discussion is less in depth, but just as important. With primary students, discuss the location of the brain and what it does: *It thinks about what you see, hear, smell, taste, and touch, and it helps you learn. We need to protect and take care of something that important.*

I find that primary students want to know how to help their brains learn, too. So, we discuss how important it is to eat good food, get enough sleep, and to have fun moving and exercising. Then we discover how the brain can change and grow new connections, a process they can't see, but which helps them get smarter. When kids try to learn new things, when they are active learners that listen, share with partners, and participate as much as they can in class, they are changing their brains and making themselves smarter every day. Even primary students can realize that school is there to help them do this. School is for them!

The Power of Mindset

What kind of mindset do students bring to their first school experience? Are they open to new learning? Do they expect to be successful? And how do those first school experiences affect their mindset? Carol Dweck has written extensively about two types of mindsets: fixed and growth, and the crucial role they play in a student's success in school. In a fixed mindset, people believe their intelligence is a fixed trait that alone leads to success. In a growth mindset, people believe that hard work will develop and improve their abilities while creating a love of learning.

It is the growth mindset that best fits the development of the unique classroom community that this book is proposing. However, just having a bulletin board that exhorts students to have a growth mindset or a lesson about growth mindset is not enough. All actions and words in the classroom must contribute to helping students feel confident and develop competence. When students feel safe to explore and learn from mistakes, to depend upon their classmates for support that deepens learning, and to understand the purpose and value of everything that happens in the classroom, a unique community comes together, one that supports a growth mindset.

In <u>Mindsets in the Classroom</u>, Mary Cay Ricci reports that rates of fixed and growth mindsets change as students progress through the grades. In kindergarten, 100% of the students have a growth mindset. By first grade it's 90%. By second grade, it's down to 82%, and by third grade, those with a growth mindset make up only 58% of the class!

> *This data sends a message loud and clear: We need to start working with educators and children as early as possible so that they can maintain a belief system that communicates that all students can succeed.*[25]   —M.C. Ricci

The ideas of this book are a blueprint to do just that. By respecting a child's dignity, making the classroom a safe place to learn, and supporting kids through the challenges of learning, we can keep that growth mindset alive.

Make Mindset Visible

Just as you can teach students about the brain, you can teach them about mindset. Display the attributes of mindset on a poster and refer to it through the year. Better yet, make that poster dynamic, and the ideas visible, by adding colorful dots or sticky notes. Each time you or a student sees evidence of growth mindset, take a dot or sticky note, put the date on it, and apply it to the poster. With each addition, the poster becomes more colorful and shows kids how much great thinking is happening in the classroom.

This strategy can also be used with any program where certain positive behaviors are taught e.g., Kelso the Frog, or Habits of Mind. In the case of Kelso, the goal is for students to use the Kelso choices to solve a social problem. After lunch or recess, you can ask students if anyone used one of those choices. If so, add a dot, along with the date, to the Kelso choice wheel. This simple action reinforces kids' problem solving skills and provides evidence to all that their skills are growing.

NOTES

Chapter 5 Key Points

See Appendix A for brain research supporting community building, active participation strategies, and formative assessment.

Students' Roles

- ☐ Think about how your active engagement in lessons and assignments benefits your brain.

- ☐ Imagine dendrites growing as you challenge yourself.

- ☐ Think about how your efforts lead to success.

- ☐ Recognize your classmates' efforts.

Teachers' Roles

- ☐ Teach students about their brain.

- ☐ Refer to benefits for the brain throughout the day.

- ☐ Notice students' efforts.

- ☐ Talk about mindset. (Make mindset visible—it is not just a poster. Notice instances where you or students are demonstrating a growth mindset. Put a "dot" on the poster!)

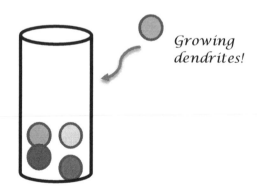

Growing dendrites!

Chapter 6: Write Goals and Community Agreements

The process of setting goals allows students to choose where they want to go in school and what they want to achieve. By knowing what they want to achieve, they know what they have to concentrate on and improve. Goal setting gives students long-term vision and short-term motivation.[26]   —D. Sasson

Overview

After students are introduced to the amazing world inside their brains, they are ready to think about goal setting. What do they want those amazing brains to be doing? Goal setting is a natural part of the classroom community in September, and its importance continues into the year. It puts kids in the driver's seat, thinking about what they want to accomplish and how to use classroom time to make that happen. It helps them recognize when goals have been met, so they can celebrate their successes, and it has a long-term component, linking the skills they are learning now with those they will need in the future.

Start the Year with Goals

Self-regulated learning is an active, constructive process whereby learners set goals for their learning and then attempt to monitor, regulate, and control their cognition, motivation, and behavior, guided and contained by their goals and the contextual features in the environment.[27]   —A. Boykin, P. Noguera.

Young children know that they are supposed to go to school, but they have only a vague notion as to why or even what this thing called learning is all about. They are not connecting the work they do in school to a career or life goal because they are just beginning to develop an idea of their *future selves.*[28] Even so, they can be introduced to the concepts of goals, planning and learning. They can also learn that what they are doing and thinking about each day affects their brains.

As students develop an understanding of the future, they can begin connecting the concepts and skills they are learning to future applications, including careers. It is not enough to just be introduced to different career choices—students need to understand the idea that what they are learning (e.g., reading informational text, writing opinion pieces, adding fractions) will be useful in their future lives. Setting a goal, planning how to reach it, and celebrating success are applicable to many aspects of life.

Begin the school year by asking, *What do you want to accomplish this year? (No, getting a new bike doesn't count!)* It may take a few days, and a little input from you, for students to decide on learning goals that they really care about. Initially, it's a good idea to brainstorm examples, and then students can choose a goal from the list or make up their own. Examples could include: I will

- learn the sounds of five letters.
- write a three-sentence story.
- read a chapter book.
- learn the multiplication facts, 0-5.
- read an informational book.
- use the scientific method in an experiment.

Kids will have greater ownership when they share their goals in pictures or words, and when you display the goals for all to see, referring to them often throughout the year.[29] It provides students with a powerful connection between the work they are currently doing and the goals they want to accomplish.

Planning Steps to Meet Goals

But goals by themselves aren't enough—without a path to success, they are merely wishes. That's why it is important to introduce students right away to the idea of planning. What steps must they take to reach their goal? Not an easy question to answer. It is challenging for children, as it is for many adults, to think of all the small steps that are needed. In a whole group setting, model the process several times. Begin by using common activities that your students engage in, such as soccer, jump rope, or basketball, and ask kids what they would have to do to become better. Guide them, if needed. For example, to become a better basketball player, someone might:

- practice dribbling up and down the court.
- dribble with either hand.
- practice making bounce passes against a wall.
- shoot 100 free throws.

Students will readily see that planning steps for academic goals work much the same way. In this case, they are actions that help move them toward a learning goal. Together as a class, take an academic goal and generate three steps that would lead to success.

For example, if the goal is: *I will increase my reading fluency by 25 words per minutes*, the plan could include:

1. I will choose books that I can read independently.
2. I will practice reading the same passage 5 times during the day.
3. I will read 30 minutes at home each night.

When you have modeled this process several times with the group, students can write their own personal goal and a three-step plan.[g] Write it on a small card, tape it to their desk, and share the plan with parents in a note or at conference time. By having the goals and planning steps on their desks, they are visible to students daily. Every week, have them reflect on their progress by sharing with partners or by writing about what they are doing.

When students think they have met a goal, they can turn their goal card over. This is a signal to you that a conference is needed to review evidence of goal attainment and to write a new goal. Equally important, it's time for students to celebrate the *success of their plans* and **to connect all the small steps and hard work they did to meet those goals—a powerful lesson**.

Community Goals: What is our vision?

Once students are clear about their own goals and plans, they are ready to learn how a community of learners can help them on the path to success. It's also time to focus on something larger: *What are the goals of the **community**? What does the **community** need to do so that everyone has their best chance to succeed? What kind of community will make each person feel valued?* Students can brainstorm with partners, then discuss as a whole group. Record their thoughts, rephrasing, if needed, any negative suggestions into positive statements. Possible goals include:

- Support the learning goals of every member.
- Recognize the efforts of each student.
- Celebrate the success of all.

---

[g] Meet with primary students individually over time to help them write their goals.

Community Agreements: How do we make it happen?

The effort of each student will make a difference in his or her own learning, and there will be many ways that students can help each other. Community agreements are one way to establish broad behavioral guidelines for the classroom that will support learning and create the kind of classroom described in their goals. These very broad agreements often include statements such as:

Respect each other.
Notice effort.
Contribute all your ideas.

Next, help students to understand what these agreements mean. How do you show respect or notice effort? Students probably understand the idea of effort better than respect, having only vague notions of this concept. They often think respect just means "be nice." How can these agreements become more than familiar words? As kids grapple with these concepts, consider using a graphic organizer that includes their words or pictures, to show what each of these agreements looks like.

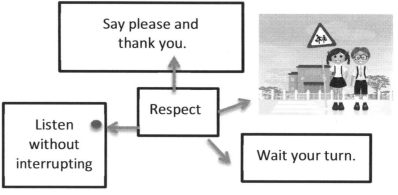

Again, when students notice a respectful behavior, put a colored dot on that poster.

Procedural Agreements: The Nitty Gritty

OK, so we've talked about goals and community agreements, but what about rules? Doesn't every classroom need them? When I began teaching, I set forth a list of rules every year that students were to follow—or else! Those rules were **my** expectations for how students should behave. But I found myself developing different sets of rules each year, because they never seemed to work as well as I expected. Worse, my students did not realize that I set out these rules for **their** benefit.

Over time, in place of teacher created rules, my students and I developed **procedural agreements**.[h] The crucial difference was that we now started with **purpose** and built a set of guidelines to help us reach our goals. We looked at *why* procedures exist, and how they are an accepted part of many day-to-day interactions. They ensure that things run smoothly and that everyone feels they are treated fairly and are safe. For example, at the grocery store or theater, we get in a line to buy our groceries or tickets. When we are at the dinner table, we pass food from person to person and let everyone have a turn to talk. These are ways we **show** respect and stay safe.

So instead of rules, we began to formulate specific procedural agreements that showed how students would carry out routines and activities to support the class's goals and community agreements. If the community agreements represented *broad guidelines* for routines and interactions, the procedural agreements nailed down the *particulars*. How could students specifically show *respect* for each other during independent work time? How could they demonstrate *responsibility* while doing partner work, or *safety* while on the playground? What would it look like and sound like? How would these procedural agreements help each of them? Procedural agreements actuate community agreements.

But I knew that developing ideas and agreements and posting them on charts wasn't enough. They needed to be dynamic. I began to refer to our community agreements throughout the year—perhaps at the end of each month or trimester or when a new student joined the class. And I made a point to review procedures before each lesson—adjusting them as needed. In Chapter 7, we will look at developing procedural agreements in much greater detail.

The Roll Out

So, we have discussed personal and community goals, broad community agreements, and the more specific procedural agreements. Obviously, the rollout will look different from class to class depending on several factors, particularly the age of your students. Let's take a closer look at what things might look like at different grade levels.

---

[h] The effective design of rules and procedures is associated with a decrease in disruptive behavior of 28 percentile points. R Marzano.

Primary Students

Start by presenting simple **community agreements** to students:

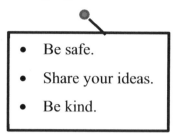

- Be safe.
- Share your ideas.
- Be kind.

For young students, community agreement words will become more meaningful as you use them in context, especially in reference to things you observe students doing. For example,

- *I noticed students taking turns getting a drink. Everyone safely got some water.*
- *I noticed everyone sharing ideas with their partner.*
- *I heard a student saying, Can I get you a yellow crayon? That is a great way to show kindness.*

Young students can learn about **goals** through the targets you present for each lesson—and by the closure provided at the end. In a kindergarten class, the teacher and students can say the target together and talk about any new words. At the end of the lesson, they can repeat the target and think about what they learned. Later, when you assess students individually— remind them of the target again and connect the work they've done to their success. For example, when conferencing with a first grader you might say:

Our target today was to make words with the "at" sound. You made 6 different words. All your practice has paid off.

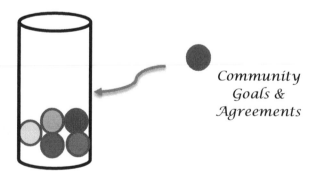

Community Goals & Agreements

Intermediate Students

When students are a little older, you can activate their prior knowledge about respect, responsibility, effort, and other concepts in their community agreements. What do these words mean to them and what could they do, for example, to show effort? Then present some possible **community agreements** such as:

> - Respect each other.
> - Share your thinking.
> - Work hard all day.

Use them in context and in reference to the students' actions you observe throughout the day. Write behaviors you notice on sticky notes and place them next to a poster of agreements.

Intermediate students will be ready to choose individual goals, as well. Initially they can choose from a class-generated list. Model how one might choose a goal—*What do I want to learn? What do I want to improve?* Show students how to generate the steps needed to achieve that goal. Later, some students may be ready to create their own goals and develop plans to achieve them. Here are examples of some 3-step goals:

Goal: I will read a chapter book.

Plan: I will:

- choose books that I can read independently.
- read a page three times to improve my fluency.
- read fifteen minutes every night at home.

Goal: I will write more neatly.

Plan: I will:

- copy a poem neatly so I can compare my later work to my best work.
- ask for help to make sure I am making each letter correctly.
- take my time when writing a story.

Goal: I will learn my multiplication facts, 0-5.

Plan: I will:

- use tiles to practice making arrays of the facts.

- practice counting by 2s, 3s………

- figure out which facts are hardest and practice those more.

For students, setting goals and formulating plans to achieve them are essential skills for success now and in later life. That same skill set may one day help them formulate a business plan, save for a major purchase, or plan a vacation. Can they suggest other situations in which planning skills are valuable? In the same way, kids need to understand how community agreements and procedural agreements help them be more successful, both now and in the future. Take time at the beginning of the year to make these connections and continue making them throughout the year. You may feel like a broken record, but these are messages that are important for students to internalize.

NOTES

Chapter 6 Key Points

Students' Roles

☐ Participate in the development of community agreements by taking advantage of thinking or response opportunities and sharing ideas.

☐ Create goals that are meaningful to you.

☐ Think about the purposes for goals and agreements.

☐ Develop and follow plans to meet goals.

☐ Connect the following of community agreements to goal achievement by all your classmates.

☐ Let the teacher know if an agreement merits revisiting.

☐ Celebrate when you achieve a goal. Think about all the steps that made this possible.

Teachers' Roles

☐ Discuss the purpose of goals and agreements.

☐ Guide students in developing goals and community agreements.

☐ Help students plan the small steps that will be needed to meet goals.

☐ Develop procedural agreements with students and refer to them often.

☐ Determine if the agreements need revision throughout the year.

☐ Recognize students for what they are doing and how hard they are working, so they make connections between their efforts and results. Say to students, *I noticed you worked the whole time*, and add, *How did that help you?*

Chapter 7: Create Procedural Agreements

One of the best ways to lower classroom stress and create a calm, peaceful learning community is to develop procedural agreements with your students. If there is a procedure or routine that will be used frequently in your classroom, take the time to develop and teach it explicitly. Your efforts early in the year will save hours of learning time that would otherwise be wasted in the months ahead.   Begin by developing a three or four-step procedure **with** your students—starting with the **benefits for them, and for you**. Kids must understand, from the outset, the purpose for procedures and how they connect to goals and community agreements. Let's take a closer look.

Student-Centered Development of Procedures

Since an important chunk of class time involves whole group lessons, how would you and your students go about developing a procedure for it? First, begin with **purpose**. Start students thinking and talking about the purpose of whole group instruction and how it aligns with their goals, their community agreements, and what they know about the brain. Your guidance for this discussion will vary, depending of course, on the age of the students. Ultimately, you want kids to realize that whole group instruction is there to help them learn, and it will include several key components. It will:

- focus on a target.
- help students add to their schema and make connections.
- include processing time (wait time, think-pair-share, table-share).
- include formative assessment, so that students and the teacher know their level of understanding.

When students recognize the importance of the whole class lesson and how it will be structured to help them learn, they are ready to develop a procedure, with your help. Here is an example of a procedural agreement for whole group lessons that you and your class might create. Note that it begins with the target— the reason for the procedure, and the steps are written as positive, engaged student behaviors:

<u>**Whole Group Procedure**</u>

Target: To add to my schema and make connections.

1. I know what the target is.
2. I listen to capture new ideas.
3. I participate to clarify my thinking.

Now let's see how this process can be used across a whole spectrum of procedures, using four basic steps.

Step 1: Start with the rationale and benefits.

With any procedure, begin by discussing with students the reasons and the benefits. Procedures have benefits for both them and their teacher. For example, a procedure for independent work benefits students because:

- They find out their level of understanding for a specific target so they know where to focus future efforts.
- They are able to concentrate better when distractions are limited.
- They know that while they work independently, small groups can receive instruction that fits their level of understanding.

And teachers benefit because:

- They are able to find out what students really know, understand, or can do **on their own**.
- They are able to work with small groups and differentiate lessons.

Check out the chart at the end of the chapter for more examples of procedures and benefits.

Step 2: List the steps.

After discussing the benefits, list the target, and help students outline possible steps for the procedure. The amount of teacher input will depend on the grade level. Younger children will need a lot of input from you, but older students are quite capable of developing steps on their own. Here are some examples of the kind of key procedures, including targets that students might develop with your help:

Walking in Line

Target: to get from point A to point B without disturbing others' learning.

I walk behind the person in front of me.
I walk silently in the halls.
I keep hands and feet to myself.

Morning Routine

Target: to get ready to learn.

I hang up my coat and backpack.
I make a lunch choice.
I put my homework on the corner of my desk.
I begin my morning work by 8:10.

Independent Learning

Target: to find out what I know

I work the whole time.
I work silently.
I try to figure things out for myself.

Partner Work

Target: to verbally rehearse a response, find out my level of understanding, and get feedback from my partner.

I am ready to share.
I speak only to my partner.
We help each other.

Small Group Cooperation

Target: to verbally rehearse a response, find out my level of understanding, and get feedback and new perspectives from my tablemates.

We take equal time to share.
I am courteous.
My actions keep the group on task.

```
┌─────────────────────────────────────────────┐
│              Dismissal Routine                │
│                                               │
│  Target: to reflect on the day and be ready   │
│                  to go home.                  │
│                                               │
│           I think about a success.            │
│                 I do my job.                  │
│  I get my desk, homework, coat, and backpack  │
│                    ready.                     │
│              I sit on the carpet.             │
└─────────────────────────────────────────────┘
```

Step 3: Model and practice the steps.

Next, it's time to try out the procedures. Start by modeling the steps yourself or having a few kids do so, while the rest of the class observes. Afterwards, ask students, *What did you notice?* and have them share their observations with partners and with the whole class. This affords students another opportunity to focus on the procedure and see what it looks like and sounds like in action. Repeat the modeling, if necessary, and when you are satisfied with their level of understanding, have the whole class try the procedure. **Stay positive and keep reinforcing what is going well.** If kids have trouble, back up and try it again, and do so in a matter-of-fact, non-judgmental way.

Once the procedure is in place, take time to review and practice it repeatedly. EVERY time students sit on the carpet, have them review the expected behaviors by reading the chart to themselves, saying the behaviors chorally, or choosing an expectation on which to work. Remind them of the rationale and the benefits for the procedure—all that takes a minute or less. You can also post the procedure, adding pictures or photos for students who are younger, English language learners, or those who have special needs.

Step 4: Monitor the procedure.

This is a step that is often left out. Being a good classroom manager means being a good observer, so step back and watch as students follow a procedure. If the procedure is partner sharing, don't just listen to one partnership—observe the whole class. Are there a few kids who need more instruction? Don't let their haphazard behavior go unchecked. In the crucial, initial weeks of school, if students learn it is OK to ignore a procedure, any procedure, they will miss out on the benefits! And they will be setting a precedent for the rest of the year. As with anything you are teaching, expect that **some** kids will need extra instruction or practice, and expect to provide that for them in a positive and discreet manner. In Chapter 12, we will take a closer look at guidelines for these kinds of private lessons.

Getting a procedure in place takes time—from four to six weeks typically, but the results are well worth it. Explicitly taught procedures, that include the reasons and benefits, help kids know what to do and why they are doing it, save teaching time, and give your classroom a sense of calm and order. Students in a classroom with clearly defined procedural agreements will develop a sense of pride in the efficient way their classroom is running.

The Roll Out

As I mentioned earlier, developing procedural agreements will look different from class to class depending on the grade level of your students.

K-1 Students: In the early grades, teach students simple 3-step procedures over the first few weeks of school. These might include procedures for whole group listening, transitioning to the carpet, sharing materials, and lining up. Model the steps, and have students practice. Observe how they are doing and provide extra lessons to kids who are having difficulty. Continue to connect procedures with benefits: increased learning, growing more dendrites, etc. (Not making you mad may seem like a benefit, but it's not one to share!) Be positive, and when you notice behaviors that are helping to actuate community agreements, point them out. Some teachers record these observations on sticky notes and post them on the procedure charts. Making connections like this reinforces the message and helps kids feel pride in their efforts.

3rd-4th Grade Students: Identify the routines and activities that are going to be used all year. Develop procedures for them with your students, using the steps outlined above. Over time, students can assume some of the teacher's roles. (e.g., line leader, person who dismisses students at the end of the day, etc.)

5th-6th Grade Students: Intermediate students are very sensitive to the difference between teacher mandated rules and the class generated procedures **they** create to support their own goals and community agreements. You reinforce this by emphasizing the benefits for them and by connecting procedural agreements with supporting learning and the brain. In some classrooms, teachers start the conversation with charts like the following. Teachers and students fill out the charts together, and then they use those ideas to develop procedures.

Partner Sharing

Looks Like	Sounds Like	Feels Like
Facing partner.	One partner talking using a positive tone.	Happy to contribute to a partner's thinking.
Giving eye-contact.	Half the class using normal voice levels.	Satisfying—able to share my thinking.

OR

Partner Sharing

Benefits to the Teacher	Benefits to the Student
Can listen to several partnerships.	Get to verbalize my thinking.
Use the time to do some observing.	Find out my level of understanding, or schema.
Use the time to think of effective questions.	Receive some feedback.
See and hear lots of learning happening.	Get to know my partner better.

Pitfalls in Teaching Procedures

The procedural agreement is the foundation of a well-run classroom, but there are many ways to get it wrong. It's easier—and arguably a lot faster—to just develop the procedures yourself and present them to the class. But then you would miss out on all the rich thinking and discussion that happens with student participation, and you'd miss the buy-in that only happens when kids are part of the process. It is easy to develop a procedure without letting the students know the purpose behind it. And it's easy to slide into negativity in the wording of a procedure or the way you reinforce it. Take a look at this example:

<u>Whole Group Instruction</u>

1. Eyes and ears on me.
2. <u>NO TALKING</u>.
3. Wait until I am done teaching to ask a question.
4. Listen so you know what the activity is.

On the surface, it seems like a perfectly fine procedure, but what's missing? First of all, there is no mention of a target. What is the purpose of this procedure? That's crucial. The target must be part of the discussion and clearly indicated on the procedure chart for all to see. Secondly, one of the steps is written using distinctly negative language: *Listen silently,* a more positive statement, could be easily substituted for NO TALKING. In addition, there is no remedy for disequilibrium if it occurs in the middle of a lesson—what do students do when they don't understand—wait until the end of the lesson? Finally, the focus of this procedure is on how to do the upcoming activity, not on the learning that should be the focus of any lesson. In general, it is best to ask for what you want instead of highlighting what you don't want. Here's another pitfall. With any procedure, there is no guarantee that students will be cognitively engaged. What do you do when things don't go well? Some teachers focus on the negative, sharing long lists of consequences to the whole class for not following a procedure. For example:

- Verbal warning.
- Hallway timeout.
- Problem solving sheet.
- Loss of recess.
- Loss of reward time.
- Phone call home.
- Referral.

Instead, I recommend first patiently re-teaching the procedure to the whole class or perhaps just the students who are having difficulty. It gets the point across, but keeps the tone positive and kids focused on learning, not punishment.[i]

---

[i] Telling students the rules and consequences for not following them has been part of classroom management strategy for decades. This style is negative from the get-go. Such a list of consequences is more appropriate as part of a private behavior plan for students who need it—such a list may also include incentives.

Great teachers are clear about their approach to student behavior. They know that if kids are not on board, it is like "pulling dead weight." Instead, they strive to have kids "walk with them." They establish clear expectations with students at the start of the year and reinforce them consistently as the year progresses. They may have predetermined and stated consequences for misbehavior, but these are clearly secondary to the expectations. They are purposeful and intentional, setting expectations and establishing good relationships with students so kids want to meet those expectations. Great teachers don't focus on "What am I going to do if students misbehave?" They expect good behavior—and generally, that's what they get. They help students see the benefits of procedures, so kids are more likely to follow them—and successfully reach their goals.[30]

As promised earlier, the following is a list of procedures and benefits. Consider it a guide as you generate your own lists with students.

Procedure	Student Benefits They are able to:	Teacher Benefits Teacher is able to:	Possible Actuated Community Agreement
Morning Routine	• Stow backpacks and coats carefully. • Make a lunch choice. • Warm up their brains with a morning task (review).	• Greet students. • Complete attendance and lunch counts. • See what skills need to be reviewed again.	• Show respect for each other. • Show responsibility. • Show effort.
Partner Work or Share	• Find out their level of understanding. • Verbally rehearse responses. • Get feedback. • Generate questions.	• Listen to get a better sense of student understanding.	• Show respect for each other. • Show responsibility. • Share ideas.

Procedure	Student Benefits They are able to:	Teacher Benefits Teacher is able to:	Possible Actuated Community Agreement
Small Group Work or Share	• Find out their level of understanding. • Verbally rehearse responses. • Get feedback. • Hear diverse thinking. • Generate questions.	• Check in with some students. • Listen to get a better sense of student understanding.	• Show respect for each other. • Show responsibility. • Share ideas.
Whole Group Lessons	• Follow the lesson sequence. • Increase their level of understanding. • Understand directions to get the most out of an activity or assignment.	• Efficiently use time to increase student learning. • Use student responses to revise or change the pace of a lesson.	• Show respect for each other. • Show responsibility. • Show effort. • Share ideas.
Dismissal Routine	• Retrieve all their belongings. • Exit the classroom on time.	• Maximize use of learning time. • Save clean up time after school.	• Show respect for each other. • Show responsibility. • Be safe.
Walking in Line	• Eliminate conflicts with other students. • Arrive at destinations on time. • Does not disturb others.	• By taking less travel time, the teacher has more time to prepare lessons.	• Respect for each other. • Show responsibility. • Be safe.

Chapter 7 Key Points

Students' Roles

- ☐ Link procedural agreements to community agreements and goal achievement. How do you they help YOU be successful?

- ☐ Help to develop procedural agreements.

- ☐ Consistently follow procedures because they increase the likelihood that everyone's goals will be met.

- ☐ Let the teacher know if a procedure needs revisiting/revising.

Teachers' Roles

- ☐ Establish a purpose for procedural agreements.

- ☐ Depending on the age of the students, include kids in developing procedures.

- ☐ Teach, practice, monitor, and reteach procedures.

- ☐ Consistently expect the class to follow them.

- ☐ Notice, share, and record when students follow procedures. Discuss the ensuing benefits.

NOTES

The Hidden Steps: Transitions

The issue: *I told my students what the rules are, but transitions are still horrible.*

—Primary Teacher

As we have discussed earlier, teaching procedures and making them stick is a multistep process—what the outside observer sees is only the tip of the iceberg. The successful adoption of any procedure requires student ownership. It begins with a discussion of the benefits for the teacher and students—and their brains. This is followed with explicit teaching, modeling, and practicing the procedure. Debriefing afterward is key. What did students notice? How did the procedure help them? Connections must be made. After the practice period, it is time to step back and see how the procedure is working and determine who might need additional private lessons. Above all, be consistent in maintaining the expectations for any procedure. So, let's review the steps for one procedure, transitions:

- Continue building community so that students know and care about each other.
- Discuss the benefits and rationale of transitions.
- Develop a 3 or 4 step-by-step procedure.
- Model and practice the transitions procedure.
- Debrief after transitions occur.
- Monitor the procedure.
- Determine who has difficulty with the procedure and provide them with private lessons.
- Be consistent! Continue monitoring transitions and reinforcing the procedure.

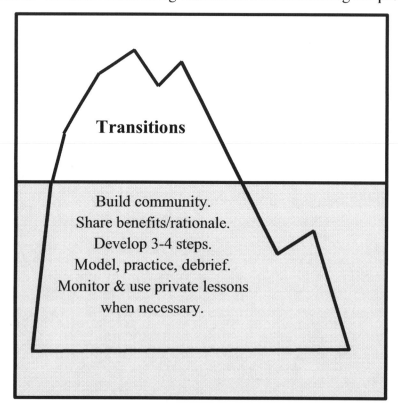

73

Hidden Steps: The Lining up Procedure

The issue: *My class is so noisy when we line up. I often make them sit down and try it again.*
—Fourth Grade Teacher

When a teacher asks me to monitor the lining up procedure, I usually discover that most students **do** follow the step-by-step directions. It is when they have to wait for a few stragglers to get in line or cease talking that many of them also begin to chat. Ideally, the line should be out the door soon after the signal for lining up has been given, but if that's not happening, here's what to do. Follow the steps for developing procedures, discussed earlier, and determine which students need private lessons to get on board. Keeping it positive, use a few minutes of their free time, i.e. recess, lunch, etc., to help these students see the connections between this procedure and saving time, respecting others, and community. Some kids many need private lessons more than once, but don't give up.

Steps:
- Keep building community so that students know and care for each other.
- Discuss the benefits and rationale of lining up.
- Develop a 3 or 4 step-by-step procedure.
- Model and practice lining up.
- Do a quick debrief after lining up, focusing on the positive.
- Determine who needs private lessons.
- Be consistent! Revisit the procedure and its rationale regularly, especially when new students join the class.

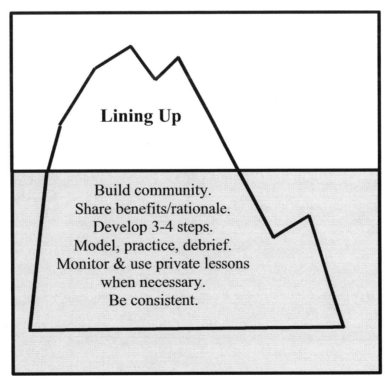

Lining Up

Build community.
Share benefits/rationale.
Develop 3-4 steps.
Model, practice, debrief.
Monitor & use private lessons
when necessary.
Be consistent.

Chapter 8: Debrief Procedures: Connect to Learning

By working the whole time, I was able to practice adding numbers.   — Second grade student

I grew more dendrites by talking about the story with Juan.   —Third grade student

In Chapter 7, we looked at the importance of teaching procedures to students and emphasizing the benefits for them and their teacher. But to maintain the integrity and purpose of these procedures, *kids must continue to make connections between their behavior and their learning.* How do you teach them to do that? One of the best ways is through the debriefing process. At the beginning of a lesson, you remind students about the procedure they will be using, and after the lesson you give them a chance to think about how their behavior helped them learn.

Let's assume your class has developed a procedure for working independently. Students have modeled and practiced the procedure, but to keep it alive, they must make a habit every time of noticing how their behavior is affecting their learning. For example, after an independent work session, resist the temptation to immediately share *your* take on how things went. Ask questions and let **them** do the thinking—a new role for many students. Start by explaining what debriefing is. For example, *At the end of many lessons, you will spend some time thinking about what you learned and how our procedures helped you. This will help you remember the purpose and importance of our procedures.*

Then provide questions, guiding kids to notice how they did, avoiding any negativity in your tone of voice. Instead of providing **your** evaluation of their behavior—*You did great!* Or, *You guys were too noisy!* —ask **them** how well they did. One simple rating system is a thumb up (*I followed the procedure*) or a thumb sideways (*I did well part of the time, or I need to work on this procedure*).

Even more important, you want students to connect their behavior to their success. So, push it a step further. Staying with our independent work example, ask your students:

- *Were you able to work the whole time? Show me with our sign for yes. Notice how much you accomplished!* (Reinforcing the positive.)[j]

---

[j] Some students may have not worked the whole time—but you will have observed that and can work with these students privately.

- *How did this help our learning?* (Connecting behavior to learning.)

- *How did this help you be successful?* (Connecting behavior to learning.)

In the beginning, and with younger children, don't wait for the end of the work period. Check-in and debrief frequently. While students are working, you can go around and whisper in their ears: *Look how you are working without stopping and look how that helps you learn!* This is especially powerful for students whose ability to work independently needs all the reinforcement it can get.

Early in the year, it helps to provide sample answers to debriefing questions at the end of a lesson. This kind of thinking is new to students, so they'll need a little coaching on how to do it. For example, if the debriefing question was, *How did listening to each other help you?* You could model possible answers like the following:

- We were able to do lots of thinking.

- Our brains made connections.

- We heard lots of different ideas!

Sentence frames also help students get started:

- I noticed _____ and that helped our learning.

- I saw students _____ and that helped our learning by _____.

Take a minute BEFORE the lesson to have students review a procedure, and one or two minutes AFTERWARD to connect the behavior to the learning. Stay positive, and enjoy teaching students who know what to do and who understand how *their* behavior can help *them* learn more!

Notice that all the teacher language suggested here is either neutral or positive in words choice and in tone. Why? Sure, it makes us and kids feel better, but there is another important reason. When you slip into negativity, get angry with students, scold, use sarcasm, or speak in a critical tone, it activates their stress response, and that's a surefire way to shut down learning. When kids sense danger, they release adrenaline and cortisol, sending fight or flight hormones to all their muscles and effectively shutting off the thinking part of their brains. In a positive classroom climate, kids feel safe, experience and celebrate success, and develop the competence and confidence to learn. You can cram all the curriculum you want into a day, but if students are in fight or flight mode, not much learning will occur. Let's see what debriefing might look like at specific grade levels.

K-1 Students: Throughout the day, help students connect their behavior to their success. Praise their efforts by **describing** what they are doing and be sure to use a positive tone of voice.[31] Point out their accomplishments, connecting that to following procedures. For example:

- *You wrote the letter 'n' ten times and worked the whole time!*
- *You turned toward your partner and now know his favorite color.*
- *All of you counted by tens so your brains are active.*

Notice that you *point out* accomplishments and *save the praise* for **effort**.

2ⁿᵈ-3ʳᵈ Grade Students: In addition to praising effort, debrief at the end of lessons and work sessions. Have students think about how following procedures helped them meet a target. Model this type of connection or use sentence frames when they are first learning and throughout the year if necessary. Have students share with their partners how following a procedure helped them learn.

4ᵗʰ-6ᵗʰ grade: Debrief at the end of lessons and work sessions. Have students think about how their level of understanding changed during a lesson or how much they accomplished during independent practice. Students can verbalize with partners and then share with the whole group. They can also jot their thinking on 3x5 cards, in journals, or on their assigned work.

Chapter 8 Key Points

Students' Roles

- ☐ Use think time and response time to connect your behaviors to learning.

- ☐ Follow procedures because you know the many ways they benefit you and your classmates.

- ☐ Connect following procedures to everyone's success.

Teachers' Roles

- ☐ Review needed procedures before a lesson.

- ☐ Debrief after a lesson to give students time to connect following procedures to a positive outcome.

- ☐ Provide sentence starters or examples of the learning that happened to help students verbalize those connections.

- ☐ Stay positive, keeping the energy on learning, and avoiding student (and teacher) stress.

NOTES

Chapter 9: Step Back and Observe Students

Students' Roles

Students take their cues from the teacher when determining their roles in the classroom. Have you ever watched children "playing school?" You learn a lot about their perceptions of the classroom—telling friends what to do, getting mad at them when they don't follow directions, assigning work. It can be a sobering reminder of what they see us do.

In a supportive classroom community, our words and actions are overwhelmingly positive, and that's what we will begin to see and hear in our students. Instead of tattling, and looking for faults in each other, they will begin emulating our words and interacting in more positive ways with each other:

- Catching fellow students following procedures.
- Using the same type of praise with each other that they hear the teacher saying.
- Making connections between procedures, hard work, and success.
- Offering suggestions for improvement to procedures or roles they could play.

Teachers' Roles

Imagine it is mid-September. Your students are conversing in small groups, and you are ready to jump in and find out what they are saying. Or maybe they are working independently, and you'd like to focus on helping a few students. Resist the urge. Particularly early on, but also periodically throughout the year, it is better instead to step back and observe. At this point, it's more important to carefully check to see if students are meeting the expectations set forth in the procedures.

So, position yourself so that you can scan all areas of the classroom. Don't turn your back on any part of the class. You can keep notes on what you notice regarding student behavior. With a clipboard and class list in hand, tell the students you are going to observe them at work, checking for all the great things they are doing. This activity helps you focus on what is right, and it allows you to feel pretty good about the large number of students who are doing well with procedures.

For example, you may want to see who can work independently without teacher reminders or redirection. Do this several times over a week and you should see a pattern—which students can or cannot follow the procedure independently? You can do the same thing for other key procedures, and I'll bet you'll see a similar pattern. It's easy to focus on what is going wrong. Instead, look for what students are doing right and let them know. At the same time, you will discover which students need a little extra coaching from you.

Let's imagine your students are working with partners. At this point early in the year, don't sit in on just one partnership and ignore the rest of the class. Check to be sure everyone has a partner—and that there is equity in sharing and working. (More about partnerships, including how to set them up, in Chapter 19.) Are students seated so they can see materials? Can they easily hear each other and converse? Are they making eye contact? If partnerships have been carefully set up and expectations modeled and practiced, it's time for students to have a go. While you observe, you might see some students:

- Taking turns.
- Commenting on their partner's thinking or conversely:
  o Not talking or facing their partner.
  o Sitting without a partner.

What if students are working in small groups? Are all of them participating equally? Is each student's behavior contributing to the success of the group? If you have set up groups carefully, modeled the process and practiced for short periods of time, using a gradual release of responsibility, it's time to step back and observe the groups in action.

Discuss with students what you noticed that was going well. The information you gathered will also inform your next steps, perhaps to:

- revise a procedure.
- practice a specific step in a procedure.
- debrief more frequently.

But here is the best part. When your students hear you share, again and again, all the positive things you observe, they start doing the same! They, too, begin noticing things going well and reinforcing each other in positive ways.[k] When that happens, you know your class is becoming the kind of caring, supportive learning community that helps everyone succeed.[32]

Formative Assessment

In the beginning, your observations are necessarily focused on behavior. Eventually though, you do want to listen to what students are saying, watch what they are doing, and check for understanding. These observations become a very useful kind of **formative assessment**.

Research shows three things that strengthen student achievement: **clear targets, formative assessment, and celebration of success.** Formative assessment is when you collect information **during** a lesson or unit to see if students are meeting a target. There are many times during the day when you can do this—and again, the clipboard is a great tool to help you out. You can jot down your observations as students are:

- Working independently. Roam around the room, observing students working and noting what they understand and what confuses them.

- Playing games at workstations. Notice if students are playing the game correctly and if they understand the concepts being taught. Which concepts are causing disequilibrium?

- Working with you in small groups. Record who is getting that letter sound or reading strategy and who needs extra help.

When students see you watching and recording your observations, they see that understanding targets and meeting expectations are important. They also realize that their work all through the day has importance and purpose.

---

[k] In *Humor, Neuroplasticity, and the Power to Change Your Mind*, Nichole Force states, "The brain gives more attention to negative experiences over positive ones because negative events pose a chance of danger. By default, the brain alerts itself to potential threats in the environment, so awareness of positive aspects takes deliberate effort."

Pitfalls in Observations

A sixth-grade teacher told his students that he would not reprimand them in public (unless he saw something unsafe.) "I will only redirect in private."

Taking the time to observe students in action seems like a relatively straightforward thing, but there are many ways to get it wrong. We could easily slip into a "gotcha" mentality—looking only for problems and publicly calling attention to misbehavior. We could share our unfavorable observations, berating the whole class for not following a procedure, when, in fact, most of the students are.[1] We could forget that the few kids having trouble need private re-teaching, not public correction.

All this has a profound influence on students. Kids whose misbehavior is corrected in front of the class will think the teacher is picking on them. Others will smile, relieved they are not the focus of another lecture on behavior. Still others will see their role as self-appointed monitors, catching their peers "breaking the rules" and then tattling. If we are not careful, we can drain all the positive energy we worked so hard to build.

This brings to mind an old Cherokee legend. In it, a man tells his grandson that there are two wolves fighting inside each of us. One is good, and one is evil. When the boy asks which one will win, the grandfather replies, *the one you feed*. Likewise, there are two forces vying for influence in the classroom climate. One is positive, and the other is negative. Which one will win in your classroom? It all depends on the one you feed.

What does teacher observation look like at different grade levels? Let's take a look.

Kindergarten Students: Methodically teach and model procedures. Students are new to the idea of school—stepping back and observing allows you to see which students need additional lessons on procedures, and to see and reinforce all the positive things that are happening.

Primary Students: As students get older, it is easy to assume that they know how to behave in the classroom and follow procedures. Do not assume—observe students to see who needs additional teaching. If your students were learning how to add doubles (6 + 6, 4 + 4, etc.), you would not assume everyone could perform this operation after only one lesson—or get

---

[1] How do you deal with the few students who were not following the procedure? See Chapter 12 for an explanation of 'private lessons.'

upset with students who couldn't. The same is true with behavior; some kids just need more time to learn. Consider acts of misbehavior as teachable moments.

Intermediate Students: In the intermediate grades, teachers sometimes assign students to observe the class, looking for misbehavior or identifying kids deserving rewards. Resist the temptation to do this. It seems like a way to empower students—but it is, in fact, just another way to maintain a teacher-controlled classroom, one that ignores the crucial connection kids must make between student behavior, and learning and growing more dendrites! Keep a clipboard handy and look for things going well to share with the class. For example, *I noticed*

- *students in Mrs. B's class kept working as we walked silently by.*
- *ten partnerships were sharing their thinking about the math problem.*
- *each student had at least one chance to share in their table group.*

At this age, kids appreciate positive feedback just as much as younger students. Just make sure it is about things they are doing, not how much they are pleasing you.

Two things are at work here, no matter the grade level—positive, public reinforcement for the whole group, and private, discreet lessons for individuals who need extra help. When you observe your students carefully and often, you will be able to do both. Find out who needs additional lessons on a procedure by collecting data over a period of time. Observe students while they are working independently.

<u>From My Experience: Determining the Scope</u>

It's easy to overreact when things aren't going smoothly. I learned to be analytical, not emotional, when problems arose. What was the scope of the problem? How many students were involved? One? A few? The whole class? Knowing that dictated my next steps. Did I need to have a whole class review? A review for just a few students? Private lessons for some? Conversations with other staff members to get more ideas?

Independent Work Procedure
Observations

	1	2	3	4	5	6	7	8	9
Sam	+	+	Abs	+	✓	✓	✓	✓	✓
Bill	+	+	✓	+	+	✓	+	+	✓
Jose	✓	✓	+	+	+	+	+	+	Abs
Megan	✓	+	+	+	✓	+	+	+	✓
Mark	✓	✓	✓	+	+	✓	✓	✓	+
Becky	+	+	+	+	Abs	+	+	+	+
Renee	✓	✓	+	+	+	✓	✓	✓	✓
Maria	+	+	✓	✓	✓	✓	+	+	✓
Noelle	+	+	+	+	+	+	+	+	+

Abs	Absent	+	OK	✓	Needs Practice

(You can also color code observations.)

Look at the data and decide who needs some re-teaching and practice working independently. Do not assume that all students need re-teaching because it "feels" like a procedure is not working. Sometimes teachers tell me that their students simply cannot work independently![m] If after observing, I note that most students are having difficulty, it is time to go over the procedure with the whole class. Usually though, I observe only a few students who need a review.

NOTES

---

[m] Sometimes the students' ideas about independent work are unclear. Some think that it is OK to get help from peers or to have conversation. Independent work must be understood as different from partner sharing or partner work.

Chapter 9 Key Points

Students' Roles

☐ Notice how the behaviors of your classmates contribute to everyone's success.

☐ Make connections between procedures, hard work, and learning.

☐ Think about the type of support you can offer classmates each day.

Teachers' Roles

☐ Observe to see who are following procedures—and who may need additional instruction.

☐ Praise students by letting them know exactly what they are doing that contributes to their own learning and to the well-being of the community.

☐ Keep the data you collect—it will show the progress students are making.

NOTES

Chapter 10: Use Language to Build Community

Greg, a friend of mine, remembers an embarrassing moment in second grade. The teacher called on a few students to join a higher-level reading group. Assuming he would be part of that group, too, Greg got up to join them. His teacher just chuckled. "Oh, not you, Greg," she said in front of the whole class. Mortified, he returned to his seat. Greg is now 70 years old, but the memory still stings.

We can all remember a teacher's words or actions that spurred us on to greater effort or left us discouraged or even embarrassed. Words and actions are powerful. And it makes sense that the language you and your students use will directly affect the sense of community you are trying to establish. This chapter deals with the many ways that small changes in language can dramatically affect the way students learn and how they feel in your classroom community.

Default Teacher Language and Actions

Computers have default settings, smart phones have them, and so do we. Anytime we respond on the fly, without first analyzing what to do or say, we are using our brain's default settings. For example, we use an automatic *Good job!* when a student masters a problem. Or we might reprimand one of our kids in public when they blurt out for the third time. Frankly, if we analyzed everything we did or said each time something occurred in the classroom, things would come to a grinding halt. Having a set of default responses is necessary. The problem is that the default responses we are likely to fall back on are the ones we have seen or heard thousands of times when *we were students*. These are not necessarily the best choices for our students. It is important to analyze what we do ahead of time and if necessary, change our automatic responses so they better fit what we are trying to accomplish.

Let's take a look at some common default responses that need to change: actions and words that persist in schools and classrooms (at every level) which stymie motivation and erode or even destroy the feeling of community.

At the top of the list are behaviors and language by teachers (and other adults) that contain subtle or not so subtle slights to individuals because of their race, gender, sexual orientation, language, disability, or perceived intelligence. There is current research about the brain, learning, and emotions that shows how detrimental these slights can be over time. Equally concerning is that others witnessing this kind of behavior begin to view it as normal and acceptable. Students are influenced by what they see and hear. They are developing their own interpersonal and intrapersonal skills and often begin "trying on different hats" that they see others wearing. Kids are checking out the kind of reaction they get from certain words or behaviors, and the responses they get influence the type of default behaviors they ultimately develop. What do we really want them to emulate?

Regrettably, there are many ways that teachers' misguided attempts to insert humor into the school day can hurt students. Traces of sarcasm, put downs, or favoritism come to mind, and all are unacceptable. In order to eliminate these behaviors, a teacher must first realize that something that may have seemed okay or funny to the class can be very destructive for an individual. For example, a teacher might say, *I am sure you will all do fine on this assignment, except for Robbie in the back who has been asleep.* Of course, students laugh—and Robbie may also chuckle. Chances are Robbie has experienced such remarks throughout his school career. But do these words motivate Robbie to work harder? Probably not.

Another unfortunate behavior that teachers sometimes employ is chastising students in front of others. The targeted students may feel embarrassed—all the while feigning they are OK or too tough to care—but not much learning is going to subsequently take place for them. They will be focusing on their hurt feelings, not reflecting on their own behavior. True, the unwanted behavior may stop for a short time, but the thinking that leads to long-term growth or behavioral change will not occur. The cumulative effect of multiple negative statements over the years is devastating for students. This does not mean that if a child acts in such a way as to hurt or endanger another that we let it go. The expectations for behavior need to be clear—but for long-term growth, reflection and discussion about the behavior are required. Let's focus now on specific examples of default words and actions that hurt students and consider some better responses to use in their place:

Public Words	What it really says	Replacement Words and Actions
Good job!	Not much. Studies show that virtually nobody takes this statement to heart.	Describe what you saw: *You worked the whole time! How did that help you?*
I am disappointed in you.	*I am bad.* Kids do not make necessary connections between behavior and results. There is no guidance to insure future change.	*Let's figure out how to help you understand this.*
I know this may seem pointless, but we have to get through it.	This is going to be quite boring and the learning, if any, will be useless.	State the target and check for understanding. Make sure the activities you include are aligned to the target.
You need to learn to work together.	*Whoops, we got the teacher's attention.* Does not lead to change in behavior and often leads to a blame game.	Teach group behaviors!
Mary, pay attention!	*I am in trouble.* The child's emotional response system kicks into gear.	Use least invasive method for re-direction; employ a continuum of responses: walk toward the student or use non-verbal signals, etc.
I like the way Fred is sitting.	*It's important to please the teacher.* This is only a short-term solution.	*Ten of you are ready to grow more dendrites!* (Give private lessons to kids who need more help learning how to focus during a lesson.)

Action	What it really does	Replacement Action
Commenting negatively or reprimanding a student publicly.	Puts students into a negative emotional state (limbic system) with cumulative effects over time that are very harmful.	Keep communication between you and your students private when talking about behavior or academic issues.
Making fun of a student to make a point to the whole class.	Confuses and humiliates students. *Does the teacher even like me?*	Avoid sarcasm, even if your students might laugh at it. Targeted students often save face by laughing along, hiding how humiliated they really feel.
Calling on students who raise their hands first or frequently.	Sends other students the message that they do not have to think or participate.	Give all students opportunities to think using wait time, partner sharing, etc. Call on students equally.
Sitting at the teacher's desk, typing on the computer, as students enter the room.	Shows the teacher is not that interested in developing relationships with students. *The teacher is not interested in me!*	Greet students at the door. A sunny *Good morning, how are you?* gets the day off to a positive start.

Just as we can reset the defaults on our electronic devises, we can reset the defaults in our own words and actions. It takes some work to do so, but the benefits are clear. In the heat of the moment, we want our automatic responses to be ones that respect students and support their learning.

I Want…I Need…

As a beginning teacher, I learned there were many times during the school day when it was necessary to give directions. But as I became more aware of the language I was using, an unfortunate pattern emerged, one that I didn't like: *I want you to come to the carpet.* *I'd like you to open your book to page 35.* *I need you to get a pencil out.* Did I want students to comply just because **I** needed them to? No, I wanted them to know the purpose of my request, and I wanted them to comply because doing so had real benefits for them. After some reflection, I came up with a different way to give directions:

- *You will be learning about the sound of two vowels, so please come over to the carpet.*
- *You will be writing a paragraph, so you will need a pencil.*
- *To be ready for reading groups, please take out your book.*
- *To be successful in math, this is what you will need…*

See the subtle difference?[33] Instead of students complying because I wanted them to, they would start connecting the needed behavior to the important learning about to take place.

The Power of "Yet"

One of the most important words in the classroom is also one of the shortest: *yet.* When students add this little word to their thinking, they begin to appreciate that perseverance, not innate ability is what produces results. More importantly, they are less likely to get discouraged when progress is not immediate. Consider how the word *yet* changes the meaning of the following sentences:

- I don't understand…*yet.*
- I haven't figured it out…*yet.*
- I can't do it…*yet.*

When you teach your students the power of yet, you help them see that learning is a process. It takes time and effort, and the only way they are sure to fail is if they give up.

Default Student Behaviors

Just like teachers, students can have default behaviors that have been learned in school and perhaps reinforced by portrayals of classroom on television. Some automatic behaviors take hold when students are in classrooms where active participation is not an expectation. For example:

- *I can be passive (or compliant but quietly unengaged).*
- *I can occupy my mind with other things instead of listening.*
- *I do not need to listen to other students. Most of the time I cannot hear them, anyway.*
- *If I am not interested, I do not need to pay attention.*

Another default behavior by students is especially detrimental to the classroom community: kids noticing misbehavior by others and tattling. Instead, students can learn that a classmate may be off-task because they do not understand a concept or know what to do. Why not teach kids to ask helpful questions instead?

- *Are you in disequilibrium?*
- *Do you need support?*
- *Are you stuck? What do you understand?*

Adopting new default behaviors that include the expectation of active cognitive engagement and positive interactions with peers takes time and requires the teaching and practice of new behaviors.

Praise from Teachers

When we describe young people's productive behavior to them without evaluation, we help them see that they can succeed.[34] . —S. Davis

Let's take a look at the subject of praise. When I was in school, it was common for my teachers to say, *Good job!* when things went well, and I used this kind of general praise when I became a teacher, too. I also prefaced many comments with the words **I like**: *I like the way Michelle is sitting,* or *I like the ending of your story.*

Consider the following commonly used teacher comments. Each is intended as praise. Read them carefully and see what you notice.

1. *You're so smart.*

2. *You kept working until you were done.*

3. *I'm proud of you.*

4. *You started right away and finished.*

5. *You are so considerate.*

6. (Privately whispered): *When you told Jennifer that you knew she could do it, you made her smile.*

7. *You make me happy. I like the way you...*

8. *You used the artist's techniques in your drawing.*

The odd numbered comments are value judgments or vague statements of praise that do little to encourage students to work hard or take pride in their own actions. The even numbered comments, on the other hand, describe specific, concrete behaviors. They may not sound like praise, but spoken in a positive tone of voice, these statements will make students look up at you and smile. Why are such statements more effective? By linking actions to outcomes, they empower students to make good choices. They put the focus on positive consequences of hard work, and not on efforts to please others. *Reinforcing language puts the focus on children's specific actions. It draws student's attention to their creativity, attention to detail, or other strength, rather than the teacher's judgment... It names for students what they're doing well.*[35]

Paula Denton (*The Power of Our Words*) describes several keys to this type of praise:

- Name concrete, **specific** behaviors.

- Emphasize description over personal approval (avoid statements such as *I like the way.........*).

- In older grades, avoid naming individuals publicly as examples for others, e.g., *See how neat Jennifer's work is.*

- Tie the behavior to results: *You learned your math facts by practicing.*[36]

With this in mind, would students benefit more from hearing, *Good job* or statements such as the following? *You*

- *are using all the primary colors in your painting.*
- *stayed focused and read 25 pages.*
- *have organized your story into three paragraphs.*
- *kept working until you were done.*
- *found all the words with the /b/ sound.*
- *used two different ways to find a solution.*
- *are carefully practicing the cursive 'c.'*
- *read for 15 minutes without stopping.*

Carol Dweck writes that when children are doing well, there is an almost irresistible urge to tell them how smart they are. *We are at a loss for other ways to show our delight and admiration. Effort praise hardly seems like an adequate substitute. But effort and strategy praise can be highly appreciative of a child's accomplishments.*[37] Initially it was hard work to change the way I praised students. As a reminder, I wrote the *keys to praise* on a card that I kept with me at the front of the room. Eventually, specific praise tied to results became second nature, and I began to observe students noticing each other's hard work and giving effective praise, too. They were internalizing the concept and multiplying the effect.

Praise from Students

Like many teachers, I encouraged students to give each other positive feedback. At first, most kids began their statements of praise with "I liked." No surprise. They'd heard that so many times themselves. Could I teach them to move beyond *I like* and actually give effective praise to each other? Could I get them to see how hard their classmates were working? I decided to try.

I started with guidelines for positive feedback and the reasoning behind them. Then we analyzed statements of praise like those at the beginning of this chapter, and looked for ones that focused on specific actions, drawing a link between behavior and success. And, we made a real effort to avoid *I like.*

Sure enough, students began changing the way they acknowledged each other. They learned to praise others in ways that reinforced effort and contributed to the positive climate in the classroom, and their words reinforced the idea that our community was there to learn. Instead of saying *I liked your story*, students began to say: *You*

- *showed the characters' emotions through their actions.*
- *described the action with lots of strong verbs.*
- *wrote a beginning, middle, and end.*

Brain research has found that positive feedback is one of the most dynamic influences on the brain's chemistry. Whisper effective words of praise to students as you pass their desks, write them notes, or speak to kids as you pass them in the hall. Remember, when you give praise, you are also modeling how to do it. Your students will take note and follow your lead when they give each other feedback. With everyone on board, the class community becomes a dynamic environment that supports positive interactions.[38]

Tone and Body Language

We can have the best of intentions when we communicate with students, yet undermine our kind intent with the tone of voice or body language we inadvertently use. Try saying the following sentences out loud several times. The first time, use a neutral tone, one that simply communicates information. Then use an encouraging voice, with real warmth. Finally, try saying the very same sentences in a reproachful tone with body language that shows clear disapproval.

- *We will start the lesson when everyone is ready.*
- *You need to keep working to finish on time.*
- *Put your finished work on my desk.*
- *As you know, we aren't starting the game until after we understand all the rules.*

As you can see, there are dramatic differences in the message conveyed, depending on how it is delivered. When you watch other adults interacting with kids, what do you notice? Do their interactions communicate caring and respect or do they show a lack of regard? Day after day, that respect, or lack thereof, adds up. It profoundly affects our students' school experience and, for good or for ill, becomes the default behavior they are likely to fall back on as adults.

Nonverbal Communication

When a teacher orally reminds a student of what she should be doing, the student unconsciously associates the teacher with the resultant feelings of having been reprimanded. When the teacher gets the student's attention and non-verbally directs her to look and follow the board's directions—this is the location of the command, instead of the teacher.[39]

—A. Kohn

Of course, there are many ways to communicate with students that involve no words at all. Nonverbal signals are effective tools to reduce public reminders, keep students engaged, raise the self-esteem of students, and preserve teacher energy. In my classroom, I knew it was time to create signals when I grew tired of telling students to do the same thing or reminding them publicly about a procedure—a habit I was working to break anyway. Since my goal was a positive classroom environment, using nonverbal signals to reduce the number of negative interactions made sense. I also wanted students to self-regulate their behavior and using signs (instead of my voice) was an intermediary step toward this goal.

Many teachers develop signs or signals for routines used daily and to help students to stay cognitively active. As with procedures, signs must be taught by discussing their purposes and benefits, modeling, practicing, and consistently expecting signs to be followed and used by students. Here are examples of signs and signals that some classes have used:

Daily Routine	Sign/Signal Examples Some signs are from American Sign Language.
Restroom use	Make an 'R' by crossing index and middle fingers.
Need a drink of water	Form the right hand into the letter W. Touch the index finger close to the mouth twice.
Straighten up the line	Touch edges of hands together.
Get into a partnership	Touch knuckles together.
Excuse table groups	Put arms on top of each other (making a flat top); excuse by table number.
Materials Needed	Hold up the materials.

Active Engagement	Sign/Signal Examples
I agree. Note: for the agree/disagree sign, have students display the signal *after* a student has finished sharing a thought. The speaker is distracted when students are signing during a response.	Move fist backwards and forwards, or have students stand up if they agree.
I disagree.	Fold arms against chest.
Please repeat.	Index finger of one hand moving up and down on open hand.
I cannot hear.	Cup an ear with hand.
Yes.	Move fist backwards and forwards.
No.	Moving fist right and left.
Show a number.	Use fingers.
Celebrate.	Open hands, fingers up, opening and closing fingers.
I am growing/not growing dendrites.	Flashing fingers of one hand vs. fist not moving.

When you develop signs and signals with your class, it is a great way to reduce nagging and keep kids dialed in, and it is more evidence of an active, engaged community. The language that is used in the classroom by students and teachers plays a major role in transforming the learning community. Being intentional about language is a learned skill that requires a high level of awareness and planning. It affects the way we offer praise, communicate expectations, ask questions, conduct lessons, and collect formative assessment—no small matter. It may be overwhelming at first to change the way we speak and interact in the classroom, but behind it all is one simple big idea: We are choosing to use language and actions that respect and empower students and get them to think.

K Students: This is a great time to influence the type of praise that students hear. Avoid using praise that begins with *I like* and focus praise on what the student is *doing* and on their *effort*. Keep your tone and body language positive and respectful. Teach students some simple signs and signals for:

- bathroom use.
- the need for a drink of water.
- think time (hand on head).
- partner share (knuckles together).
- choral response (move hand off head and point to the audience.)

Primary Students: Continue with praise that focuses on doing and effort. Teach students the power of *yet*. Teach students additional signals:

- Agree or disagree, or yes and no.
- I can't hear (someone speaking).
- Please repeat.

Intermediate Students: Teach students how to give praise to each other—what to look for and what words or sentence stems to use. Expand the number of signs and signals students use to communicate.

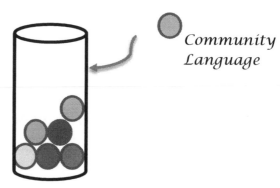

Community Language

Chapter 10 Key Points

Students' Roles

☐ Use concrete, specific praise that recognizes your peers' efforts.

☐ Use non-verbal signs and signals to stay actively engaged.

☐ Understand the power of *yet* as you reflect on your progress.

☐ Use respectful tone and body language when you interact with others.

Teachers' Roles

☐ Work to reset your default responses so they better support and respect students.

☐ Use praise that recognizes student effort and show kids how to praise each other.

☐ Keep your tone of voice and body language positive or at least neutral.

☐ Teach students non-verbal signs and signals.

☐ Replace *I want* and *I need* with more useful instructions that link behavior to learning.

From My Experience: Subtle Reinforcement of Self-Concept

While most of us are pretty good at avoiding obvious negativity with our students, it is often the accumulation of small, subtle facial expressions and posture that signal to students whether you believe in them. Smiling or frowning, hands on hips or to the side, showing patience or impatience all add up to reinforce or challenge what students think of themselves.

NOTES

Chapter 11: Respond to Misbehavior with Kind Intent

When students are apt to notice misbehavior they often want to point it out. Instead, they can learn that a classmate may be off-task because they do not know what to do. They can simply ask, "Do you need support?" —G. Peterson

Students and Behavioral Responses

Kids take note of how we respond to classroom problems, and they often mirror our actions. If someone is called out again and again for problem behavior, the rest of the class will find it easier to treat that student poorly, and to "pile on" more negative attention. They may start providing loud reminders to those not following procedures or running up to the teacher to report them. Clearly, this is not evidence of a supportive community.

A behavioral response continuum can help students learn more constructive ways to address problems, and there are well-known conflict management programs that do the same (e.g., Kelso the Frog). Let students in on what you are doing: using gentle, quiet (and the least invasive) reminders to help them refocus. Tell them what "least invasive" means and what your goal is. You are not trying to catch them misbehaving or "get them into trouble." A true community of learners cannot be teacher versus students. Students know that *their* long-term goal is to be able to manage their own behavior (to self-regulate) and these are tools to help them do just that.

In the classroom community, we welcome students taking ownership of the class's procedures. Kids can be taught to use the quietest, least invasive, form of a reminder when they sense a problem—for example, a non-verbal signal given with kind intent. Take some time to talk with your students about this and decide together on some discrete interventions they can use to help and remind each other about procedures.

And just as we are looking for positive behaviors—those that help the community and each student succeed, students can be doing the same. Teach them to notice when others do well. It helps them feel good about their class and become more open to working cooperatively with others. It also helps students realize something important —being positive and helping each other contributes to their own success, and the success of all.

A Continuum of Responses

Let's say you've taught key procedures, established debriefing as an expected and natural part of lessons, and are careful to use language of community as you interact with students. Any realist knows: kids are still going to mess up.

So, what do you do then? Before you jump in, keep the big picture in mind—you want *students* to learn to control their own behavior. The goal is change, not punishment; so, think of their indiscretions as teachable moments. No matter what the behavioral mistake, strive to ensure that student and teacher dignity remains intact. Grace under pressure is a powerful model for students—a model they may not see in other adults in their lives. And it helps kids focus on the behavior in question, not your reaction to it.

Consistency is important, too. Be aware of everything going on in your classroom. And when you say something, mean it. If you have a signal for students to get quiet—and several students continue to whisper—you have inadvertently given the message that the signal is not for everyone. Careful observation will help you identify problems early and address them. There is a continuum of responses a teacher can use when offenses are small. Begin with "the look" or pause the lesson briefly, and progress to proximity, a non-verbal signal, and a whisper, before resorting to additional consequences. Doing things in a neutral, non-judgmental way keeps the message on the behavior and makes it more likely that students will comply. Let's look at one such continuum. What do you notice?

Situation	Teacher response
Student(s) losing focus, e.g., conversing with partner.	Pause or look.
Behavior continues.	Move unobtrusively toward student.
Student not focusing on task.	Whisper in their ear, then walk away.
Student not following procedure.	***May I make an observation?*** Tell student privately what you noticed. Let them connect the behavior with how much learning they were able to do.
Student consistently not following a procedure.	Have student review the procedure and its rationale privately.
Student continues to have difficulty.	Use private lessons as needed.
Student's inability to follow a procedure is disruptive to the classroom community.	Brainstorm ideas with colleagues. Develop a plan and inform all staff members who interact with the student, so that responses to misbehavior are consistent. Notice when the student IS following procedures (use a non-verbal signal).

As you can see, in this continuum, teacher responses are discrete and at least initially, nonverbal. This is not the time to make an example of anyone. The goal of an intervention is always learning—not chastisement. When you take care of problems in the most unobtrusive way possible and avoid calling attention to issues in front of the whole class, kids find it easier to change their behavior. And just as important, you preserve the teacher-student relationship and avoid eroding the positive classroom climate you are trying to build.

There are other considerations as well in responding to behavioral issues. Ask yourself why the student is acting out. What happens just before the misbehavior? Is the assignment or task appropriate?

In one classroom, three students were consistently not following the 'lining up procedure.' Their teacher tried several non-verbal reminders, but to no avail. These kids just weren't getting on board, and the teacher didn't want to start nagging them in front of the whole class. She decided to give them private lessons on their next recess. That's when she discovered that two of the students didn't actually understand the procedure (one was an English language learner), and needed more direct teaching and practice. The third student could not remember all of the steps. The teacher gave him a 3x5 card with the steps illustrated, and he used the card to successfully follow the steps for lining up. Eventually he didn't need the card at all. None of these interventions involved nagging, shaming, or singling out anyone in front of the class. The problem was addressed, with the students' dignity intact and their relationship with the teacher strengthened.

Using the language that promotes community will also help as you tackle problems. We looked at this in greater detail in Chapter 10. As discussed earlier, giving students opportunities to think and make better decisions is always a good idea. When an intermediate teacher I know, notices some "off-task" behavior, she often asks the students a question: *May I make an observation?* She wants to tell students what she noticed rather than reprimand them. Here are a couple of situations illustrating this approach.

- Connecting behavior to results*: I noticed you talking to Gabriel, and you did not complete your story. What might help you complete your story?* versus *You wasted the whole time.*

- Using empathy: *I noticed you were distracting Elijah, and he did not complete his assignment. Such a bummer. I trust that you can figure out what to do.*[40] Or, *What will you try next time to be more successful?*

Let's not forget one of the most powerful strategies of all: catching students behaving correctly, particularly those who are often "caught" behaving incorrectly.[n] When you keep noticing all the positive things a student does, it's hard for them to continue thinking of themselves as the class goof off.

Primary Students: Kindergartners bring their growth mindset to school, and it is our job to help them keep it. Help them develop a positive attitude about school as a place of learning, celebration, and collaboration. As a teacher, I realized that my students would potentially imitate everything I did. I worked hard to avoid chastising children in public, to teach expected behaviors (not assuming they would already know), and to use a positive tone of voice. Not surprisingly, I rarely had time to sit at my desk when students were present. I needed to be up and about, observing and assessing, and using the continuum of helpful responses when necessary.

Intermediate Students: With older children, you can begin telling kids about the different ways you will quietly help them to follow procedures, so they can learn more. You want students to view such reminders as beneficial to them. When a student sees you using a reminder directed at them in a non-judgmental, unobtrusive way, they may give you a non-verbal thank you. When that happens, you can tell they see you as someone looking out for their best interests. A more sophisticated level of student behavior happens when they begin to use quiet, respectful reminders with each other.

My Experience: Noticing and Recognizing

It's easy to forget about reinforcing behavior when things are going well. However, I learned to keep my vision of classroom community at the forefront of my thinking. I wrote myself reminders to look for and recognize positive behavior, and I kept a clipboard and class list to record what I observed.

---

[n] When observing in classrooms, I often learned the names of just a few students—those whose behavior was corrected publicly by the teacher. We have to remember that classmates are also hearing these names in a negative context over and over, year after year.

Chapter 11 Key Points

Students' Roles

☐ Remind a friend about a procedure, using words or signals that are positive and do not hurt feelings.

☐ Give specific compliments to your peers.

☐ Learn from behavior mistakes (just as you learn from math mistakes).

☐ Connect and celebrate behaviors that contribute to the success of yourself and the community.

Teachers' Roles

☐ Use the "least invasive" reminder to correct student behavior.

☐ Keep in mind that the primary goal is to teach behaviors and the purpose of procedures.

☐ Teach students to use a continuum of responses with each other when issues arise.

☐ Connect and celebrate behaviors that contribute to the success of the community.

NOTES

Chapter 12: Analyze Common Challenges

If a student had trouble with long division, we would naturally want to help him understand the procedure (and its rationale), rather than seeking to punish him. So, if a student instead had trouble, say, controlling her temper, our response again ought to be, How can we help?— not, What consequence should you suffer? We would ask, in other words, What can we do for you?—not, What can we do to you? —A. Kohn

Teaching procedures, discussing their benefits and purpose, using positive language, nurturing a community of learners—all these go a long way toward heading off behavior issues. But that is not to say problems won't occur. There will always be challenges, and this chapter addresses some of the most common ones that teachers face: recalcitrant students, blurting out, and transitions. In a fear-based classroom, the focus is too often on negative consequences for misbehaving students—*I'm going to make these kids do what they should do!* But instead of devising punishments, let's look at strategies that move students in a more positive direction.

Private Lessons

When you teach routines and procedures well, most students get on board. There are always a few, however, who don't realize, or don't want to accept, that all this applies to them. They are the ones that need **private lessons**. Without investing a great deal of time, you can use private lessons to successfully address many classroom management issues.

Explain to students the purpose of private lessons—they are not punishment, but another learning opportunity. Classroom procedures are designed to maximize the time for *them* to learn. Tell students you'll help them out during your break (their recess) for a couple of minutes. During private lessons, kids review and practice a procedure for a minute or two and then head out to the playground. Here is how one teacher did it:

(Privately) *Hey, Sam, I noticed you had trouble with our partner sharing in class today. Take a minute and think about the steps for our procedure.* She pointed to a chart listing the steps.

OK, now tell me what the steps are. Sam did so without a problem.

Okay, let's practice. Think about what you like about…cats or dogs. After a few seconds, she continued, *Sam you go first. Share with me.* He did so, and the teacher then shared her thinking.

I knew you could do it. In the future, if I spot you following the procedure, I'll give you a thumbs-up. If you follow the procedure without a reminder, you give me a thumbs up. And with a high five and a smile, she excused him to recess.

As you can see, this teacher made her point, and sent the student out on a positive note to enjoy the rest of his break. No lectures, no punishments.

During the lesson, she noticed that Sam needed a little help with conversation starters and extenders. She suspected that others in the class might be having trouble, too, so later she did a mini-lesson on this very subject, posting a list of helpful phrases, and inviting students to add their own suggestions.

- *Do you want to share first?*
- *That's an interesting idea.*
- *Here's what I think.*

Checklists

Do you have students who have difficulty following a routine or a sequence of directions? Checklists are an effective way to provide more scaffolding for students who need it. Again, this is not a punishment but an aid to help them be successful. A morning routine checklist might be a series of pictures or a list like this:

- ☐ Hang up your coat and backpack.
- ☐ Make a lunch choice.
- ☐ Put your homework in the basket.
- ☐ Complete morning work.

The list can be illustrated and laminated, and the student can check off each task with an erasable marker when completed.

Student Goal Setting

As discussed in an earlier chapter, students can set goals to help them develop habits and behaviors that enhance learning. Using any classroom procedure poster, they can select what to work on, write it on a 3x5 card, and tape it to their desk. Every once in a while, ask students to write about progress they are making toward their goal and how that is helping them be more successful learners. Some may want to share their progress with parents, a partner, or the rest of the class.

Doing More Than Apologizing

Of course, self-management is the ultimate goal for all students, and our job is to provide the teaching and guided practice kids need to replace misbehavior with positive actions. This is particularly true when one student causes a problem for another. *I'm sorry*, a typical but often insincere apology, is rarely enough to compensate for unkind words or actions. But what is? Having the student answer that question gets them to think and begin to empathize with the person they wronged. With a little help, even young students can come up with something to make amends for their mistakes.[o] Here are some examples:

Student Behavior	Action
Splashing water on another student at the sink.	Get that student a paper towel.
Calling a student a "name."	Give that person three compliments during the day.
Spilling another student's box of crayons, breaking one.	Help pick up the crayons; find a new crayon to replace the broken one.

As you can see, actions are far more meaningful than mumbled, hollow words like, "Sorry." They give the offending student a chance to make things right and to think about how their actions have consequences for themselves and the community.

The Blurt Epidemic

A student in a fourth/fifth grade class said to his class: "I am not going to blurt out answers. I now know everyone needs their think time." How did he come to that realization?

Has this happened in your classroom? You are in the middle of a lesson, and several students blurt out answers or comments. The flow of the lesson is interrupted, and the pace grinds to a near halt. When I saw this happening in my classroom, I realized some of the blame was mine. First, I had responded to these interruptions in different ways. Sometimes I ignored them, sometimes I reminded students to raise their hands, and sometimes I even responded,

---

[o] *The Responsive Classroom* describes such an act as an Apology of Action. See https://www.responsiveclassroom.org/

Good thinking! Second, I realized I had skipped a step at the beginning of the lesson—reviewing my expectations. Finally, I had not trained students how to respond during a lesson.

Once I admitted these shortcomings, I needed to determine the scope of the problem—was it just a few students or the whole class? If it was few students, I could meet with them for **private lessons**, as discussed earlier. If it was the majority of the class, a whole class review was in order. Over time, I made myself a list of strategies I could use to extinguish the blurting epidemic:

- Increase awareness of what blurting is and talk to students about it as a problem you are going to solve <u>together</u>. Talk about how blurting hurts the community. Some students automatically give an answer to a question— a learned response. But if there are 15 interruptions during a lesson, it is harder for everyone to stay engaged. Tell students you will let them know **when** an answer is required and **how** those answers will be shared: raised hands, signals, partner talk, choral response, etc.

- Students have been trained to listen for question words, *Who knows...? What is...?* These question starters cue some kids to immediately shout out an answer. Instead, begin with action words*: **Think** about... **Share** with your partner... **Wonder** about...*

- Let students know that after a question, you will give them think time (five seconds at least), and then let them share with a neighbor, or you will call on someone randomly.

- Practice for short periods of time, three to five minutes at first. Read a story and ask questions. After every question, wait five seconds or more. Look at the clock—a reminder for you and your students that you will be waiting. Alternate between pair sharing and choosing a raised hand.

- Debrief at the end of the lesson. *How many of you were able to think for five seconds, and share without blurting?*

- Be consistent. Consider using signals to remind students to wait and think before responding out loud. (e.g., put your hand on top of your head)—and expect to stay very consistent over a long period of time to retrain students who developed bad habits in the past.

Don't be discouraged if your students don't respond immediately. It takes time to change bad habits—yours and theirs.

All throughout the year you will be talking to students about community and their roles in developing one. Don't be afraid to be a broken record about it. In this case, students can discuss what happens to the community when someone blurts a response without giving everyone else a chance to think.[p] They can also share how the community is strengthened when everyone's thinking time is respected.

Transitions: Teachers and Students

If you could track all the opportunities for wasted time in the school day, transitions would surely be near the top of the list. Get a jump on time management by teaching your students how to change activities quickly and efficiently. You can begin by explaining to students what a transition is.

1. **What is a transition?**

A transition is the time between the end of one activity and the start of a new one. Explain to students that: *During the day, there will be different things to learn. We might be helping our brains learn about reading and then need to switch to numbers or math. This change or switch is called a transition. I will let you know when a transition is near, so you can wrap up your work or thinking. We will then talk about what you just did before moving on to something new. Sometimes we will take a movement break before starting the new activity.* [q]

2. **Give students a 2-minute warning.**

Don't expect students to stop an activity and transition to a new subject immediately. Let them know when they have a few more minutes to finish. Some teachers set an overhead or visual timer to help students keep track. After this time has passed, use a signal (verbal or nonverbal) or a music cue that lets students know it is time to clean up. You can also give additional directions—but wait until you have every student's attention. Part of your routine

---

[p] *The rate of retrieval is independent of intelligence.* It is more closely tied to how and where the information was stored originally. *Teaching with the Brain in Mind*, E. Jensen.

[q] Standing appears to provide a 5-15% greater flow of blood and oxygen to the brain, thereby creating more arousal of attention. See *Connecting Brain Research with Effective Teaching*, M. Hardiman.

might include having kids come to the carpet for a debriefing (closure) of academic or behavioral expectations.

3. **Develop a procedure for direction giving.**

Develop a procedure for transitions with a rationale, benefits for the teacher and students, and a step-by-step routine that is modeled and practiced. For example:

1. Stand and look after the transition signal.
2. Listen for directions.

Teach students a protocol for directions—and practice, practice, practice. When giving instructions, teachers often start with a verb: *Put away..., Get out..., Pass your papers....* Once students hear this action word, many begin before the directions are completed. I often hear teachers react by saying, *Stop. Hold on. I'm not done giving directions!*

Instead, teach students that you will give them the exact number of directions and use the word "Go" as a signal to start. For example, for a transition from seatwork to a lesson on the carpet, tell students, *I have 3 directions for you:*

1. *Put pencils away.*
2. *Put paper in table basket.*
3. *Come to carpet in 2 minutes. Go.*

4. **Insert movement breaks.**

Sometimes students just need to move. Before beginning a new activity, give kids movement opportunities such as a games or songs. Simon Says (where no one is out), jumping jacks, running in place, stretching, or moving to a song, these work for all grade levels, and they inject a little fun in the school day. After this break, let students know the next lesson's target and review or practice the behavioral expectations for the next activity.

Students should notice an explicit break between the completed activity and a new activity. After you have given your signal, or directions, remain in one spot and look for students following the routine. Scan the whole room. Don't get distracted by students coming up to you for conversation. They can wait. If your attention is not focused on the routine, students will think you are not really serious about it.

Primary Students

At this level, the emphasis must be on modeling and teaching behaviors. Young children are keen observers of their teacher and peers. They are also excited about learning and many will impulsively shout out their thoughts. So how can you not squash that enthusiasm, while making sure students have equal opportunities to think and respond? Signs and signals help. Explain to students what think time is and its connection to the brain. Try this: Anytime you ask a question, put your hand on your head, signaling them to wait while they consider their answer. Then teach students signals for the three ways they will be responding:

- Partner share (knuckles together)
- Choral Response (hand out)
- Hand up (will call on someone randomly)

I have noticed that effective transitions for primary students include these crucial elements:

- The teacher knows exactly the sequence of steps needed for the transition to occur smoothly.
- The class models and practices those steps.
- Steps that are not working well are adjusted or practiced again.
- The teacher monitors the transition and provides private lessons, as needed, to students having difficulty.
- Music and songs are frequently used to help kids stick to the transition sequence.

Intermediate Grade Students

It may take longer to overcome bad habits in the intermediate grades, making it particularly important to teach procedures well and be consistent about monitoring behavior. In addition, many students have learned to be passive learners, doing work without understanding why, just trying to stay out of trouble without seeing the powerful and positive role they could play in their own learning. It is critical to stay positive and hang in there. Your belief in their ability to change will gradually affect their mindsets, and students will grow into more self-directed, active learners. But older students are also quite capable of assuming responsibilities for many aspects of routines and the classroom environment. Students can lead lines, take care of the class library, straighten desks, and collect and pass out papers. All of these jobs contribute to the feeling that this is *their* learning community, and they make a difference.

My Experience: Doing the Opposite

The situation: students were in small groups sharing their thinking about a story, but a few groups were off task and getting noisy. My first impulse was to raise my voice and say, "Quiet down!" But scolding is a negative response and not always effective, so instead I did the opposite. I gave the attention signal so the class would freeze. "What did you notice about the green group." In that group, kids were leaning forward, one person at a time talking, while the others listened. I also shared my positive observations. It only took a minute, but when students returned to work, all groups were noticeably more on task.

Chapter 12 Key Points

Students' Roles

☐ When you hurt someone's feelings, think of an action to help them feel better— and notice the effect.

☐ Use the procedures the class has developed to respond to questions.

☐ Think about how your words and actions help the classroom community.

☐ Notice when it is time to change activities and follow the directions given by the teacher. Consider how much time that saves for learning.

Teachers' Roles

☐ Teach expected behaviors and use private lessons when needed.

☐ Teach the procedures that guide student responses. Discuss with students the negative effects of blurting on thinking.

☐ Teach procedures for transitions and learn to give precise directions.

☐ Include periodic movement breaks for students.

Chapter 13: Value Relationship Over Rewards

There is a negative correlation between the use of rewards and punishments by teachers and the amount of task engagement by students.[41]   —A. Boykin & P. Noguera

It is our nature to want students to behave and work hard. After all, it's the right thing to do, and it benefits them in the long run. But what if they aren't there yet? Is it wrong to use extrinsic motivation to insure good behavior? Will they get "hooked" on rewards and never become intrinsically motivated learners? These are important questions to consider.

Although I discourage the use of rewards systems now, during my teaching career I tried just about every system known to man before realizing there was a better way. I used to joke that the perfect teacher accessory was a **reward belt**. It would have pockets to hold every kind of incentive you could want: Candy! Stickers! Tickets! Tokens! etc. With it, you could immediately reinforce any positive behavior you might see. When I retired, a colleague made a reward belt just like that and gave it to me for a gift. We both laughed, but maybe someday, someone will take that idea and make a fortune selling it to desperate teachers.

Desperate Measures: Reward Systems

Remember that vision I had when I first began teaching—great lessons, kids happily complying with instructions? When things didn't work out, I became disillusioned and desperate to turn things around. Like many teachers, I thought a reward/punishment system would help, and I assumed that if I could just explain it well enough, students would get on board. So, I gave it a shot. Overall, student behavior did improve a little, but not the way I expected. Most students were conforming, but they were doing so because they didn't want to get into trouble, or they wanted to collect more points, tokens, etc. And the behavior of challenging students hadn't changed much at all, especially when my attention was focused elsewhere. My students weren't becoming the intrinsically motivated learners I wanted to see. It wasn't until I started to work on developing community, establishing procedures, and analyzing students' needs, that I began to see real change. Rewards and punishments were no substitute for a community of learners when it came to getting kids on board.

Develop Relationships: Teacher-To-Student

One study found that students who felt unconditionally accepted by their teachers were more likely to be genuinely interested in learning to enjoy challenging academic tasks.[42]

—A. Kohn

Developing a community of learners takes time, but it begins with one crucial relationship—the relationship between teacher and student. The teacher establishes the tone, provides a vision, and models the kind of interactions that help students feel included, influential, safe to take risks and make mistakes. There are many things teachers can do to forge bonds with students and contribute to their sense of well-being:

- Greet students by name at the door each morning.

- Find out what students are doing outside of school. They will feel that you care about them and are interested in them. Attend student sporting events or recitals.

- Write positive notes—students really value this private communication, and some will save your correspondence until it falls apart. Even at the end of a tough day, I tried to write positive notes to at least five students. It made me focus on the many positive things that had occurred during the day, and reading these notes was a great way for my students to start the next day.

- Debrief lessons, having students recognize all the positive behaviors that contributed to lots of learning.

- Have lunch occasionally with a small group of students. (Everyone gets an invitation sometime during the year.)

- Send positive notes home or make a phone call, recognizing a student's progress, hard work or achievement. Parents love this, and for some, it may be the first positive phone call they've ever received for their child.

- Design lessons that engage students by using active participation techniques. (Section 2)

- Celebrate student work. Give them opportunities to share their work with the principal, custodian, secretary, parents, or another class.

- Surprise the whole class with a treat.

- Laugh; use humor.

- Establish traditions: making bread in the classroom once a month, having hot cocoa every Friday, or singing songs at the end of the day.

Building relationships and respect is key. Eric Jensen writes, *Students don't care how much you know until they know how much you care. Teacher student relationships have a whopping 0.72 effect size when it comes to student achievement.*[43]

Student-to-Student Relationships

If you want academic excellence, you have to attend to how children feel about school and about each other.[44] — A. Kohn

In building community, establishing a positive relationship with students is a crucial first step, but it is not enough. Kids can have a great relationship with you, but struggle with the interactions they have with each other. Dissent and disrespect among students can quickly undermine all the good work you do, so it is essential to teach students **how** to work with and to care about one other. That starts with kids getting to know each other. Many students interact rarely, if at all, with others outside their small group of friends, and some may not even know the names of other kids in the class. How can they work together easily and solve the inevitable problems that arise if that is the case? We can provide activities such as the following, to help students bridge the relationship gap and get to know each other.[r]

Morning Circle: Roxanne Kriete, in *The Morning Meeting Book* describes get-together where students greet each other in different ways. Some teachers have students partner up each day with someone new and talk about a given topic. It helps kids expand their circle of friends and learn interesting things they might not have known about each other.

Community Building Activities: The *Tribes*[s] book is full of activities that allow students to work together to accomplish a task. In the process, they learn valuable group skills and opportunities to deal constructively with problems that come up. Each activity is designed to help students practice key group behaviors.

---

[r] Review Chapter 3 about building community.
[s] *Tribes* by Jeanne Gibbs

Group Work: In the book, *Designing Groupwork* (Cohen, Goodlad), there are cooperative group tasks that teach specific collaborative skills such as:

- Pay attention to what other group members need[45]
- No one is done until everyone is done.
- Help students do things for themselves.
- Explain by telling how.
- Everybody helps.
- Find out what others think.
- Telling why.

Add these three great books to your teacher toolkit and you will have plenty of strategies for developing teamwork and community.

Compliments: Post compliments that students receive from other adults. Teach students how to compliment each other's efforts and to connect effort with learning. (See Chapter 10) Allow time for oral compliments after lessons and activities. What do all these activities have in common? They help students forge working relationships with each other, teach them the skills they need to be successful in group work, and help them see the value of other students' contributions.

Positive Portfolios: *Almost everyone remembers negative things more strongly and in more detail.*[46] —A. Tugend

To help students remember their successes and positive moments, create a "positive portfolio" for each student. They can keep work showing their growth and success and positive notes they have received. Give students a weekly opportunity to look through their folders.

Students don't always SEE the progress they are making. To ensure that mine did, I got a milk crate and filled it with hanging folders, one for each student. Next to that crate I placed a basket. When I had samples of student work that I wanted to save, I put them in the basket. Sometime during the day, a student helper filed everything in the correct folders. Kids could also save work they were especially proud of by placing it in the basket. This small change made them much more likely to produce work that was "folder worthy." Every once in a while, I had students look through their portfolios and compare recent work with previous assignments. I wanted them to notice the differences and reflect on how much they had improved—and why.

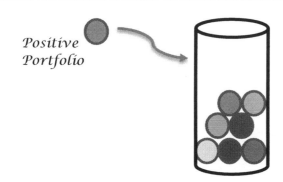

Positive Portfolio

Using Reward Systems

Why is community building superior to rewards systems? To answer that question, let's look at the variety of rewards systems teachers often use and some of the pitfalls we find in their implementation. Those systems might include:

- Class Points: Negative and positive tally marks for the whole class.

- Table Points: Groups of students earn points.

- Clip up and clip down systems: Children's names are on clothespins and they move up and down on a behavior continuum. Students are told to move their clip up or down— from Great Day (highest) to Call Parents (lowest). There can be up to 6 levels.

- Warning, or red cards (negative consequences) for individuals if problems occur.

- Class money or tokens: "Dollars" are distributed to students for good behavior which can be used later to buy items.

- School-wide tickets: Tickets given to students for a drawing held each week for prizes.

To understand the pitfalls of such systems, consider the use of Table Points, a popular behavior modification system used by many teachers. The purpose of table points is to help students feel good as they work together in groups, earning points toward a reward. Nothing wrong with that. But point systems can be tricky. How do you monitor **every** table group, **every** minute of the day while you are busy doing the myriad other things teachers must do?

Perched in the back of the classroom, one can easily observe things an instructor might miss, things that undermine the effectiveness of the system. Here's what I saw on one occasion in my classroom observations: One table group was off task every time the teacher looked away. As soon as he turned around, they were model students and subsequently earned quite a few points. What lesson did they learn? On another occasion, I saw a girl burst into tears. Her group had become quiet quickly when asked—but didn't earn a point. Again, what was the lesson for her, and what can we as teachers learn from this?

Behavior modification proponents say that for a system to work, the expected behavior must be very clear to students, the consequence (positive or negative) must be meaningful to them, and, most importantly, the reinforcement must be consistently and equitably applied throughout the day.[47] There must be a close relationship (time-wise) between the behavior and the reward or punishment. No small task in a classroom of 30 students!
Too often, this is what actually happens:

- Teachers, busy with instruction, assisting students, and answering questions, hand out rewards haphazardly. Some students who are meeting a behavioral standard receive a reward, and others don't. Sometimes kids who do not deserve a reward receive one.

- Students don't always know why they receive a reward. When asked, they might respond, *I was good.* But what does that mean? Are they making a real connection between the expected behavior and the reward?

- Well-behaved students most fear getting a red card, moving their clothespin down a behavior continuum, or being punished. But the more challenging students do not significantly modify their behavior, often due to inconsistent application of the system.

Behavior Modification for a Few

You may have a few students who struggle with behavior and would benefit from a reward system. Focusing on one or two students is manageable, and a little extrinsic motivation might nudge them in a more positive direction. Hopefully, as the year progresses and as the students mature, their need for rewards will wane. In the end, we want kids to be successful learners, intrinsically motivated, because it's the right thing to do and it benefits them.

Making Community Visible

An Alternative Point System

Use a point system **without** a tangible reward and start building intrinsic motivation. Tally up points for the whole class as you notice procedure adherence each day and celebrate how well everyone did. Keep point totals for each week and establish "class records." Here are a few examples of "point worthy" behaviors. Notice how in each case they are connected to their impact on learning:

- *All of you worked independently so my small group was able to spend the whole-time learning.*
- *You walked to the library silently so that other students were able to keep learning.*
- *All of you shared with your partner to clarify your thinking.[t]*

Deciding Whether to Use a Reward System

If you are considering a reward system for your classroom, but aren't sure whether to go forward, here is a strategy to help you decide. Imagine a behavioral continuum such as the one below, and mentally place each of your students on it. Where do the majority of kids fall on the continuum? The answer to this question will tell you whether your whole class or just a few students would benefit from a rewards system.

$$\longleftrightarrow$$

Extrinsic Motivation   Intrinsic Motivation

---

[t] Eliminate threat from point giving by avoiding statements such as: *If John had not run in the hall, you would have earned a point;* or *You came so close to earning a point for listening.*

If you decide to go forward, here are some questions to consider when choosing a system and evaluating its effectiveness:

- Does the system contribute to your vision of community?
- Are behavioral expectations clear to each student?
- Have students been involved in the creation/rationale of the system? Should they be involved?
- Is the system manageable?
- What is the student perception of the system?
- Is the connection between the reward (or punishment) and behavior crystal clear?
- Is the system getting the intended results? Is behavior changing?
- Is it working with the more challenging students?
- Are rewards and punishments dispensed equitably? Do students *perceive* the system as being equitable (fair)?

Primary Students

Students' beliefs about school and what it is all about begin with their first experiences. It is imperative to establish a learning community on day one, by teaching procedures and expected behaviors, connecting behavior and learning, and re-teaching and using private lessons when necessary. Let students know what they are learning and celebrate small successes. Students who are continually exposed to clear, expectations (that are taught), positive language, and opportunities to actively engage, do not need candy, stamps, stickers, and tokens.

Intermediate Students

In one classroom, a fifth-grade girl was very skeptical. She just didn't believe it when her teacher said, "I'm here for all students." This girl was even reluctant to shake her teacher's hand at the door in the morning. After two months of being immersed in community words and actions, though, she came around, surprising her teacher one day with a heartfelt side-hug. After that, she became one of the hardest working students in the class, coming in with a smile every day and getting her "side-hug."

If older students come into your classroom with the collaborative experiences described earlier, the old norm of an authoritarian teacher handing out positive and negative consequences will have already been replaced by the new norm of community. You can build on that and continue to empower students and connect their behavior to results.

But if students come into your classroom having experienced the old norm, you must start the process of transforming the community at the outset. There might be a tendency to rush to a reward system, but hold off. Do the hard work of community building, and save the reward systems for specific situations, if necessary.

Chapter 13 Key Points

Students' Roles

- ☐ Think about behaviors that benefit you and your classmates, changing your brains and brightening your futures.

- ☐ Think about the benefits and purposes of classroom procedures.

- ☐ Use positive language. Notice its effects on your peers.

- ☐ Notice how the good feeling that comes from learning is the best reward.

- ☐ Celebrate your classmates' successes and your own.

Teachers' Roles

There are many aspects of teaching and learning to consider before implementing a whole class reward system:

- ☐ Develop positive relationships with students—and give them opportunities to do the same with each other.

- ☐ Use positive language.

- ☐ Teach procedures.

- ☐ Celebrate success.

- ☐ Use active participation strategies: Students who are not engaged in a lesson—or not able to access the lesson or an assignment—are more likely to misbehave.

- ☐ Save the reward system for the few students who might really need one.

Section II: Engage the Community of Learners

Chapter 14: The Tired Trifecta

If you had the luxury to observe a good number of classrooms over the course of a school
year, what teaching strategies would you be most likely to see? I'd wager that you'd see a lot
of I.R.E., round robin reading, and worksheets. I call them the Tired Trifecta—strategies we
all experienced as students and that continue to be used far too often with today's students. In
some classrooms, these practices take up a majority of the school day. With an abundance of
alternative strategies at our disposal, are these three still worth the time spent on them? Let's
take a closer look, and you decide.

1. I.R.E.: Lecture/Call on Student Hands

When the Initiate, Respond, and Evaluate strategy (I.R.E.)[u] is used in the course of a lesson, the teacher intermittently asks questions, calls on students who have raised their hands, and evaluates responses.

The intent of *I.R.E.*: The teacher presents information, often through lecture, and students are expected to learn by listening. Occasionally, the instructor asks questions, and kids raise their hands to answer. Students are called upon one at a time, and the teacher comments on the accuracy of each answer as it is given.

The reality: This "conduit model" of teaching and learning has remained the instructional strategy of choice in schools for decades, if not centuries. It is based on the idea that in order to learn, all students need to do is listen and remember. There are several fallacies with this assumption. First, research on the efficacy of lecturing is mixed, much of it concluding that traditional lectures result in low levels of information retention.[48] Second, "the human brain is poor at nonstop attention. Working memory is active for preadolescents for about 5 to 10 minutes, for adolescents and adults for 10 to 20 minutes, after which the average person loses focus."[49] Neuroscience tells us that learners need time to process new information, and they can't do that if the teacher continues talking nonstop. Teachers "can either have their learners" attention or they can be making meaning, but never both at the same time."[50] Processing happens best, not with long stretches of passive listening, but with frequent breaks for active engagement. Such active learning not only enhances educational outcomes but results in chemical changes in the brain.[51]

What does all this mean in practice? We need to respect the age and attention span of our students by limiting "air time" when presenting new material. Just as important, we need to interject processing opportunities such as think time, partner sharing, written responses, etc. throughout our lessons so all students stay engaged, not just the ones with their hands up. Unfortunately, the traditional I.R.E. model does neither of these things.

---

[u] Also, referred to as I.R.F (Initiate—Respond—Feedback) or Triadic Dialogue.

2. Round Robin Reading

*Using round robin reading, I soon learned that many kids were actively participating only when it was their turn. While one student read, the others were taking a **brain break**. Having "read" only their portion of the text, they were not able to retell the story or answer questions!* —Third Grade Teacher

The intent: In a small reading group, each student gets a turn to practice reading aloud, while the teacher assesses strengths and weaknesses. The other students are following along and comprehending the text. In a whole group setting, round robin reading is a way to cover large amounts of content text (e.g., social studies). It is a brain-active strategy because all students are following along. The teacher can periodically check for understanding by pausing and asking questions.

The reality: Unfortunately, all the students are not following along. A few are reading ahead while others are mentally checked out. Some only pay attention to the text when it is their turn. In addition, students' stress levels can rise significantly as they await their turns, and this is true particularly for struggling readers. It is actually more difficult to comprehend text when it is read in small chunks by different readers with different styles and paces.

3. Worksheets

The intent: Students work on a paper and pencil task that is aligned with material presented in a lesson. The teacher reads the directions and models completion of some of the tasks. Often the worksheets come with purchased curriculum programs. By completing these tasks, students are developing a work ethic.

Worksheets can be used in any subject:

- Complete math problems & facts (math).
- Fill in the blanks (vocabulary/spelling).
- Answer questions (social studies or reading).
- Match pictures and sounds (phonics).
- Find words (word search—vocabulary/spelling).

I have seen whole lessons based on worksheets—students completing pages together as the teacher calls on volunteers to provide solutions to problems or questions. Answers are sometimes read aloud, displayed on a screen, or checked by the teacher and returned to students the next day. Students look at the worksheet corrections and revise answers, learning from their mistakes.

The reality: Thousands of dollars are spent each year on published workbooks and the reams of paper used to run off worksheets, but they are not without issues. Consider the following:

- Too often students *do not* connect their work to the academic target. Instead they think the point of the lesson is to complete the worksheet.

- I have seen adults working with students on worksheets—making sure all the answers are correct. The emphasis is not on knowing, understanding, or using the target concept or skills, but once again on finishing the worksheet.

- Students rarely reflect on corrected work, stuffing the pages in their backpacks, later throwing them away.

- Sometimes worksheet directions are so convoluted that the skill to be practiced gets lost.

- Often, all students are completing the same worksheet. Some finish in a few minutes, while others need additional time or help, perhaps staying in at recess to complete the task.

There are ways to use worksheets that make them more effective, and there are alternative paper and pencil tasks that require more thinking from students and give teachers better information about kids' levels of understanding. In Chapter 24, we consider the uses of and alternatives to worksheets in greater depth. Meanwhile the takeaway: worksheets have a place in the classroom, but they must be used strategically, not as routine busy work. There are plenty of other strategies in our toolbox, and just because textbooks provide worksheets, doesn't mean we have to use them all.

Alternatives to the Tired Trifecta

1. Processing time: Instead of lecturing to students for long periods of time, interrupted only by asking questions and calling on a few volunteers, limit teacher talk and give students frequent processing time by having them **share with a partner *first*.** When working with students or adults, if I ask a question and then ask for volunteers to provide answers, I do not see many hands go up. There is not much enthusiasm. In fact, there is a passive feeling tone. If I ask a question and then give participants a chance to share with partners, I get many more students eager to share their thinking because they have activated previous knowledge and organized their thoughts.

There are many strategies for getting kids involved and exercising their brains in a lesson, and when things work, it's a wonderful thing to see. Recently, I was in a fifth-grade classroom, watching a student present his solution to a math problem. When he was done, the rest of the students were given an opportunity to work in partnerships, trying to solve a new problem using the solution path their classmate had just presented. Afterwards, students were given the opportunity to ask questions of the original speaker. A spirited debate ensued about whether you always had to start on the right when using a subtraction algorithm. Where was the teacher? Seated in the corner with a smile on her face. How did she elicit this level of math conversation? She was willing to step out of the spotlight, let students grapple with a concept, and not stop the thinking by giving away answers. It also came about because of her patience and clear expectations.

As teachers, our job is to set up lessons so that students have multiple opportunities to verbalize, write, share, and clarify their own thinking. This is based on the concept of **constructivism**: no matter how many times you explain something (or how loudly or dramatically), there is no guarantee that kids will understand. They have to construct their **own** meaning.

2. 100% participation: With all its drawbacks, why is the round robin protocol still used in so many classrooms? And for what purpose? After all, when adults read newspapers, novels, or take tests, with few exceptions, they don't take turns reading aloud. They read silently. For starters, we could let proficient readers read silently and provide them with checks for understanding. When we do need to support students' reading skills or provide assistance with challenging content area texts, we can choose from many viable alternatives to round robin reading. Unquestionably, there is a place for reading out loud in the classroom—it's an important assessment tool for teachers, and it gives kids a chance to practice and hone their reading skills. Done right, it keeps them actively engaged. The trick is to choose the best strategies to accomplish those goals. The following is a menu of options proven highly effective for doing just that. Some can be implemented with the whole class, while others are better used one on one or with partners.

- **Assessment**: Reading out loud is best used as an assessment tool by teachers, particularly for primary students. The teacher listens to individual students one on one, checking their fluency and helping with decoding skills and/or comprehension.

- **Cloze reading**: The teacher reads out loud, pausing at times for students to fill in a word. (Requires 100% participation).

- **Choral read**: Everyone reads together out loud, at a pace set by the teacher.

- **Partner read**: Two students take turns reading a designated amount (e.g., a paragraph). At the end of each page, they restate their understanding of the text.

- **Assisted reading rehearsal**: The student reads a passage several times out loud to an audience—an adult volunteer, an older student, a classmate, even a stuffed animal! The goal is to build confidence and increase fluency.

- **Individual reading rehearsal**: Students read quietly into "whisper phones." These are commercially available, or you can make your own with a piece of PVC pipe and a PVC elbow at either end. Using their "phones," many students can practice reading aloud at the same time.

- **Teacher read aloud**: The teacher models a reading pace and from time to time, uses self-talk to explain what she is thinking while she reads. This is also an opportunity to incorporate other reading targets: discussing characters, setting, or plot, for example. After modeling several times, teachers can invite students to do the same with partners.

Why are these strategies superior to round robin reading? Because they require overt participation by students and include targeted instruction. To make literacy time really count, we have to keep kids actively involved and provide a mix of targeted strategies that keep things interesting. Reading class is for building better readers, not time for kids to be taking brain breaks!

Round Robin Reading in Content Areas

Teachers often choose to cover social studies or science material by having students take turns reading paragraphs or pages out loud. This is a sure way to kill any enthusiasm for these subjects. Content area reading is very vocabulary and schema dependent—think about a fifth grader's understanding of the American Revolution versus that of someone who has read several books on the subject. There is no comparison! Moreover, social studies texts often cover big ideas and events in just a few pages, summarizing content that requires a lot of previous knowledge.

Before you launch a unit, it is important to decide what you want students to know or understand about a historical event or scientific point. What exactly are your targets? Then introduce needed vocabulary and help kids build schema with read alouds, video clips, science experiments, and other experiences. When you determine that students are ready to read the texts, use some of the techniques described above.

3. __The un-worksheet__

Here's a simple but versatile strategy that can be used again and again across the curriculum. It starts with paper folding and saves reams of worksheet copies. Have students fold a blank piece of paper into 4 or 8 sections. This gives them separate spaces to solve problems, answer questions, or show their understanding of concepts or vocabulary. Here's how it can be used:

Math:

- Instead of students completing a whole page of problems, they can make up four of their own that meet certain criteria—2-digit addition that requires one act of regrouping, for example, or story problems using multiplication. Creating their own problems requires kids to use a higher level of thinking. They can solve the problems themselves or switch papers with another student. When they discuss their work in partnerships, it challenges them to clarify their thinking even more.

Phonics:

- In each space, students can draw pictures that represent a sound or word family they are studying. For example, they might draw things in each space that begin with the letter b—*ball, bean, bun,* etc., or draw pictures of things in a word family, such as *cat, mat, bat,* etc., labeling each.

Social Studies/Science:

- Students can show the sequence of events in an historical period, sketch the life cycle of an animal they are studying, or illustrate subject specific terms.

Reading:

- Kids can show the sequence of events from a story, show cause and effect, or illustrate new vocabulary words. Using folded paper helps with differentiating tasks. Even when students are reading different books, they can use this method.

Chapter 14 Key Points

Students' Roles

☐ Use processing time to think of a response to a question or to check your understanding with a partner.

☐ Anytime your teacher gives you an opportunity to participate, take it!

☐ Use assignments to practice and check if you understand the target.

Teachers' Roles

☐ Choose instructional strategies that cause all students to think and participate.

☐ Give students time to process their thinking individually or by sharing with a partner.

☐ Check to make sure 100% of the students are using active participation strategies.

☐ Consider the purpose of assignments—and how well they align to the target.

NOTES

Chapter 15: Engage Students

Often, focus is on the lesson and not the students. Kids are seen as either compliant enough so that the lesson proceeds or they are obstacles to completion of the lesson.   —G. Peterson

Until now, we have been focusing on community—building relationships, and teaching procedures—preparing the groundwork for learning. In this section, we'll examine a second crucial element for student success—instruction. Which instructional strategies get students actively involved, and which shut down learning? Not surprisingly, the level of student engagement in a classroom is powerfully influenced by the strategies a teacher employs. To illustrate this point, consider the following two scenarios. The students are first-year teachers gathered in the library for professional development, and while the lesson targets are identical, the teaching strategies employed are markedly different.

Scenario One

Instructor: *Take about 10 minutes and read the article in front of you.*[v]

Teachers began reading. Some began to chat.

Instructor: *This is an independent activity. Please read without any conversation.*

After 10 minutes: *OK, stop reading. Who can tell me what one dimension of student engagement is?* (Immediately called on a teacher).

Teacher1: *Um, um. Relationships?*

Instructor: *Who can elaborate on that? You?* (Pointed to another teacher.)

Teacher 2 began to look at paper.

Instructor: *Just tell me. You don't need to look at the paper.*

Teacher 2: *Students feel you care about them?*

Instructor: *Right. So, what is another dimension?* (Immediately called on a third teacher who had raised her hand.)

Teacher 3: *Relevance. Is this learning significant outside of my school?*

Instructor: *The answer is actually authenticity. Someone else?* (Immediately called on a fourth teacher).

---

[v] Washor, Elliott & Mojkowski, Charles. "Student Disengagement: It's Deeper Than You Think." *Phi Delta Kappan*, May 2014. Vol. 95, #8, p. 8-10.

I was the instructor that day, giving teachers a taste of the kind of teaching that stifles engagement. As soon as I began calling on them (without wait time), I could feel the tension in the room rise. Teachers became noticeably uncomfortable. They avoided eye contact, and gave responses that were hesitant and guarded. In our debriefing afterward, teachers also said:

- *I didn't want to be called on.*

- *I wondered, "What is going on?"*

- *I wanted this to end.*

- *I didn't know why I was reading this article.*

Sounds a lot more like fear than engagement, doesn't it? Sadly, the strategies demonstrated here are common, and their unfortunate effect is to suppress, not foster thinking. I wanted to give teachers a visceral understanding of why the instructional model in scenario one was counterproductive.

Then I taught the lesson again, this time using the strategies advocated in this book:

Scenario Two

Instructor: *Let's do some thinking about student engagement and how students are feeling in a lesson. What might they be thinking? What would help them stay engaged? Those are the targets for this session. Read the article in front of you and choose three dimensions of student engagement that you think are important. You will be sharing your choices with a partner.*

Teachers began to read, highlighting, and making notes on the article. After about 10 minutes, I gave them a protocol to use during their partner sharing time:

- Partner 1 shares one choice.

- Partner 2 responds.

- Partner 2 shares one choice.

- Partner 1 responds.

This cycle was repeated 3 times.

Afterward, there was whole group sharing. *Did anyone have an "aha" during their sharing time?* Teachers stood to share their thoughts. Occasionally, I asked them to respond to one of the whole group comments with their partner. Other teachers asked questions of the speaker. At the conclusion of the lesson, we debriefed once again. This time I heard:

- *I was focused on the article and the topic of engagement.*

- *By sharing with my partner, I was able to clarify and deepen my thinking.*

- *I was not tense this time around, and I felt comfortable sharing my thinking.*

- *I got some good feedback from my partner.*

The results were clear. Compared with the first scenario, the second take on the lesson resulted in dramatically more engagement, and the level of thinking that occurred was infinitely richer because teachers had the freedom to explore ideas without judgment. Clearly the instructional strategies that we use in the classroom matter.

What Is the Evidence That Students Are Engaged?

One study found that one in six students were bored in every single class, and almost half experienced boredom and disengagement every day. Students reported that they were in a state of apathy for more than 25 percent of the day.[52]   —E. Jensen.

How can teachers determine if students are actively learning and not just quietly conforming? Equally important, how can students themselves recognize when they are engaged? Engagement is something that is fostered by the teaching strategies we use, as demonstrated in the previous scenario. But it is also something that can be taught. First, we need to be clear what it looks like and sounds like, using a list of indicators such as the following. Engaged students:

- have their heads up, looking at whomever is speaking.

- share with partners on cue.

- ask clarifying questions.

- respond to questions.

- display some emotion—e.g., they smile, appear genuinely interested, puzzled, or perhaps confused.

- read and take notes.

- use non-verbal signals.

There is an absence of off-topic chatter, aimless roaming around the classroom, heads on desks, and students not participating. How do we get there? Let's take a look at two factors that vastly increase student participation: teaching kids how to be engaged and intentionally providing active learning opportunities.

Engagement from the Student's Perspective

"Keep quiet, behave, listen, and then react to my factual closed questions when I ask you." Interaction means: "Tell me what I have just said so that I can check that you were listening, and then I can continue talking"[53]   —J. Hattie

Kids don't automatically know what it means to be engaged—because they are used to "keeping quiet and listening to the teacher." They need to be taught—too often a rare occurrence. Statements such as, *You guys are having an off day,* or *You're not paying attention,* don't help. Here is a better way:

1. Discuss the idea of engagement and give examples. Get specific about what it looks like and sounds like.
2. Have students give examples, too.
3. Connect engagement to its effects on the brain and the benefits for them.
4. Discuss the benefits of engagement for the whole community of learners.
5. During the day, have kids share a time when they realized they were engaged!
6. Create a non-verbal signal for students to use when they realize they are engaged.
7. Develop criteria for different levels of engagement.
8. Connect evidence of engagement to students' accomplishments when you debrief a lesson.

Another way for students to internalize the message of engagement is through positive statements. Kids can read or chant together phrases such as:

- I know what I am supposed to learn.
- I am engaged.
- I know the purpose of work.
- I listen to learn.
- I use think time to create a response.
- I know by sharing, I will clarify my thinking.

- I want feedback from others.

- I want to add to my schema.

- I know my level of understanding.

- I want to help everyone understand.

- I am not afraid to share my disequilibrium.

- I try to capture the thinking of others.

- I want to know what questions I need to ask.

- I persist and work through disequilibrium.

When lots of discussion, modeling, and practice have occurred, students will be ready to develop criteria that describe various levels of engagement. Here is an example created by one group of students and their teacher:

EVIDENCE OF ENGAGEMENT	
Level 1 Celebrate	I am giving my full attention.
	I am committed to growing my brain.
	I embrace challenge.
	I do not need reminders to remain engaged.
	I use non-verbal signals to show my thinking.
Level 2 Practice	I am following the teacher's directions.
	I am committed to finishing.
	I sometimes freeze when I feel challenged.
	I may need an occasional reminder.
	I use non-verbal signals some of the time.
Level 3 More Teaching	I am having trouble staying engaged.
	I am committed to the bare minimum.
	I quit when I feel challenged.
	I need frequent reminders.
	I rarely use non-verbal signals.

This same teacher spends time discussing what is going on in his students' brains when they are actively participating, and he wants to increase kids' awareness of their levels of engagement. His students are discovering how important it is to be actively involved. If a few students are off task, he speaks to them privately, reinforcing the benefits of engagement.

Maximize Your Turns

Getting Students Actively Engaged: Taking Their Turns[w]

Students seem to come to school to watch teachers work. — J. Hattie

Imagine that all your students have light bulbs on the top of their heads. When their brains are thinking, the light bulbs turn on. We know that those light bulbs are more likely to be lit if students are emotionally OK and feel a part of the classroom community. At the same time, it is our job to make sure we give students opportunities throughout the day to think, and they take advantage of those chances.

Opportunities to think can be called "**TURNS**"—and we want students to take as many turns as possible each day. You might ask them to echo or choral read, share with a partner, discuss an idea as a group or write their thinking in a journal. In each case, your students are taking **TURNS**, or opportunities, to engage. If some are reluctant, talk to them about the benefits of cognitive activity: their brain gets smarter, constructs more scaffolding, and makes more connections.

When these thinking **TURNS** are happening, students should look and sound like they are engaged. From the back of the room, watch your students as they work independently, with partners, or in small groups. Are those bulbs lighting up? Students' body language is evidence of a commitment to learning. Which way are knees pointed? Knees, facial expressions, hands, and eyes all tell a tale. In the whole group, if students are seated in groups or at round tables, have them turn their chairs to face the speaker. Teach them to automatically change body and eye position when the speaker moves or another person begins

---

[w] Chapters 15 through 19 have detailed discussions about partner sharing, student speaker and audience responsibilities, and whole group active engagement strategies.

talking from a new location. Model and practice until it becomes second nature and periodically review throughout the year.

When students are on the carpet, make sure each one has his own space. It's hard for kids to take turns when they are hiding in a corner or crouching under a desk. Students should be facing the direction of the speaker. By listening to each other and processing ideas, kid are taking turns and switching on their light bulbs.

In partnerships, everyone needs to have a partner! Unless the classroom community has evolved to the point where students make sure, on their own, that no one lacks a partner, assign them. Students are eye-to-eye, knee-to-knee (even in chairs). They should speak in courteous tones and listen to each other. In small groups, students are leaning in, using a normal voice volume. One person speaks at a time, and interruptions occur politely.

Being picky pays off. Chances are, if students look and sound like productive and cooperative learners, they are. In the process, they will learn what it **feels** like to be engaged. All this takes lots of modeling and practice, but the payoff is big.

Primary Students

Some of my happiest, most rewarding moments as an educator have been hearing what comes out of learners' mouths when I get out of the way.[54] —E. City

Even very young children can have discussions about the brain, engagement, and learning. When students are interested in a learning target, engagement happens naturally, and kids experience what true focus feels like. It's tricky in the classroom, though, because not all targets are interesting to all students. So how do you keep them engaged?

Lessons presented to younger students should be brief—the attention span of a typical five-year-old is only about five minutes. Despite this, many teachers talk to kids much longer. There is a lot of material to cover, after all. Unfortunately, longer isn't better, and if kids start to mentally check out, the additional instruction time is wasted. This is where short focused presentations and active participation strategies can help:

- Think in terms of 5-minute time limits for continuous presentation of information (teacher talk) before giving processing time.

- Allow for think time: Give students frequent processing time. *Students need to hear the information, process it, and provide a response. Actively providing at least four to five seconds of think time is an essential component of lesson planning.*[55]

- Give students time to verbalize their thinking with partners.

- Intersperse movement, hand motions, singing or music into a lesson. You can use old stand-bys like *Simon Says* or calisthenics. The key is to plan ahead. Be ready when kids get the wiggles!

- Make sure concepts are broken down into manageable steps for students. By listening to their responses and gauging their level of engagement you will know if they are able to access the lesson.

Initially, your goal is to focus on *evidence* of student engagement and understanding—and worry less about covering the material. A major job for teachers is planning and assessment, with a big emphasis on the planning part. Decide ahead of time which active participation techniques you are going to use and write yourself reminders. Eventually, they will become second nature. The lessons are the fun part—observing and listening to students to see what they have to say, which is an indication of their level of understanding.

Intermediate Students

Teachers talk between 70 and 80% of class time on average. Teachers talking increases as the year level rises and class size decreases.[56] — J. Hattie

Long, droning lectures get a bum rap, and rightfully so, but teacher talk is not inherently bad. For the most part, teachers are presenting information that students need to know. The 'aha' I had early on was that when I talked to my students for extended periods, I was focusing on *my* understanding and *my* grasp of the material, not theirs. In my teacher-centered classroom, I was getting better every year at understanding the material and explaining it. I was engaged and working hard, but what about my students? Over time, I began to realize that the real measure of effective instruction was not how much time **I** was spending on the material—it was how much time my **students** were engaged.

So, I learned to include lots of "**TURNS**" and processing time. I had students partner share, and taught them how to have class discussions not just with me, but also with each other. We also developed non-verbal signals to show our responses. In short, I began to focus on *their* understanding, not mine.

Intermediate students are ready to think about engagement in greater depth than younger students, and their discussions will be richer. Consider some of the following strategies to facilitate their thinking:

- Discuss with students what "processing time" is. Why is it important? What is their responsibility when you give them processing time? How does this help them get smarter?

- Let them know the forms of processing time:
    - Think (or wait) time
    - Sharing with a partner
    - Writing or drawing their thoughts

- Give students reflection time to think about their level of engagement during whole group lessons, partner shares, or independent assignments. Have them share evidence verbally or in written form.

- Talk about factors that might make it more difficult to be engaged—and how those challenges can be overcome.

- Develop a *Levels of Engagement* chart. Sure, you can use the one shown earlier in the chapter, but kids do more thinking when they develop their own. Once you have the chart, there are multiple uses for the information it conveys. For example, you can look for evidence of students operating at a certain level. Without using specific names, tell students what you noticed. For example, *I noticed students*
    - *asking each other questions.*
    - *turning intently toward their partner and trying to solve a problem.*
    - *being so engaged they did not realize it was time for recess!*

- Continue adding descriptors to the engagement chart throughout the year.

- <u>Connect engagement to accomplishment.</u> Don't assume that students who are engaged understand how strongly their commitment to learning is leading to their success. Point it out and see the power of reinforcing their hard work. Likewise, students who are not successful may not realize that a lack of engagement may be the cause. Take the opportunity to conference with those students privately, in a nonjudgmental way, making the connection and getting them back on track.

- <u>Make time for private lessons.</u> If a student is having difficulty staying engaged, have a <u>private discussion</u>. By keeping the conversation private, you are demonstrating that you care about the student, and in the process, you may also determine the cause of the disengagement. Often the student is having difficulty understanding—important information for you to know and address.

Levels of engagement will fluctuate, based on a number of factors, but many of them are under our control. Keep in mind the following components of good instruction, and the likelihood of student engagement will markedly increase:

- A clear target that is accessible by students.
- The pace of the lesson—concepts and skills presented in chunks.
- Lesson design—planning that includes visual, oral, and kinesthetic modes for variety, processing time formats that have been taught, movement breaks, and checks for understanding (teacher and students).

Desk Configuration and Student Engagement

Of the many factors affecting student engagement, one obvious one, the direction kids face, is often overlooked. Picture this: a teacher is at the front of the classroom giving background information as part of a lesson. Many students are focusing on her, but some are looking out the window, at other kids, or entertaining themselves with engaging activities such as rotating rulers on pencils (helicopters), tearing paper, reaching into their desks, etc. Which students are more likely to be learning something in this lesson? The answer is obvious. When students **look** like they are engaged, they are much more likely to **be** engaged.

You can teach students how by introducing the procedure:

1. Turn toward the speaker.

2. Give eye contact

To understand the value of this procedure, consider the situation created by desk configurations seen in many classrooms. In the following diagram, arrows show the direction students are facing when seated in commonly used rectangular or circular table groups. It's hard to teach a whole group lesson when students are facing so many different directions. If kids in the front or on the side do try to focus on the teacher, they will feel stress building in their neck muscles, or give up and face their partner instead. I call this the **dining room formation**, because it feels like students are eating together and conversation is permitted. It's a social, collaborative formation, and the focus is on other students, not a whole group lesson.

Teacher at front of the classroom

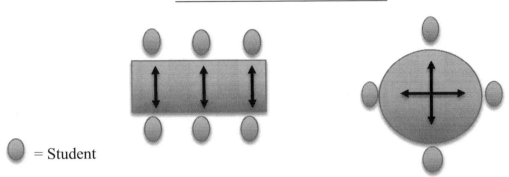

= Student

With one crucial change, the same desk configuration can work for whole group lessons, partner sharing, or small group conversations. In the case of whole group lessons, students simply turn their chairs so they are facing the teacher. I call this **audience style**. When we go to the movies, we do not sit facing the left or right side of the theater. We face front. By turning their chairs, students set themselves up to focus on the lesson, and no one gets a stiff neck!

<u>Teacher at front the classroom</u>

(Audience style for whole group lessons: Chairs face speaker)

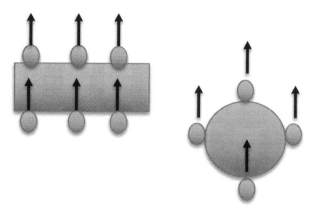

When students partner share, they turn their bodies or quickly move chairs so they are facing their elbow partner or the person across from them. In small group work, the direction students turn depends on the sharing protocol being used. (More on this in Chapter 19.)

If, instead of tables, students have individual desks, the same flexibility can be achieved. Simply teach kids to move their desks to match the intended activity. Keep desks separate for independent work and whole group lessons:

Push them together for partner work:

Push more desks together for small group work:

With a bit of practice, students can learn to quickly transition to the configuration required.

Of course, not every situation requires moving desks or chairs. Sometimes students need only pivot in their seats in order to face whomever is speaking, for example during class discussions. Regardless of the activity, when kids face the speaker and give eye contact, it helps them get dialed in. Remember, when students **look** like they are engaged, they are much more likely to **be** engaged.

NOTES

Evidence of Classroom Engagement Levels

Most teachers were themselves taught in classrooms with little opportunity for engagement, a reason why so many of us fall back into the old instructional model. It's our comfort zone. But classroom instruction can be so much more. Look at the following descriptions to see what different levels of classroom engagement look like.

LEAST EFFECTIVE INSTRUCTION

- The teacher asks questions and calls on one student at a time.

- He/she immediately judges the correctness of responses.

- Students are given little or no wait/think time after a question.

MORE EFFECTIVE INSTRUCTION

- The teacher follows questions with wait time.

- Students have some opportunities to share at tables and with partners, but they could be given more.

- Kids are called on randomly. (...using a random generator or pulling sticks with student names out of a cup).

- Teacher and students use signals and sign to show thinking.

- Students respond chorally.

MOST EFFECTIVE INSTRUCTION

- Students stand and speak to the <u>class</u>, not just the teacher.

- Kids respond to each other's thinking and conduct discussions <u>without</u> the teacher.

- The teacher refers student answers or questions back to the class: *Talk to your partner about Maria's answer.*

- Students share in small groups using protocols. For example, each one might have 90 seconds to share his or her solution to a problem, followed by a general discussion.

- Students use signals. (For example, *I agree with you, I can't hear, Please repeat,* etc.)

- Listeners and speakers understand that they have responsibilities. (See Chapter 16)

Chapter 15 Key Points

Students' Roles

- ☐ Define engagement in your own words and give evidence of high and low focus.
- ☐ Determine your level of engagement using a class-developed rubric.
- ☐ Maximize your **"TURNS"**—using every opportunity to engage in a lesson.
- ☐ Connect your successes to engagement.
- ☐ Let the teacher know when you are in disequilibrium by asking for more think time, processing time, or more explanation.

Teachers' Roles

- ☐ Discuss the concept of engagement, its benefits, and link it to the brain.
- ☐ Plan carefully: think about limiting teacher talk and giving students plenty of processing time.
- ☐ Develop criteria for judging levels of engagement.
- ☐ Give students multiple opportunities to actively engage in a variety of ways during a lesson.
- ☐ Teach kids to ask for more think time or more time to process information when they need it.
- ☐ Use different desk formations or audience styles appropriate to where students should be attending.

Engagement: Take your TURNS!

Chapter 16: Listen and Capture Thinking

Students must be just as interested in capturing other's thinking as in sharing their own.
—G. Peterson

Research tells us that students derive significant benefit by participating in class discussions. When they hear diverse points of view and consider multiple solution paths to problems, they expand and clarify their understanding. But if kids can't hear each other, or worse, are not even listening, the best sharing in the world is nothing but a wasted opportunity. In this chapter, we tackle some of the stumbling blocks to effective class discussions and consider ways to address them.

What problems commonly arise when students speak to the whole group?

- No one can hear them.

- They mumble or speak at a low volume.

- There is an assumption that students are just talking to the teacher.

- Kids stay seated. It is hard to tell who is speaking.

- The audience disengages (heads on desks).

- Students react negatively to the speaker (do not differentiate between the "idea" being presented and the 'person' expressing it).

- No one asks questions or requests clarifications.

- It's like blank air-time (blah, blah, blah).

- Some explanations are too long and circuitous.

- Certain students' responses become more valued.

What are some keys to getting students to really listen to each other?

It's important to establish at the outset that students' ideas have value—not just for you, but also for the whole class. Start by developing a rationale for students listening to each other.

- *You may be able to add to your schema.*

- *You may hear something you never thought about—and have a question.*

- *It is a way of showing (actuating) the idea of respect.*

Discuss, model, and practice the "what it looks like, sounds like, and feels like" when that happens. Once you've established the groundwork, expect students to listen to each other. Tell them their job is to capture each other's thinking. You can pretend to grab an idea and pull it toward your heart to make the idea more concrete. At the end of a math lesson, a second grader, with a big grin, once told me, *I captured everyone's thinking!* Finally, reinforce the concept: debrief often at the end of sessions, celebrating behaviors that supported learning. *How many of you were able to capture someone's thinking? How did that help you learn more?*

Creating the conditions for vibrant class discussions involves a few changes in teacher behavior, too. Resist the urge to respond immediately after students share. If you respond, why should they? Let kids know you will avoid giving cues, spoken or unspoken, on the correctness/incorrectness of their ideas—you are leaving that for them to weigh and discuss. Encourage students to call on each other and grapple with ideas together. Then stand back and be amazed at the depth of their thinking.

Procedures and Mindsets to Help Students Listen to Each Other

Here are a few considerations to keep in mind as you teach your students how to listen to each other:

1. Teach students to **stand** and face the majority of the audience.[x] The class must be able to see and hear the speaker. Its sends an unspoken and important message: *My thoughts are part of a conversation with the whole class, not just the teacher.* Members of the audience should show the speaker they are listening by turning toward him or her.

2. When someone is speaking, students must refrain from raising their hand—*and instead focus on capturing the thinking.*

3. Speakers will, over time, improve the clarity and volume of their explanations. That doesn't mean nagging quiet students to speak up, but reinforcing instances where students *can* be heard. As students gain confidence, their volume will increase.

---

[x] Some teachers have students get up on their knees when it is their turn to speak on the carpet. The point is for students to know clearly who the speaker is.

4. Use practices that give kids opportunities to think about other students' understanding. You can:

1. Wait after a student response, giving everyone a chance to process what was just said. (Essentially a second wait time.)

2. Have partners restate the thinking of the speaker to each other.

3. Select a student randomly to restate the thinking. The presenter then OK's the restatement as being on target or has a chance to clarify their ideas.

4. Avoid repeating what a student says. *Why should kids listen if the teacher repeats everything?*

5. Refer student answers back to the class, and ask them what they think.

6. Give students opportunities to:

   - Ask questions of each other.

   - Write in their journals, restating another's thinking or trying to solve a new problem using a presenter's solution path.

   - Share in table groups, using small group protocols.

   - Use nonverbal signals after a speaker shares, indicating they processed the information. (For example, showing that they agree, disagree, can't hear, or need something repeated).

All this takes time to teach and weeks of consistent practice. But if you are having students talk to each other, they need to learn how to make that time really worthwhile. The result is a rich conversation that deepens student understanding and reinforces the bonds of your classroom community. The following charts may be useful while you are teaching procedures initially or revisiting them periodically.

<u>**Primary Students**</u>

<u>**Responsibilities of the Speaker and Listener**</u>

The speaker will:

- Stand to talk, facing the audience.

- Talk loudly enough for all to hear.

- Try to be clear.

The listener will:

- Look at the speaker.

- Be ready to share with a partner what the speaker said.

- Think of questions.

<u>**Intermediate Students**</u>

<u>**Responsibilities of the Speaker and Listener**</u>

The speaker will:

- Stand to talk, facing the audience.

- Talk loudly enough for all to hear.

- Try to be clear and succinct.

The listener will:

- Focus on the speaker.

- Process what the speaker is saying.

- Formulate questions.

- Be ready to paraphrase what the speaker said.

<u>**Teachers' Roles**</u>

In a typical classroom, what happens when students answer questions? Everyone looks at the teacher to see if the response given is correct, right? But must the teacher be the only judge? Share the role, and you will nudge students to stop being passive audience members, to listen more closely to one other, and to start developing evaluative skills of their own. That's not something you can accomplish in a business as usual classroom. If you want to give high

148

priority to students listening to each other and engaging in constructive class discussions, you may have to break some habits. Here are the worst offenders:

- Asking questions and calling on the first raised hand.

- Telling students right away whether a response is the one you are looking for, or if an answer to a problem is correct.

- Giving **nonverbal** reactions—a smile, a frown, etc., to student responses. Kids will either relax (*The answer was right!*) and stop trying to puzzle things out or get ready to raise their hands with a different answer (*The answer was wrong!).*

- Repeating student responses.

- Not giving kids enough time to process or capture the thinking of their peers.

- Assuming the rest of the class is following the discussion.

Using the techniques presented in this book, you will avoid most of these pitfalls.

This is not to say that you never respond to students in class discussions. There are those who argue that teachers should always correct students or respond immediately in some way. True, sometimes you should. But how do you decide? A teacher's judgment is crucial here. When a student responds, you have three questions to answer in a split second:

- Does this response push the conversation in the planned direction? If so, you can continue, using wait time, partner sharing, non-verbal responses, and other inclusive strategies.

- Is the response letting the teacher know that some students do not understand the target? Time to step back and adjust!

- Should I pose a different question (or problem) to redirect the conversation?

All this takes a lot of skill on the part of the teacher. It requires careful listening to student responses, and a willingness to adjust when things are going in the wrong direction.

Empower Students

Listening to others is a skill that begins in kindergarten. It starts with students standing to share with the whole group, facing their audience, and it is fostered by teachers who expect students to respect each other's thinking. Kids quickly learn whether their comments are valued in the learning community.

- Young students must first be expected to give attention to their peers' responses. As time goes on, and with teacher guidance, they can learn to think about their peers' responses instead of just their own.

- As kids get older, they can be expected to think about a peer response and react to it—agreeing, disagreeing (with evidence), paraphrasing, elaborating, or questioning.

When students are just as interested in capturing the thinking of others as they are in their own thinking, they will be adding more "building material" to their schema.

Chapter 16 Key Points

Students' Roles

☐ Remember that the teacher and other students are providing building materials that can help you construct your understanding of a target.

☐ Stand to share your response.

☐ Listen and process what your classmates are saying.

☐ Ask for time to clarify fragile understanding with a partner.

☐ Ask a student to repeat their response if you did not hear it.

Teachers' Roles

☐ Teach students the responsibilities of the speaker and audience. Discuss, model, and practice their roles.

☐ Avoid behaviors and responses that shut down thinking.

☐ Teach students to stand when responding.

☐ Give students opportunities to respond to each other's thinking.

NOTES

Hidden Steps: Listen and Capture Thinking

The issue: *When I ask students what a classmate just said, most of the time they respond with "I don't know," or "I couldn't hear."*   — Intermediate Teacher

In my long career in education, I've heard the same complaint from teachers every year — kids talk too much!   I would argue that kids don't talk enough…about their learning. Let's channel that talking energy into discussions that get them grappling with ideas and stretching their thinking. The first, and easiest step, is to have kids stand up when they share with the whole group. If you, the teacher, are sitting down, it focuses even more attention on the student speaking. Teach kids to turn and look at the speaker, use signs to show whether they agree or disagree, and with a partner, share their thinking about what was just said. Give students reasons to listen to each other, and connect the benefits to their own brain and learning. Here are the hidden steps that make this strategy successful:

- Build community so that students know and care for each other.
- Develop a visual for learning or adding to schema.
- Let students know that their job is to capture others' thinking to add to their schema.
- Teach students to stand when sharing.
- Teach them to give the speaker their attention.
- Give students turns to signal or share their responses verbally when they hear others share.
- Connect the benefits of these procedures to student success.

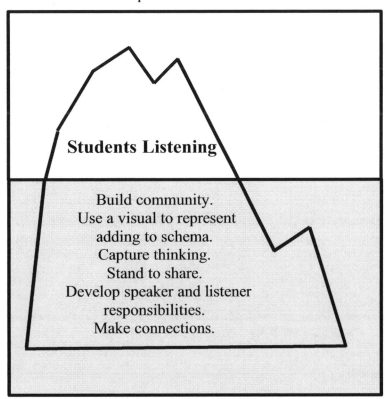

Chapter 17: Engage Whole Groups:
Active Participation Techniques

Putting Students in the Spotlight

At the end of the day, when the kids leave, the buses pull away, and the after-school activities finish, the classroom is a peaceful place. As a teacher, I spent that time preparing for the next day and mulling over how things went. It gave me an opportunity to feel good about things that worked, plan next steps, and come up with ways to tackle any issues that had come up. But it was also a time to look at the big picture. And it was during these reflections that I came to an important but uncomfortable realization—one that ultimately changed the way I taught: I was doing a lot of talking **at** my students, reinforcing **my** own thinking and learning. But who was doing most of the work? Who was doing most of the thinking?

I began to wonder, is school just a place where kids go to watch teachers work? How could I get my students more involved, put **them** in the driver's seat when it came to learning? Eventually, I discovered things that really worked, and that's what this book is about.

A Visual for Building Understanding

My definition of a good teacher has since changed from "one who explains things so well that students understand" to "one who gets students to explain things so well that they can be understood.[57] —S.C. Reinhart

The fun part about teaching is seeing and hearing what students are thinking and what they understand. Be curious about how they are translating your words, the activities, and feedback into early notions of the target.

I like to tell kids their brains are like construction zones. As they grapple with new concepts, their brains are busily trying to construct meaning. They start with what they know and build on that, erecting pieces of mental scaffolding in the process. This scaffolding provides nascent support for new thinking, and new scaffolding is added every time students use think time, process what the teacher and other students say, share with partners, get feedback, focus on learning activities, ask questions when confused, and are otherwise actively involved.

Some of the scaffolding will be tenuously placed, moved elsewhere, or even discarded as thinking evolves. Some of the scaffolding will provide connections to other construction sites within the brain as students connect new learning to other things they are studying. But in every case, the work of learning builds smarter, more resilient thinking. That's why it is so important to get kids involved in lessons. When they are actively participating, they are also building their brain.

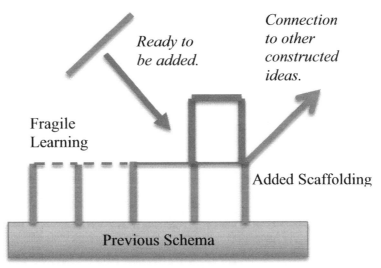

Planning the Lesson:

Kids need to get their thinking out of their heads to see how it sounds and if it makes sense.
—G. Peterson

Lesson planning involves more than determining the schedule for each subject, the pages of a text to be covered, and a worksheet to be completed. It includes a game plan to get students engaged. As you plan lessons, consider when students might need think time, processing time, and formative assessment. If this is a new way of thinking, pick a subject and start planning with these questions in mind:

- When in the lesson will students need processing time?
- Which active participation techniques will most help them engage and learn?
- At what point might students need a short break?
- How can I determine if kids are getting the target?

154

Think or Wait Time

Brain research tells us that students cannot pay attention to the "sage on the stage" for great lengths of time. Remember, while you are talking—you are moving around and speaking about subjects on which you have volumes of schema. Meanwhile, students are expected to sit still and construct understanding of unfamiliar concepts. They are, in fact, using more cognitive energy than you are. Doesn't it make more sense to get kids involved? When you are teaching, pause every few minutes, and allow students to connect, process, and be actively involved.

Giving them enough time to think after a question is an important first step in establishing active participation. The average time that teachers wait before calling on students is a surprising 0.7 to 1.4 seconds![58] That's not much time for kids to gather their thoughts! Extend the wait time to 5-10 seconds, so more students have time to retrieve information or synthesize a response.

Second Wait Time

When you do call on a student, what happens after they respond? A lot of kids give *you* that *Did-I-get-it-right?* look. They are scrutinizing your face and waiting for your response. What's happening with the rest of the class in the meantime? Do they care? Are they weighing the correctness of the answer or waiting for you to do it for them? It's tempting to respond, but if you pass judgment on an answer, no one else has to think.

A better response is to say nothing at all and let the answer hang there in space. Give it some wait time and silently count to ten if you have to. Let students ponder, and let them decide together on its correctness. A wrong answer can be the springboard for an interesting discussion. An 'aha' moment for me was discovering that second wait time. I found that if I waited again after a student answered, I could expose misunderstandings and nudge the class to deeper thinking. So, let the answer sit there. Let students ponder, share with each other, and ask questions. Keep the thinking going.

5 Steps

If you are like most of us, these techniques are very different from the ones you experienced in school, and it will take a while to feel comfortable with them. Try using the following 5-step whole group participation protocol as a way to get started:

Step 1: Give students wait time after a question.

Step 2: Have partners share.

Step 3: Choose a student randomly to share. He stands.

Step 4: Students turn toward the speaker. The teacher sits down (audience responsibility).

Step 5: Have students partner share in response to the thinking just expressed.

After a partner share, it is not necessary to always call on a student to report to the whole group. What is important is that each student "got their thinking out of their head," thought about their level of understanding, and got some feedback. When you listen in to some partnerships, you may hear some thinking that everyone would benefit from hearing. You can be strategic about whom to call on

Mix it up

Partner sharing and class discussions are great strategies for keeping kids dialed in, but they aren't the only ones. During a whole group lesson, include a mix of opportunities for students to think and reflect. (**TURNS!**) This also helps with the pace of the lesson and keeps things interesting. Even when we need to present information, we can give time to process and discuss.

Active participation techniques include:

- Using **wait time** after a question to think.

- **Sharing with a partner**: after a question, students are given an opportunity to think, discuss with a partner, and then share with the whole group.

- **Re-voicing**: a student or the teacher restates another person's thinking (that everyone heard!). This can also be done in partnerships.

- Responding with **nonverbal signals**: students can display answers with fingers, signal that they agree or disagree, or mime the meaning of a new vocabulary word.

- **Responding as a group**. (100% must chorally vocalize.)

- **Writing** on a whiteboard <u>during</u> the lesson: write a response, hold up the white board when the teacher says "Show," and/or share with a partner. Students can also sketch or write their thinking in journals or on 3x5 cards which you later collect.

- **Showing cards** (prepared by the teacher or by students) with printed responses:
  - Yes/No
  - Agree/Disagree
  - A/B/C
  - True/False
  - Numbers 0-9

- **Standing**: when students are sharing their thinking, they stand so that other students know where to focus. They <u>can</u> also call on the next speaker.

- Putting **heads together**: students in small groups share thinking. Each student must be given a chance to share.

- Using **"Go Around" protocols**: each student in a group has an opportunity to share—one idea or more—for a given amount of time.

- Calling on students **randomly**: kids' names are called. (Pull sticks with student names out of a cup.)

- **Singing**: It's surprising how quickly students learn multiplication tables, science information, and other facts when they practice them in songs. Plus, singing is a fun activity to do when kids need a break.[59]

What a shift from traditional classroom practice! In a single lesson, students might read, draw, write, sing, think-pair-share, signal responses, use a small group protocol, and listen to you. Plan ahead which techniques you will use. Mix it up, keep the pace productive, and students will be engaged.

Planned Lesson Alternatives

We've all had plenty of experience with typical lesson design: explain the concept, give students a chance to practice, ask if there are any questions, and end with independent work. That's fine if all kids are able to grasp the concept simply through listening and watching and are ready to apply what they learn immediately. But this doesn't work for all students and doesn't take into account all the research about how the brain learns, how the student's levels of understanding evolve throughout lessons, and how teachers must make adjustments during lessons based on feedback from students. To change this paradigm requires intentionality that can only come from creating lessons that focus on the students' learning instead of just the teacher's role.

Changing our teaching practice takes time and commitment. Start by choosing one subject and write out several lessons in detail, including strategies to ensure student thinking and participation. When you actually teach the lessons, the strategies you use may change, depending on the needs of your class, but the plan will give you a starting point and force you to think about including active participation opportunities. Of course, we don't have time to plan all our lessons this thoroughly. But by thinking through some key lessons in this way, you will begin incorporating active participation as a matter of habit, and those habits will eventually become second nature. Let's see how a lesson plan might look as you begin building in opportunities for student participation.

Example: A Plan for the Teacher and Students

Posted target: I will be able to add 2-digit numbers with regrouping (using my understanding of place value).

Text: Pages 192-193

Think time: *What do you understand about place value?*

Partner Share: Students take turns sharing ideas with their partner.

Teacher: Call on students (who stand) to share. Other students can show they agree or disagree using sign language. Record their ideas on a chart or board.[y]

Teacher: Have students use place value pieces to make two 2-digit numbers using numerals less than 5. Have students compare their models.

Teacher: Observe & notice students' models. What are they understanding or misunderstanding? Which models might I have students share? Is more practice needed? Moving on:

Teacher: Have students make two 2-digit numbers, again using numerals less than 5, and combine them. Have students compare their models and solution steps. Observe and notice students' models. Choose some for sharing.

Teacher asks: *What did you notice?* Call on random students. Record their thinking. Continue to show and combine 2-digit numbers as needed. Begin to use larger numbers so that some problems require regrouping. Students compare models and solutions with partners and with the whole group.

Teacher: Show 2 problems—one that requires regrouping and one that does not. Students continue to solve problems, sharing the differences in the two types of problems.

---

[y] Reason for recording: it is difficult for students to follow oral statements, particularly for new material. By writing down student comments, you make it easier for them to follow, and you have 'footprints' of thinking that can be referred to later for revision and reflection.

Exit Tasks

Partner Share: *Revisit and revise definitions of place value. Ask: How would you now define place value?* Have students share with the whole group. Record changes to thinking.

Exit Cards ^z

Give students 3 problems to solve on a 3x5 card, two with regrouping and one without.

Another way to ensure that students have processing time and active participation opportunities is to jot symbols right into the textbook lesson sequence. For example:

PS:	Partner share
WT:	Wait (or think) time
TS:	Table share
W:	Write
R:	Re-voice (students)
A/D:	Agree/disagree
HS:	Hand signal
SS:	Stand to speak
GR:	Go around (the table) protocol
T:	Teacher
S:	Student
Q:	Question to ask:
S:	Song

These symbols serve as reminders to get kids involved and to give them opportunities to find out if they are moving toward the target.

During the Lesson

Of course, the plans you make for student participation are only a guide. Once the lesson begins, you may need to shift gears, change strategies, or try something different, but the plan will give you a good starting point. As the lesson progresses in real time, look for evidence of students needing more processing time or practice, having disequilibrium, or needing a break, and adjust as necessary.

---

^z An exit card is, for example, a 3x5 card on which students solve a couple of problems or answer a question relevant to the target. The responses provide a quick check (formative assessment) on levels of understanding. (More on this in Chapter 24.)

Disequilibrium and Mistakes

Error is the difference between what we know and can do, and what we aim to know and do.[60]

—J. Hattie

Let's talk a minute about disequilibrium. Disequilibrium is that uneasy feeling we all get when things don't make sense, or we fear we're never going to "get it." Kids experience it every day in our classrooms (and elsewhere), and well-meaning adults often jump in too soon to take that discomfort away. But disequilibrium is not the enemy; it is an indication that our brains are trying to learn something new. I would argue that instead of taking away disequilibrium, let's help kids see it as natural part of the process. After all, there is little need for learning to occur without it. So, talk with students about disequilibrium: *Sure, it feels uncomfortable and makes us uneasy, but it means our brains are working, and if we persevere, we will learn and make sense of things. Our disequilibrium is just a state of "not yet"—we have not yet figured something out.* When students are successful, talk with them about how good that feels, and how rewarding it is to work *through* disequilibrium and reach understanding.

Learning is messy—we make mistakes, we get confused—it's all part of the package. When you teach students to accept this reality, you must also make it OK for them to talk about their mistakes and confusion without fearing they will be unfairly judged. It is easy to give lip service to words on a poster: *In this classroom, it is OK to make errors. They are opportunities to learn.* But if you are not careful, you or your students can sabotage this important principle in subtle and not so subtle ways. We've all seen examples of a teacher's impatient body language or tone of voice, students groaning or laughing when someone makes a mistake, or outright sarcasm when someone isn't getting it. Ouch. How do we ensure a sense of safety where the inevitable struggles to learn are respected?

There are several things teachers can do to create that "Mistakes are OK" environment:

1. First and foremost, model the behavior. Kids take their cues from the teacher: if you avoid the above actions that contradict a "Mistakes are OK" environment, your students will begin to do so, also.

2. Mistakes are part of the learning process, right? All our bald pencils are living proof! But why do we rush to erase our mistakes? If you think of them as evidence of thinking and how it evolves, leaving mistakes in place makes more sense. It lets us see the progression of learning and allows us to compare earlier efforts with later, more accurate ones. Consider these attempts by one student to solve a tricky (for him) math problem

$$
\begin{array}{r} 34 \\ +39 \\ \hline 613 \end{array}
\qquad
\begin{array}{r} 1 \\ 34 \\ +\ 39 \\ \hline 73 \end{array}
$$

or to spell a troublesome word:

ketch cetch catch

When the attempts were left in place, this student could consider which sum made more sense and why. And he could easily see which spelling looked right. If you are truly okay with mistakes, have your kids do some of their work using pencils without erasers! Even better, use those errors to generate class discussions, not to shame anyone, but to deepen everyone's understanding. A strong classroom community makes this possible. In such a community, kids learn it's okay to share their errors, and they start to realize how valuable mistakes can be.

3. Use the scaffolding diagram presented earlier in this chapter to help students think about the fits and starts that inevitably occur on the way to understanding.

4. Let students know learning is a marathon that everyone can finish. *Get better today than you were yesterday in whatever needs to be learned.*[61]

5. Present or brainstorm words that students can use when they don't know or are confused. For example:

- *I am not sure YET and will keep working.*
- *Would you ask the question again, or in a different way?*
- *I became confused at this step: _____.*
- *I need some more think time. Please call on me later.*
- *I need more practice.*

As a teacher, I knew it was critical that my students' misconceptions bubbled to the surface over the course of a lesson. It gave me a chance to adjust how I was conducting the lesson and what I was having students do. Think about it—if we don't have this information (because students are uncomfortable sharing disequilibrium or they don't how), we are teaching blindly. We could be assuming understanding that just isn't there, and we could be presenting information or using activities which don't match the place where most students are at that moment. This is an inefficient way to teach, to say the very least.

Teaching to the whole group is an instructional choice made by the teacher. It does not mean, however, that students sit by passively without thinking about the lesson target or gauging their level of understanding. Fill a whole group lesson with multiple opportunities for students to take "TURNS" (actively participate). Let kids own their disequilibrium without judgment, and let their misperceptions guide your teaching during the lesson.

Primary Students

Establishing students' role in their own learning is set early in their school career. Will they listen passively, keep quiet, and hope the teacher does, or does not, call on them? Or will they learn to be active participants?

Here's what you can do with younger students:

- Talk to them about the importance of taking "TURNS." You can connect this to their emerging understanding of how the brain works.
- Teach them how to use think time and partner share.
- Teach them nonverbal signals for showing their thinking.
- Tell them the target (what they will be learning) at the outset.
- Point out evidence of that learning and encourage them to recognize it, too.

Intermediate Students

Older students come in with habits already in place, and often that means teaching them to take on a new, more participatory role. Start with the above, but, in addition, explain to students what you will be doing during whole-group lessons:

- Giving think time (to think about the target or a question).
- Giving time to verbalize their thinking with a partner.

- Teaching them signals to help stay engaged.

- Having students stand to share with the whole group and explaining why this benefits them: so, they can process what is being said and potentially add to their understanding.

- Providing TURNS—opportunities to activate their brains, add to scaffolding, increase depth of understanding, and make connections.

From My Experience: Collecting Building Material.

Any good message bears repeating. I reminded students every day that their hard work on targets meant they were collecting building material for their brain's schema. "Use every opportunity you can to learn, and it will make your brain smarter!"

NOTES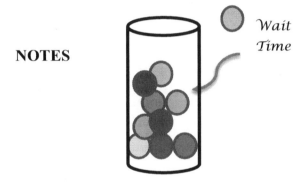

The Importance of Disequilibrium and First Tries

Learning is a process. Sometimes it happens very quickly, but more often, it follows a path like the one shown below. Disequilibrium is the natural starting point. Our first tries may result in mistakes and more disequilibrium, but they get us moving along the path. Many subsequent tries may be needed before true equilibrium and understanding are reached, but if we persevere, we will get there. Showing a continuum like this to kids, perhaps adding pictures for younger students, can help them understand the process of learning and help them be patient with themselves and others along the way.

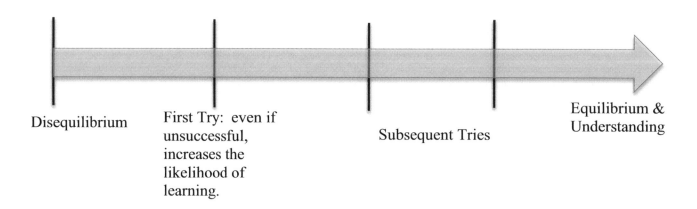

Disequilibrium

First Try: even if unsuccessful, increases the likelihood of learning.

Subsequent Tries

Equilibrium & Understanding

Wrong answers—aren't merely random failures. Rather, the attempts themselves alter how we think about, and store, the information contained in the questions.

The Surprising Truth About How We Learn and Why It Happens (Benedict Carey)

Chapter 17 Key Points

Students' Roles

☐ Think about how you are adding to your schema by processing information.

☐ Use wait time and second wait time to think.

☐ Understand what disequilibrium is and how errors help us learn.

☐ Help (and be patient) as peers work through their disequilibrium.

☐ Even if you are not sure about a solution to a problem, share it with a partner or the class.

☐ Let the teacher know if you need more practice.

Teachers' Roles

☐ Plan ahead which active participation strategies to use.

☐ Give students plenty of wait time—and second wait time.

☐ Teach students about the benefits of taking TURNS and building scaffolding of understanding.

☐ Develop a community of learners where disequilibrium is accepted and errors are valued. Recognize and appreciate when students let you know they are in disequilibrium.

☐ Teach students ways they can let you know they are in disequilibrium.

Hidden Steps: Whole Group Participation

Through consistent practice, students will learn new protocols for sharing their ideas. They will expect wait time for coming up with a response, time to share their thinking with partners or group members, opportunities to write down their ideas, or chances to signal they are listening and have a response to a speaker. Let students know that in most lessons you will be presenting some background knowledge or modeling a strategy, and that they will get processing time after 5-10 minutes of listening. Steps:

- Build community so that students know and care for each other.
- Let students know what the target of a lesson is.
- Teach students how to use wait time and share with a partner.
- Let students know that after 5–10 minutes of listening they will get an opportunity to process information or practice a skill.
- Teach students signs to show their thinking and engagement while they are listening.
- Connect all of these processes to learning and student success.

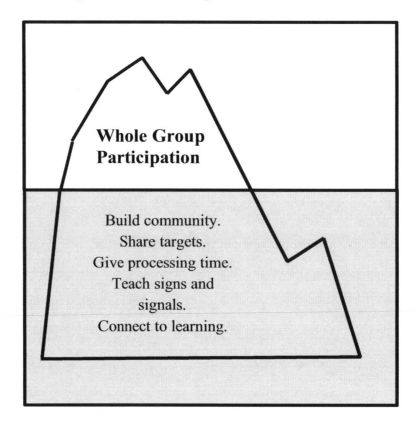

Hidden Steps: Active Participation Techniques

The issue: *My students are so passive. After I ask a question there is silence. I eventually call on one of the few students who raises his hand.*   —Intermediate Teacher

It is a big deal to raise your hand and share an idea with a group of people, and it puts you in a vulnerable position. *What if I am wrong? What if someone laughs? What if I realize I don't know?* Hence, the importance of developing a community of learners where it is safe to share thinking, say *I am not sure yet*, or that *I am in disequilibrium*. Give students a chance to retrieve answers from their brains or synthesize ideas using wait time, and then give them time to share with a partner to rehearse an answer, find out their level of understanding, or get feedback. The goal is 100% participation, and when only a few hands are called on, as is traditionally the case, we fall far short of this goal. Give every student a chance to share, using strategies such as:

- Partner sharing
- Written responses
- Whiteboards
- Nonverbal signals
- Cards with responses
- Small group protocol

Steps:

- Build community, so students know and care for each other, and are kind when others struggle.
- Discuss how mistakes and disequilibrium are a natural part of the learning process.
- Notice and recognize when wrong answers shorten the road to right answers.
- Teach multiple ways for students to share their thinking.
- Reduce hand-raising as the go-to procedure students use to indicate they want to share.

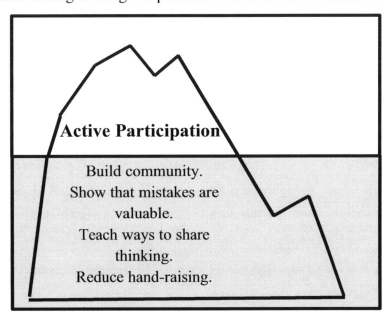

Chapter 18: Guide Students Toward Independence

If you're a going to be a good teacher, you have to believe in malleable intelligence. And character is equally malleable. You teach kids to pay attention to character, then their character will transform.[62]   —Paul Tough

Non-Cognitive Skills

As a teacher, it's easy to assume that students know how to do what you ask of them. For example:

1. *Finish problems 1-15. You have 30 minutes.*

2. *You are going to do a report on a South American country. Here is a list of all the things you need to include. You will have 2 weeks.*

3. *For homework tonight, write a story about an animal.*

4. *In your group, look up the definitions for this list of words.*

5. *With your partner, create a poster about the book we just finished.*

But do they know how? Let's look at each of the five tasks above and consider what students must be able to do in order to complete them successfully.

Task #1—Manage Time. If there are 15 problems, about 7 should be finished after 15 minutes. Kids should skip any troublesome problems and come back to them later.

Task #2—Make a two-week timeline for completion of the project and know how to find resources, take notes, write information in their own words, and format a report.

Task #3—Designate a time to complete homework at home (assuming students have needed materials and the schema to write a story).

Task #4—Collaborate with group members to accomplish a task.

Task #5—Work with a partner, brainstorm possibilities together, make decisions, and divide up the tasks.

When these skills are missing or not well developed, kids have a tough time being successful. There are numerous reasons that some children, particularly children in poverty, come to school lacking these skills, but the end result is the same: students without them are at a real disadvantage. A more comprehensive list of non-cognitive skills important for student success would surely include:

grit, resilience
self-control, self-discipline, self-regulation
zest, motivation
gratitude
optimism
curiosity
perseverance, persistence
effort, diligence
time management
work habits[63]

Clearly, it's not enough to just teach academics. We need to include and recognize character traits during instruction every day. This does not mean having an isolated lesson on one skill: *Today we will talk about grit.* Instead, we plan **dual-purpose instruction,** where we make explicit talk about character traits a component of every lesson.[64] Part of breaking things down for students is to ensure that they are developing the non-cognitive skills necessary to succeed, and when we embed the teaching of such skills into daily activities and assignments, we help them do just that.

Dual Purpose Instruction:

To facilitate acquisition of these skills, look for opportunities to reinforce behaviors that will help students be successful:

- Talk to students about non-cognitive skills. Knowing that they may not have some of the skills necessary to complete an assignment lets them focus on acquiring those skills as you teach them rather than concluding, *I can't do this,* or *I'm not smart enough.*

- Notice and praise students for effort and working continuously to solve a challenging problem. (***Persistence***)

- Model positive language that includes overtly thanking others and showing ***gratitude.*** This skill is especially helpful in partnerships and small groups.

- Display a "can do attitude." *I know that you can do this."* Remember, Henry Ford said, *If you think you can or think you can't, you're right.* (***Optimism***)

- Start lessons with "wondering" questions—yours and theirs. *I wonder what would happen if we added salt to the water. Would the egg float?* (***Curiosity***)

- Notice and recognize when students solve their own social problems. (***Self-Regulation***)

- Show students how to manage time. If students have 20 minutes to solve some math problems, help them figure out how much time they have for each problem. (***Time Management***).

- Teach students how to complete homework.[aa] Homework must be purposeful, not busy work, and students must have the understanding necessary to complete the homework independently. Large packets assigned on Monday and due Friday often lack these two qualities. At the beginning of the school year, talk about the purpose of different kinds of homework, and make sure kids have the necessary supplies. If students are not accustomed to doing homework, you can reserve the last 15 minutes of the day for them to complete an assignment. Then have them put their paper into the "Homework Basket." Students need to know how it feels to complete and turn in homework. Gradually give them less in-class time to finish the work, moving the responsibility of completion to home. And it's a good idea to track homework completion and see if it actually correlates with academic success. If not, take time to rethink the kind of work you assign. (***Work Habits***)

Throughout the day, be alert to students displaying non-cognitive skills and be ready to reinforce them. Above all, think through each activity and assignment that students will be doing in the course of a day, including homework. Do they have all the necessary skills? If not, address those skills when they are relevant in a lesson.

[aa] The jury is out on the effectiveness of homework. *In fact, for elementary school-age children, there is no measureable academic advantage to homework.*
http://www.greatschools.org/gk/articles/what-research-says-about-homework/

Gradual Release of Responsibility

Early in my teaching career I used to teach a lesson, give my students a task to complete, and then be disappointed with the results. Their work didn't come close to meeting my expectations—couldn't they see that? Over time, I realized that my students either didn't fully understand my expectations or didn't have enough schema or background knowledge to complete the task. When I learned about the gradual release of responsibility model, I knew I'd found the missing link. Douglas Fisher and Nancy Frey, in *Releasing Responsibility,* say:

> *Newly or barely learned tasks do not make for good independent learning activities. Unfortunately, educators often ask students to assume full responsibility for their learning prematurely in the instructional cycle. Teachers should reserve independent work for review and reinforcement of concepts that have been previously taught.*[65]

So, don't make the same rookie mistake I did, asking students to complete a task or use a strategy independently before they are ready. Wait until they have seen the task modeled or demonstrated, listened to a teacher "think aloud," practiced with partners or in small groups with teacher support, and tried the strategy with teacher feedback. Here are the four steps in gradual release of responsibility instruction:

1. Modeling/Demonstrating (while thinking aloud)

Model the task while explaining aloud what you are thinking. At this point, you are assuming all the responsibility for the task. Imagine you are teaching text-to-self connections. While reading a story, stop for a moment, put the book down, and let students in on your thinking— the connections you are making between the story and your own life. Model the strategy with a variety of texts—fiction, nonfiction, and poetry.

2. Partner Practice

Give the students opportunities to practice a strategy or complete part of the task with partners or in small groups. Continuing our example, read stories, share your connections, and invite students to add theirs. Use familiar books and also texts that are new to students. At this point, you are beginning to release some responsibility to them.

3. Guided Thinking/Practice

Gradually give more responsibility for the strategy or task to the students. Pause as you read and have students share their thinking with the whole group, in partnerships or in small groups, while you provide feedback and support. If they are practicing text-to-self connections with a familiar story, you can point out how those connections enrich their understanding.

4. Independent Application

At this stage, students assume all the responsibility for the task or strategy.

> *Well-structured independent learning tasks are the ultimate way to build self-esteem through competence. By the time a student has reached this phase, he or she should be working at the level of competent novice; the purpose for additional work is to refine skills and become expert. Isn't this how many of us learned to be good teachers?*[66]

In the text-to-self example, students would now look for connections during independent reading, recording them on sticky notes for later sharing.

It is important to listen closely to students to determine when they are ready to assume more responsibility. When things don't go well, it's usually because we cut short the release of responsibility process. It's not an indictment on us, just a signal that we need to back up and revisit the missing steps.

Guided or Independent Practice?

Before assigning a task, you must decide its purpose and how much responsibility to give students. If you want to "assess" students (find out what they understand on their own), then you don't want to provide any help. After all, if you give an independent assignment and then go to individuals to "reteach," it isn't independent work!

However, if your purpose is to give students time for guided practice, then you can provide assistance or encourage partner collaboration. Make sure students are working silently before you begin. Alternatively, you can structure an independent/guided practice hybrid. Ask students to work independently for 10 minutes (to find out what they understand) after which you or partners can provide help if needed.

One caveat: when you tell students it's OK to help each other, some will think they can talk about anything. That's why it's important to teach students what peer assistance looks and sounds like: A student whispering to a neighbor, conferring briefly, and getting back to work immediately. It's not students whispering to each other for an extended period or two students sharing their work and doing a lot of giggling. Their responsibility is to work continuously, seeking the help of a neighbor only when needed, and doing so in a focused, productive way. When you intentionally teach, model and practice peer assistance routines, kids will be able to use their time more wisely and limit interruptions to their valuable work time.

Practice Considerations

When I observe classrooms, I often see every student in the room working on the same fill-in-the-blank worksheet. Some kids are finishing quickly, others are working quietly, and a few are spending their time staring at a blank page. Most math and reading adoptions include pages and pages of such worksheets, and busy teachers rely on them for independent work assignments. These worksheets are not without issues, however, especially when they are used without regard for differentiation. In addition, they can provide too much or too little practice for kids or directions may be confusing, even impossible for some students to read.

When students are applying new skills, the kind of practice they engage in is critical. Worksheets have their place, but you can often design assignments for students that provide differentiation, maximize practice, and at the same time avoid unnecessary repetition. Here are some examples to show what I mean:

Math:

- If students are truly at the practice stage, they do not need to complete 25 problems to demonstrate proficiency. You (or they) can choose five problems that demonstrate their understanding of a skill or strategy.

- If students are practicing reading large numbers, have them randomly choose from a stack of number cards a certain number of digits—and then read the number to a partner. Partners could read dozens of numbers in a just a few minutes.

Language Arts:

- In reading, journals are an effective tool where students can answer open-ended questions and can apply a variety of reading skills discussed previously in class— sequence, inference, drawing conclusions, and author's purpose, to name a few.

- In language arts, if students are studying apostrophes, they can collect words with apostrophes (and a couple of surrounding words) on a bookmark as they read. These words can later be sorted according to the reason the apostrophe is used.

Social Studies:

- Students can create timelines, maps, or sketches of events. This open-ended assignment requires them to think carefully about what to include and what to omit.

Bottom line: think about the *actual* amount of practice students are getting from the work you assign and the level of thinking it requires.

Post-Independent Work

In many classes, students are given paper and pencil tasks to complete as part of morning routine. Then teachers solve all the problems or have students come up front to share their solutions. Over the course of a school year, morning work can consume a fair amount of class time. So, it's worth asking, is it time well spent? Are kids sufficiently engaged? Are they spending too much time on problems they already understand? By changing up a few key aspects of morning work, you can get a lot more bang for your buck. Let me explain.

To squeeze the most out of morning work or indeed any assignment, have students compare answers with a designated partner when they are done or after a predetermined amount of time. It keeps them engaged, and by explaining their reasoning, kids will clarify their thinking. Teach students how to have a discussion around disagreements and have them highlight answers that differ. While they are working, go around and look at their work. Strategically select those students whose solution path you want the whole class to see. If you have a learning community that values all thinking, you can choose work from a student whose answer is incorrect, and use that as a springboard for discussion. After each student shares, resist the temptation to weigh in. Instead, ask the class:

- *What do you think?*
- *Agree or disagree?*
- *Talk to your partner about this way to solve the problem.*

By observing students and looking at the highlighted areas of their work, you will determine which problems or concepts need to be revisited. You can get a lot of mileage out of a short assignment, ascertain students' levels of understanding, and save a great deal of correcting time later!

The Independent Work Routine

Of all the academic routines, one of the most important to teach students is how to work independently. Let kids know up front the purposes and benefits both for you and for them:

- When working by themselves, students can find out whether or not they are getting it.

- You can more accurately assess your students' understanding when you see what they do unaided.

- You can work with individuals or small groups while other students practice skills.

Unfortunately, independent work time can easily fall short. When I observe classrooms, I typically see one of two scenarios taking place:

Scenario 1:

The teacher finishes a lesson and excuses students to work independently at their tables. He begins conferencing with a needy student immediately. After five minutes or so, a handful of kids have begun earnestly working. The teacher continues to assist students, keeping his back to the rest of the class, and the noise level continues to rise. After ten minutes, about half of the students are now focused on their assignment; the others are still visiting or gathering materials. After about fifteen minutes, and multiple reminders, most of the students are working; but a few are still not yet engaged.

Scenario 2:

The teacher finishes a lesson; then he tells and writes the directions for an independent assignment. Students know the routine for independent work, because it has been explicitly taught. After being excused, they immediately head back to their tables and get out needed materials, as the teacher observes, noting who is getting right to work. All students begin to work silently.

At the end of scenario 2, the whole class was working independently and silently, without help. Independent work means just that—students are on their own, and for a period of time, no help is available. It is a chance for students and you to assess levels of understanding. We care about kids, and it is very tempting to jump in immediately and help a struggling student, but wait! Let them experience what independence really is.

Accountability

The implicit message in scenario two is that the teacher expects students to use their time efficiently, understanding their responsibilities during work times and realizing that practicing skills benefits them. Just as important, we want students to feel the **success of accomplishment**—that feeling spurs them on to work even harder. Some students will fritter away a 30-minute writing period, write three words, and then head out to recess—without realizing they just wasted another opportunity to learn. We must hold students accountable, and help them connect effort to success. Check in with each student to gauge work completed; celebrate when a student writes one more sentence or one more paragraph today than yesterday. Students must know that you notice what they do and have high expectations for efficient use of time.

Here are some guidelines for independent work:

- Start by reviewing the target. Give all the directions up front—orally, visually (words & pictures), and even kinesthetically. (Pretend you are writing!) Students can refer to written directions during work time if they need clarification. They can also repeat the directions to partners. Include in your directions what to do when finished.

- Give a specific amount of time for the assignment (use a timer).

- Tell students they will be finding out what they really understand!

- After giving students directions, observe carefully to see that they are following them. If you expect kids to get right to work, that is exactly what they should do!

- If someone doesn't know what to do—point to your directions on the overhead and leave. (You want them to learn to pay attention to directions the first time.)

- Monitor and assess: As students are working, carry a clipboard. Note what kids seem to know and not know. This informs future lessons—and kids learn they are responsible for working on their own.

- Debrief afterward, guiding students to make connections between that behavior and their ability to accomplish tasks, meet the target, and learn.

It takes clear expectations, careful monitoring, and lots of practice for most students to really work independently. After you teach kids what it looks like and sounds like, give them opportunities to practice for short periods of time. Gradually they will be able to stay focused for longer periods. Expect it to take at least six weeks to put this protocol in place—and don't give up if students need even more time. Revisit the procedure periodically, especially when new students join the class.

Working Independently at Stations

Once students can work independently, you can begin to work with individuals and small groups, knowing the rest of the group will respect your teaching time. Teachers often set up stations with tasks to be completed without assistance. In that case, it is essential they be assigned tasks that are meaningful, and provide practice for concepts and skills that have been already taught and can be completed independently. Here are some guidelines:

- Each station must have a clear learning target and a routine that is thoroughly understood and practiced.

- Start with a limited number of stations, perhaps two or three.

- Packets of worksheets are problematic and should be avoided. Often, students are not able to decipher directions when there are multiple pages. Consider using only one worksheet. Upon completion, students can compare answers with each other or with an answer sheet.

- Create reading or math stations where the logistics are the same, but the words or numbers change. For example, students might be expected to write sentences or stories, using certain vocabulary words. The expectation stays the same each week, but the words change.

- Stations need to change periodically to maintain interest and to focus on new concepts or strategies. Introduce a new station to the whole class first, explicitly teaching and practicing the activity. When students understand the new task and are comfortable doing it independently, you can add it to the rotation. Above all, do not introduce a new batch of stations to the whole group just before station time.

- There must be an expectation for amount of work completed. Some students can spend 15 or 20 minutes at a station and accomplish very little. Here are some ways to insure accountability:
  - In between station rotations, collect work from students.
  - As part of the transition, have some children share what they did.
  - As kids are leaving for recess, collect an assignment.
  - Have students keep work in folders; check it when they come to a reading group.

When students know you will be looking at their work or that they will be sharing what they did, they feel a greater responsibility to be productive.

As you can see, anytime students work independently or in guided practice situations, tasks must be carefully designed and expectations explicitly taught. When students understand their responsibilities and connect them to achievement, they begin to develop lifelong skills, skills that will make them successful learners and productive citizens. Just as important, they begin to genuinely value their own learning time.

Students' Perspectives

A major factor in a student's math achievement is his level of confidence.[67]   —J. Hattie

I once had a conversation with a colleague about students who were failing. His contention— some kids just come to school and try not to learn. I would argue there are lots of factors that contribute to students giving up. Some are out of our control, but it is our job to create a classroom environment where students will want to learn. Learning feels good. Success feels good. Observe young children trying to climb a small rock wall at a playground. They keep trying and trying until they reach the top. And often, like my granddaughter, they celebrate with a big "ta-da!" when they succeed. That's what we want kids to do in school—work hard, persevere, and feel those "ta-da!" moments. When students experience failure after failure in the classroom, though, they respond very differently. Some act out. Some choose to become the class clown, diverting attention away from their academic failure, and gaining positive recognition from classmates. Others just give up. They become lethargic, putting their heads down on their desks, and essentially checking out.

How do we help these students? We start by transforming the learning community, purposefully creating a positive, supportive learning classroom. We find out what students already know, and go from there. John Hattie states that, *The most important single factor influencing learning is what the learner already knows.*[68] We use target ladders with rungs spaced closely enough together so kids can climb up. (More on this in Chapter 22.) We teach the non-cognitive skills they need to succeed. And we use a gradual release of responsibility, actively engaging kids, and assessing frequently to inform next steps. Our goal is to help students succeed, one step at a time, building their confidence and helping them become independent learners.

NOTES

Chapter 18 Key Points

Students' Roles

☐ Learn about non-cognitive skills. Recognize when you or your peers are exhibiting them—for example, persistence or grit—or managing your time well.

☐ Use your level of understanding to determine if you need more modeling, guided practice, or independent work.

☐ Choose work at stations that will challenge you and add to your schema.

Teachers' Roles

☐ Model non-cognitive skills. Notice and recognize student effort, for example, effort that exemplifies persistence.

☐ Use a gradual release of responsibility framework for instruction.

☐ As you proceed through lessons, determine whether more whole group modeling/demonstrating is needed, students are ready for guided or independent practice, or if small group differentiation is the next step.

☐ Formatively assess students frequently, in order to make the above decisions based on data.

☐ Carefully plan and teach station work, making sure it meets the needs of each student spending time there.

☐ Help students recognize their many small successes along the way.

NOTES

Hidden Steps: Independent Work

The issue: *As soon as I give students an assignment to work on, hands go up and the talking starts.*   —Intermediate Teacher

Independent work for students must always be at their practice level. If it's not, you'll find yourself running around the classroom re-teaching multiple times and getting generally frustrated. In addition, kids should know the procedure for independent work as well as its benefits. Students can self-check their work or check with a partner and then determine their level of understanding.

Here are the hidden steps that make this strategy work:

- Build community.
- Embed non-cognitive strategies into lessons.
- Use modeling, guided practice, and partner work to prepare students for independent work.
- Discuss the purpose and benefits of independent work.
- Develop the procedure.
- Teach students how to self- or partner-check.
- Use three levels of understanding to determine who is ready for independent practice. (See Chapter 24.)

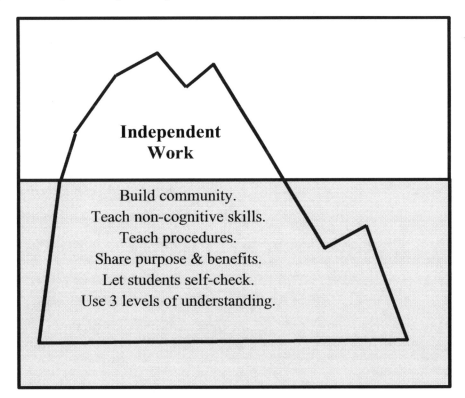

Chapter 19: Deepen Thinking with Partnerships and Small Groups

Brain research tells us we learn best through challenge and feedback. We need tasks that stretch us a bit, and we need feedback on our thinking, in order to revise and fine-tune our understanding. Partnerships and small groups provide rich opportunities for this kind of feedback. In addition, when students share with each other, they are able to verbalize and clarify their own understanding. They also have the opportunity to "capture" someone else's thinking, adding it to their own schema. Giving students turns to share may take more time, but the long-term benefits are well worth it.

So, which is better, partnerships or small groups? Partnerships give more chances to share; small groups provide more diversity of thought. They are equally powerful vehicles for feedback, so why not make use of both? Let's start with partnerships.

Partnership Considerations

Some teachers hesitate to use partner sharing at all. They worry it will degenerate into unstructured time where students all talk at once, socialize off target, and the room will be chaotic and noisy. They don't want to lose control of the class—w*hat will the principal think?* Besides, students talk too much anyway. Why open the door to more chatter?

Partner sharing, however, is anything but unstructured and chaotic. It is focused time, carefully taught, using protocols. Getting there is a step-by-step process, with lots of modeling and practice. We don't assume all our students come to us understanding how to share in a respectful and productive manner, but we do assume we can teach them, and they can all learn. The goal is self-regulation—students eventually having an internal structure, where they self-monitor because they understand the benefits of sharing. Recently, I had the pleasure of seeing this in action in a friend's classroom. His fifth-grade students were sharing characters they had created for a writing assignment, and, scanning the room, he and I witnessed the unmistakable look and sound of learning—something he called *productive chatter.* He interrupted the group briefly to give them a compliment. It was also a great opportunity, I thought, to ask the students how they felt during this sharing time—and to help them connect engagement and focus with productivity and community.

PHASE 1

Here is a blueprint to follow as you establish partnership procedures:

1) **Have a discussion with students about the purpose of partner sharing.** As suggested in previous chapters, help students connect their sharing with learning and the brain. Give them reasons for sharing:

   a) <u>Verbal rehearsal</u>: Students get to "hear" what their thinking sounds like, and they are rehearsing for a possible share with the whole group.

   b) <u>Level of Understanding</u>: The ease or difficulty of explaining their thinking can give students clues about their level of understanding. *If you can't explain yourself easily, maybe your understanding is shaky, and that's important for you to know.* In an upcoming chapter, we will delve deeper into this topic.

   c) <u>Feedback</u>: Students will receive feedback or scaffolding that they can add to the construction of their understanding. The feedback could reinforce, or conversely, put into disequilibrium their previous thinking.

2) In the beginning, whether students are working at desks or on the carpet, take the time to assign partners. Avoid the situation where some kids end up without a partner, time after time.

3) Change partnerships every four to six weeks. This builds community, nudging students to have discussions and build working relationships with others they may not know as well.

4) Teach children the <u>partner sharing routine</u>. It can include designating each partner as 'A' or 'B' and setting a time limit. For example,

   a) *At the signal, turn your knees toward your partner.*
   b) *Partner A share for 15 seconds.*
   c) *Partner B share for 15 seconds.*
   d) *Turn back.*

5) Model and practice the steps several times initially, and don't be afraid to revisit the protocols later, especially when new students join the class.

6) Debrief after partner sharing. *How did that help you succeed?* Encourage students to notice when their thinking changed due to a partner exchange. It's a sign of new learning!

Monitor carefully to make sure every student has a partner and is following the protocol; your job is to make sure each student has an opportunity to share. This includes teaching them what to do when their partner is absent—for example,

- *Stand and look for another student standing.*
- *Get together with that person.*
- *If there is an odd number of students without partners, form triads.*

Of course, some students will need extra practice in order to be successful in partnerships. You can provide that practice in small groups or with private lessons.

PHASE 2

Teach children how to have conversations, listen to ideas, and respond to each other. Many of them have never experienced the give and take of a real conversation. Some teachers I know show a film clip of people sharing (initially without sound) so their students can analyze what conversation looks like and later what it sounds like. You could also videotape students who are having effective conversations to show future classes.

Primary Students

With younger children, focus on the listening aspect of partner sharing. Use simple questions with more convergent responses and give a purpose to the sharing. For example:

Question: *What is your favorite kind of pet? Listen to your partner's answer.*

After sharing: *How many of you named the same pet?*

This last question causes students to think about their partner's answer, not just their own.

Another strategy to help students carefully listen to each other's responses is:

- Partner A thinks about a response to a question.
- Partner B *does not think* about a response.
- Partner A shares.
- Partner B actively listens and summarizes the response.
- Partner A gives feedback as to the accuracy of B's summary.

Here is a progression of partner sharing goals for students. I can:

1. Listen to my partner's answer to a question.

2. Remember my partner's answer.

3. Know if my partner's answer was the same as mine or different.

4. Agree or disagree with that answer.

5. Tell why I agreed or disagreed.

A lot of students benefit from sentence starters. After listening to a partner, they say:

- *I agree because _____.*

- *I'm not sure. Would you explain _____ again?*

- *I disagree because _____.*

- *Would you tell me more about _____?*

All these sharing strategies require a significant amount of modeling and practice. Demonstrate by listening to one of the students and then giving feedback, using the sentence starters above. While you demonstrate, let students know what you are thinking and how you come up with responses. As time goes on, ask partner-sharing questions that allow more divergent thinking.

Intermediate Students

If older students have not previously experienced carefully taught partner sharing protocols and expectations, begin with the recommendations above for primary students. On the other hand, if they are ready for more rigorous expectations, give them opportunities to build on their partner sharing skills.

Regardless, begin by stressing the real benefits of partner sharing—it enriches kids' thinking and helps them learn. When you debrief after lessons, celebrate the aha's that happened, as students listened and received feedback or when they gave feedback to others. Here is a continuation of the progression of partner sharing goals begun earlier in Chapter 22. *I can*:

1. *add to my schema (or scaffolding) by listening to my partner.*

2. *share math answers and solution paths.*

3. *use my partner's solution path to solve a problem.*

4. *compare my answer to a reading question with my partner's.*

5. *find evidence to support my answer and share that with my partner.*

6. *understand and use my partner's viewpoint to answer a question.*

Sentence starters, introduced in primary grades, also benefit intermediate students. They move the conversation along and help kids focus on comprehending their partner's thinking. After listening to partners, students can respond with:

- *This is what I heard you say:* _____ .
- *I understood the first part. Could you explain* _____ ?
- *Would you repeat your answer?*
- *Can you tell me more about* _____ ?
- *I agree because* _____ .
- *I disagree because* _____ .
- *Could you say that again in a different way?*

Model listening and responding to a partner, using these sentence starters, then ask a few student partnerships to do the same. Let the class observe, and afterward, ask them what they noticed. Doing this shows kids what real partner sharing looks like and sounds like. After such careful modeling, chances are they will all be able to partner share in a constructive, productive manner.

From My Experience: Finding a Partner

If I had not assigned partners, I used this protocol: *Students touched hands with or pointed to a potential partner. Those without a partner stood and looked for someone who also needed one.*

Small Group Considerations (Grades 3-6)

In one of my observations, a fifth-grade class was studying explorers as part of their social studies curriculum. At one point, the teacher asked an important question, "Why did Marco Polo explore China? Talk about that in your groups." At several tables, no discussion occurred at all, and in one group, a single student dominated the entire conversation. Frustrated, the teacher confided later, "This is the reason I don't like kids sharing at tables!"

If your target is to encourage more divergent thinking, having students talk in small groups is a strategy to consider. Small groups are also useful when you want kids to experience collaborative completion of a project. The larger the group, the less opportunity for participation per student, but the greater the possibility of diverse thinking and collaborative interactions. I find a group of four is ideal. As with partnerships, however, the protocols that allow groups to be successful must be carefully taught. If they're not, you're likely to end up with problems like the ones in the example above.

Begin by discussing how small groups and partnerships have different purposes, and consider drawing up a chart such as the following with your students:

Partner Share	Small Group Share or Work
I get more turns and time to share.	I hear more viewpoints.
It's easier to practice listening to just one person.	I see more ways to arrive at opinions or solutions.
It's easier to stay engaged.	I get to know more people.
I get to know my partner very well.	Each member has different strengths.
I get immediate feedback.	There are more people to answer questions if I am stuck or confused.

Next, develop the small group share procedure. What does it look, sound, and feel like? For example,

- Each person gets the same number of responses or time to share.
- If we use a protocol, we will stick to it!
- Only one person speaks at a time.

Finally, provide multiple opportunities for practice, using simple, easily accomplished tasks. You want the focus to be on learning the procedure more than on the activity itself. Once the procedure is in place, revisit the expectations each time it is used: *Let's review our procedure. Do we need to add or take off anything on the list? Choose something on the list you want to focus on today and be ready at the end to evaluate how you did.*

If students are going to share answers or opinions, use protocols to ensure equitable opportunities to participate. At first, protocols might seem stilted or contrived, but they quickly become comfortable routines for sharing. They also offer a key advantage: protocols help groups avoid situations in which one or two students dominate while others say little or nothing at all.

A simple protocol to start with is **Whip Around**. In Whip Around, each student takes a turn sharing one idea. If time is left, the group can continue taking turns around the circle or have a general discussion. Students can skip their turn—but because of previous discussions, they know how much the community benefits when everyone adds their two cents. Here is a sampling of other protocols that work well:

1. Save the Last Word for Me[69]

- Each participant independently reads an article, identifying significant ideas and aha's.
- Person #1 identifies what was significant and reads it out loud to the group.
- The other 3 participants have one minute each to respond.
- Person #1 has 3 minutes to respond to what the group members said.
- Follow the same pattern for all group members.

2. All the Thinking

- Person #1 reports all of their thinking.

- Other members do not comment or interrupt.

- When person #1 is finished, person #2 shares all of their thinking.

- Continue until all members have shared.

- If time is left, a general discussion can occur.

3. Timed Rotation

- Person #1 shares for a predetermined number of minutes or seconds.

- A timer in the group warns person #1 when their time is about up.

- Person #2 shares for the same amount of time.

- Continue until all members have had time to share.

Debrief at the end of each sharing, referring to expectations. Comments should be positive. Instead of asking, *How did it go?* (which can invite negative responses), ask, *How many of you were able to participate in your group?* Or *How did that help you learn more?* Groups can also self-evaluate, using specific criteria you develop together.

Small Group Collaboration

Teachers often assign small group projects and have students present their products to the whole class. For example:

- Create a poster showing how the group solved a math problem.

- Create a poster showing a concept that was researched, e.g., water cycle, metamorphosis, scientific method, or order of operations in a math equation.

- Research a Latin American country: geography, culture, government, and economy.

It's surprising how often students are given multi-step projects such as these with little or no instruction on *how* to do them. Consider the complexities involved: students must know how to work together, delegate tasks, manage time, understand project expectations, etc., etc. Some students complain because they end up doing most of the work. Others slide by, doing little to contribute to the group's success. There are many benefits to be gained by assigning group projects, but there are pitfalls, too, so before you begin, set the groundwork.

Small group projects are not busy work. They help students increase academic understanding, and the task assigned must be worthy of time required. Equally important, they build collaboration skills. While you teach concepts, you will also be teaching what collaboration is and what strategies ensure that groups are able to work successfully toward a target and product.

A great resource for this is *Designing Groupwork*, a book by Elizabeth Cohen and John I. Goodlad. The book includes small group games that teach the behaviors students should exhibit during group work.[70] These behaviors make sense in almost all group work situations:

- Pay attention to what other group members need.
- No one is done until everyone is done.
- Help other students do things for themselves.
- Explain by telling how.
- Everybody helps.
- Find out what others think.
- Tell why. (You made a certain decision.)

Small Group Collaboration: Setting Kids up for Success

Let's examine how you can lay the foundation for the kinds of skills students need to collaborate successfully. The following strategies and activities have a dual purpose: they give kids opportunities to practice group collaboration and provide enough structure to ensure success.

Purpose: Get to Know Each Other

At the beginning of the year, or when new students join the class, or when you just want to mix things up a bit, give students an interesting question to ponder. Let them take turns sharing their thoughts in small groups. I bet you can think of lots of great questions, but here are a few to get you started:

- *Which planet would you like to visit and why?*
- *What two sports could be combined into one?*
- *What country would you like to visit and why?*
- *What two foods could be combined to make a delicious new entree?*

Purpose: Share Thinking

If you want students to hear a variety of answers to questions you pose or to share solutions to math problems that were independently solved, use a small group protocol. This can be effective in lieu of always having one student present their answer or solution to the whole class. The expectations for the sharing time must be taught and practiced, however. For example, in a four-member group:

1. After one student presents, each group member has a turn to ask a question, agree or disagree and state why, or make a connection.
2. Person #1 then comments on changes to his thinking resulting from the feedback received.
3. The process is repeated with each additional group member.

Purpose: Brainstorm

When you want kids to brainstorm ideas, use a small group protocol such as **Whip Around.** There are many opportunities to use brainstorming in the classroom; for example, kids could generate lists of:

- synonyms for slow and fast.
- different emotions.
- ideas for a Harvest Party.
- games to play at recess.

If you give kids a chance to think of their answers individually first, the group brainstorming will be that much richer. Each student then gets a turn to share with the group, while one student records.

Purpose: Share Opinions

If you want students to hear different opinions about an article that each has read, use the **Save the Last Word for Me**[71] protocol. Students highlight what they think is the most important passage in the piece. One student reads aloud their passage and other members take turns responding with their opinions and connections to that passage. The first student concludes round one with his thoughts on the responses.

<u>Purpose: Review</u>

When you want kids to review concepts or vocabulary, give them a question to consider or a word to define. After some think time, which may include writing or illustrating their thoughts, students get together and share responses. After each student gives an answer, the other members can take turns giving feedback.

As you can see, giving a bit of think time before collaborations is often helpful. When adults hold a meeting, they are more productive if they've had time to consider the issues ahead of time. The same is true for kids. Give your students the opportunity to do some pre-thinking, perhaps by drawing, writing, or problem solving, before meeting in small groups. Then, when they get together, each student will be more prepared and more likely to participate. If students struggle when working independently, they have even more reason to collaborate.

<u>Purpose: Short Term Project</u>

If you want small groups of students to create a chart that explains something, such as a math concept, make sure they have had plenty of practice with the above exercises beforehand. For this one-time product:

1. Have a clear purpose for the chart. How is it going to further everyone's learning? Discuss this with students so they understand that the target is learning, not just completing the chart.

2. Have clear expectations for the chart. For example, what should be on it? What size should numbers and letters be? Should the students in the back of the room be able to see the numbers?

3. Show examples of effective charts and some charts missing elements. Present, or develop with students, a rubric for evaluating the chart based on what they noticed.

Rubric for Chart			
Score	**5**	**3**	**1**
Product Completion	All requirements met.	Most requirements met.	Some requirements met.
Ease of Reading	Easy to follow concept.	Part of the chart is challenging to understand.	The chart is difficult to follow and understand.
Member Participation	All members participated equally.	There was not equal participation.	Not everyone participated.

4. Give students time to develop a rough draft of the chart—independently.

5. When students meet as a group, they should use a protocol to share their ideas and drafts. One of the criteria for chart completion should be that it includes at least one idea from each student.

6. Some teachers assign each student a job in their group, e.g., materials manager, reader, speaker, writer. The purpose of each job and the specific responsibilities that go along with it must be taught. Students can also use different color markers for writing their portion of the chart so it's clear who contributed what.

7. Give students a specific amount of time in which to complete the project. Help kids with time management by letting them know how much time has passed. For example, "half time," ten minutes left, two minutes left. Eventually, each group can have their own timekeeper to take on this responsibility.

8. Have students evaluate their own chart using a rubric you develop. (See the example.) Consider saving some of the best charts to show future classes.

9. If you want students to present their charts to the class, be sure to teach them a presentation protocol and give them time to rehearse multiple times.

Steps might include:

    a. How to stand so that all students can see the poster and the presenters can easily refer to it.

    b. What to include in the presentation.

    c. How to break the poster down into component parts and decide which part each student will present.

10. Using the rubric, decide what the audience will look for as groups present. Rather than having audience members clap absentmindedly after each performance, have kids provide specific and constructive feedback based on that focus.

Purpose: Long-Term Project

In another observation, I was in a classroom talking to a small group of students who were completing a report on a country. One member was able to tell me that the report should include information on the culture, economy, history, and government. However, none of the students could tell me what those things were.

The long-term project is the most complex of the small group assignments. If students have had many opportunities to participate in the activities described above, and they are ready for the more challenging experience of working on complex, multi-step projects with peers, here are some important things to consider:

- Choose a broad topic that is familiar to students. If kids are researching animals, for example, they should have experience with typical subtopics that are included in an animal report. During a previous science unit, students should have learned about animal habitats, special survival adaptations, and methods of getting food. In their small group, they choose an animal the group finds interesting, and research those same areas—perhaps adding one of their own. The project criteria thus limit the scope of the study and focus on important aspects of the animal.

- Over the course of the project, make connections to skills students learned previously in language arts lessons, such as how to read informational texts, how to take notes, and how to write paragraphs based on those notes.

- The project should have clear targets and product expectations. For example, the group will:

  o Write a report with one to three paragraphs addressing each subtopic.

  o Create one artifact, such as a chart. Expectations for what is included in the chart must be explicit. (Show students models of exemplary charts. Do not assume that they know how to place writing, photos, and other artifacts on a chart in an effective way.)

  o Present their information to the class. Expectations for this presentation must be clear. For example:

    - The presentation will be 5-10 minutes.
    - Each group member will speak.
    - Use notes; do not read the written report.
    - When speaking, refer to the group's chart.

- Create a rubric to evaluate the project that includes criteria for the product **and** the effectiveness of group collaboration. Students should have a copy of this rubric as they work together, refer to it periodically, and use it for frequent self-evaluation.

- Do not assume that students know how to plot a time line for completion of a project; create such a time line with them. This exercise will help students see how to break down multistep projects into manageable chunks, and they will eventually be able to do this independently. Here is a template to get you started:

  Day 1: Decide on topic. Collect resources.
  Day 2: Assign each person part of the research.
  Day 3-4: Research the topic, taking notes.
  Day 5: Present research to each other, using a group protocol.
  Day 6: Each person writes one paragraph about their subtopic.
  Day 7: Students work in partnerships to edit and proofread the paragraphs.
  Day 8: As a group, students write an introductory and a concluding paragraph.
  Day 9: Students complete final drafts of all paragraphs.
  Day 10: Use a protocol to brainstorm ideas for the artifact, e.g., chart.
  　　　　Each person chooses something to add to the chart.
  Day 11-12: Work on chart.
  Day 13-14: Rehearse Final Presentation.

Students check off each step on the timeline as it is completed, and each day can end with a debriefing about success and progress. This is a wonderful time for you to connect collaboration and working in groups to all the new learning that is occurring. It takes a lot of planning to set students up for success working in small groups, but the results are worth it, and think of the life skills kids are developing along the way!

From My Experience: <u>Giving Independent Time First</u>

Before my students shared or brainstormed in partnerships or small groups, I gave them time to work on the assignment or brainstorm ideas independently. It gave them a chance to activate prior knowledge and think creatively on their own. They were subsequently more prepared to join in and their sharing was far more rich and diverse.

NOTES

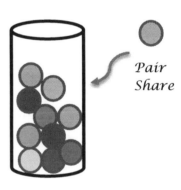

Pair Share

Chapter 19 Key Points

Students' Roles

☐ Follow small group protocols.

☐ Connect sharing with your partner or small group to learning and the brain.

☐ Take your turn to share with a partner or a small group.

☐ Make sure there are equitable opportunities for the students in your partnership or small group to participate.

Teachers' Roles

☐ Put partner share opportunities into lesson plans.

☐ Develop questions for partnerships to consider.

☐ Teach a partner share procedure.

☐ Gradually teach students about processing what they hear from their partner. Give them opportunities to give specific kinds of feedback.

☐ Connect partner sharing to learning and the brain.

☐ Decide if a learning situation would benefit from a small group format.

☐ Decide on the purpose of small group work, teach protocols, and provide opportunities for students to learn how to work together.

☐ Connect small group work to learning and the brain.

Hidden Steps: Partner Share

The issue: *I told my students to talk with their partners. Some kids shared. Some did not. Some didn't even find a partner. Help!*   —Primary Teacher

Even young children learn early on that they can stay hidden in the classroom. Perhaps they have not been in classrooms where partner sharing is a norm. Or initially, it may be hard for them to retrieve ideas to share. To move kids in the right direction, building community activities must be a part of the weekly schedule. They give students a chance to participate in non-threatening ways. Explicitly teach, model, and practice partner share protocols, beginning with simple questions to which students respond: favorite colors, animals, books— and why. Observe carefully and check for 100% participation. Teach a protocol for finding a partner if someone is absent.

Remind students that sharing is a way to offer building material (schema) for the community to capture.

- Build community.
- Discuss benefits of sharing:
  - Feedback
  - Find level of understanding
  - Verbal rehearsal
- Discuss benefits for the brain.
- Teach how to find a partner (if not assigned).
- Teach how to partner share.
- Scaffold sharing, beginning with easier questions.
- Teach ways to share: A to B, B to A, only A, only B, A to B to A (feedback)
- Use sentence frames.
- Sometimes have students share with the whole group.
- Debrief the experience, connecting to learning.
- Celebrate!

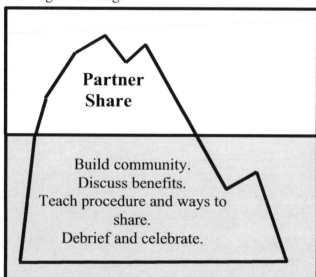

Partner Share

Build community.
Discuss benefits.
Teach procedure and ways to share.
Debrief and celebrate.

Hidden Steps: Table Talk

I can remember being disappointed when students did not cooperate or collaborate well when I gave them an assignment to complete as a group. Of course, that was before I realized how important it was to teach them the needed group social skills and protocols that would set them up for equal sharing opportunities. Don't make the same mistake I did. Start with a discussion of the rationale and the benefits for table sharing. Teach students a protocol for equitable sharing and debrief afterward. Ask, *How did that feel? What did you learn from your tablemates? Did everyone get equal turns?*

Steps:

- Build community so that students know and care for each other.
- Teach students that during group sharing, they will be adding building material to their schema.
- Discuss benefits to the brain.
- Teach table talk protocols.
- Debrief afterward.
- Empower students: have some share with the whole group.

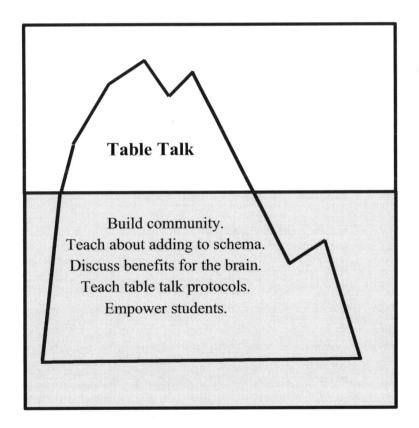

Table Talk

Build community.
Teach about adding to schema.
Discuss benefits for the brain.
Teach table talk protocols.
Empower students.

Section III: Plan for and Assess a Community of Learners

Introduction

In part three, we tackle the essentials of lesson planning and assessment. It may seem odd to include assessment in a book about creating a community of learners. The word assessment typically calls to mind things like grade books, unit testing, report cards, state assessments, etc., all necessary parts of a teacher's job. But assessment can be so much more. In fact, the word assessment comes from the Latin, **assidere**: *to sit beside*. In the context of teaching: to *"sit beside"* someone in order to understand their thinking. Assessment can be a tool that informs teaching and supports and motivates students, helping them understand what they know and what they need to do to reach learning targets. It is, in fact, one of the key components of a transformed learning community.

Traditional assessment is **summative** in nature. It occurs at the end of a unit, a term, or a school year, long after lessons and daily work are completed—often so long afterward that students don't connect daily effort to grades. They open their report cards and are elated or disappointed, as if grades were purely arbitrary: *What, a C? I don't deserve a C! How did I get a C?* Or, *Yay, I got an A! My parents will be so happy!*

A better way to do business is to focus on **formative assessment**. Formative assessment is ongoing feedback that helps students determine their level of understanding and see where their next efforts should be focused. It can show small increments of improvement that might otherwise be missed—little victories for students to celebrate, motivating them and reinforcing their hard work. Formative assessment is also an important tool for teachers. Those frequent checks of kids' understanding provide key information for planning upcoming lessons.

In addition to formative assessment, the following chapters focus on several important keys to good instruction:

- Giving purpose to classroom activities and student work—so kids connect what they are doing in class to learning a target.
- Writing targets in student language so students know the goal of their lessons.
- Composing lessons using a 4-component template for ease of planning.
- Breaking down targets into smaller steps (target ladders).
- Using three levels of understanding to differentiate lessons.
- Guiding students toward independence.
- Planning for differentiation.

Chapter 20: Give Purpose to Student Work

Work, work, recess, work, work, lunch, work, dismissal—and then homework! That's the perception many students have of the school day. They think the purpose of school is just to do work. As a teacher, I even had a chart on the wall labeled "Missing Work." However, as we've seen in the previous two sections of this book, what happens in the classroom is not just work. It is work with purpose. When kids understand purpose, they are much more likely to get on board, realizing the work exists to help them learn and make them smarter. Through the course of my teaching career, this realization became clearer and clearer to me.

Students' Perspectives

In my observations, I often ask students why they are working on a particular assignment. They typically respond, "Because the teacher told me to," or "I don't know." They seem to completely miss the larger purpose of classwork—to help them learn!   —G. Peterson

As teachers, we can give students a different perspective about school. We can help them see it's not just a place to do work. It's a place to learn, and the work they do is purposeful, so that when they are asked why they are completing an assignment, they will say something like, "*I am learning how to add fractions, so I am practicing.*"

Kids' views about school begin forming on the first day of kindergarten and probably even before. This first year of school is an opportunity to guide students in seeing and *feeling* that school is a place where they go to learn. They can see exactly what they are learning—*the lesson target*, and how they are doing—through *formative assessment*. Even very young children can understand targets, if they are presented in a way kids can comprehend—with pictures, symbols, or simple words they are able to read. Students can realize that each activity or assignment relates to that target, and that their hard work has an important payoff: to change their brains and make them smarter. They can learn that frequent assessment is not a means to pass judgment on them, but a way to show how they are progressing. It helps them and us decide what steps need to come next in their learning.

Activity Focus

When I first began teaching, I was basically an ***activity teacher***. I gave my students work to keep them interested, keep them busy, and to fill up the school day. The goals of these activities and the connections to other learning were unclear, sometimes even to me, and a lot of my teacher talk was spent giving instructions. Examples of assignments, depending on the grade level, were:

- Draw a picture of the main character.

- Make a speech about a book you just read.

- Create a diorama.

- Write a report about Paraguay.

- Do the homework 2.1 on page 73.

- Complete the phonics packet.

I bet you've seen assignments just like these in the teacher editions of your students' textbooks.

Coverage Focus

As I became more familiar with the curriculum, I changed to a ***coverage teacher***. I spent a lot of time talking to kids and mentioning all the state standards. My goal was to cover all the material in the textbooks, and before long I was mired in frustration. I just couldn't get to everything, and I couldn't give my students the depth of experience they really needed in order to learn. With the emphasis in recent years on common core standards and testing, today's educators feel increasing pressure now, as I did then, to prioritize covering the curriculum over student learning. In *How to Build a Better Teacher*, Elizabeth Green refers to one teacher's dilemma: *In third grade, students were supposed to master fractions, but [the teacher] never found enough time to get them to really understand. They moved on to fourth grade able to master the state test, but with very little idea of what kind of number a fraction actually represented.*[72]

It didn't take long before I began to question the "coverage" approach. It just didn't make sense for my students, and I worried it was leaving kids in a constant state of disequilibrium.

Target Focus

Finally, though, I found what I was looking for: a **target** focus. I began by letting students in on my targets…not just jotting a few objectives in a lesson plan book for the benefit of my principal, but posting them for kids to see. After all, the students were the ones who really needed to know what they were. My goal became providing activities and assignments to assist students in reaching clear targets. And I started using frequent formative assessment to inform my students and me on how clear their understanding was at any given point.

I started first with targets so my students could see the purpose of lessons. If they were giving a speech about a book, I wanted them to see it as a chance to practice oral presentation skills and to verbalize/clarify their comprehension of the book—it wasn't just something to keep them busy. I wanted to make sure fourth graders understood that doing the problems on page 73 gave them a chance to see how well they understood the difference between area and perimeter. And I wanted second graders to make the connection between phonics and the ultimate goal of reading—comprehension. I began to question how making a diorama demonstrated reading comprehension. And I realized that a report on Paraguay required a lot of schema (history? economics?) that students didn't yet have. With clear targets, it was easy to see that not every assignment was a good fit.

So, what do targets actually look like? Targets are written in student language, using explicit wording, and posted for all to see. They begin with words such as:

- I know… (vocabulary, basic facts, etc.),
- I understand… (content knowledge), or
- I am able to… (a process).

You can also include language targets for English language learners.

As you can see, the words you begin with indicate the level of thinking you want to elicit from students. Here are some sample targets for specific content areas:

Math:

- I know the definition of sum and addend.
- I understand how to use place value and regrouping to add 2-digit numbers.
- I am able to solve problems that require adding numbers.

Social Studies:

- I know the names of important European explorers.

- I understand two reasons why these European explorers came to the New World.

- I am able to compare and contrast two European explorers and the purposes of their missions.

Science:

- I know the life cycle of a butterfly.

- I understand the purpose for each stage.

- I am able to use resources to determine the life cycle of other insects.

Very young children may need pictures or symbols, rather than words, to indicate the target, but even nonreaders need to know that lessons have learning goals. Each day, post your target and call attention to it. You can take a moment to discuss the vocabulary used, or have students chorally read the target to change things up. The key point is that *students* are able to tell you what they are learning.

As I changed my view of instruction, I also discovered that my understanding of curriculum became clearer. Instead of teaching students a laundry list of curricular objectives, I could focus on the biggest idea of all—getting them to think and including them as partners in their learning.

Next, I tackled formative assessment. I didn't want to get buried under stacks of papers with no time to really analyze my students' work, so I found ways that were easy to use, yet gave solid feedback into their thinking. It became second nature to include these quick checks during and after lessons, and my students soon realized I was using the information to guide our next steps, not to penalize them with low scores if they didn't understand a concept. In Chapter 23, we will explore formative assessment in greater depth.

Chapter 20 Key Points

Students' Roles

☐ Think about how each activity or assignment you do is connected to a learning target.

☐ If you do not know what the target is—or understand the target—ask for more clarification.

☐ Ask: *How will I know if I meet the target?*

Teachers' Roles

☐ Understand the purpose of every classroom activity and share that with kids.

☐ Guide students in developing a purposeful view of school.

☐ Write targets in student language and post them prominently.

NOTES

Chapter 21: Design Lessons with Four Components

Americans hold the notion that good teaching comes through artful and spontaneous interactions with students during lessons.... Such views minimize the importance of planning increasingly effective lessons and lend credence to the folk belief that good teachers are born, not made.[73]   —J. Stigler & J. Hiebert

Once we teach the procedures and get students actively engaging in lessons so important for a strong community of learners, our most important focus shifts to **planning and assessment**. Lesson planning starts with an informed "guess." Based on assessment evidence, we design lessons that we think will help students meet the next target. Then, during the actual lessons, we observe carefully and assess how things are going. We listen to student responses and watch kids work, seeing how our "guess" is working, and deciding what adjustments to make and/or what new questions to ask.

Students' Perspectives

Too often, students growing up in typical classroom environments become passive learners. They rarely wonder…

- *What is the target of this lesson?*
- *How will I know if meet the target?*
- *How does it connect to my previous work?*[74]

Their idea of the lesson objective is, not surprisingly, short sighted also. Students will tell you that they are trying to:

- finish a worksheet.
- not get in trouble.
- get the right answers.
- get the work done so they can go out to recess.

While all those things may have some value, at least to them, the real purpose of a lesson is something far more important—to learn! That's why it is critical to show students exactly what the lesson targets are. They need to know **why** you are asking them to engage.

In the Beginning...

After earning a teaching license, many beginning teachers breathe a sigh of relief, "Thank goodness I don't have to turn in any more lesson plans with objectives!" It's easy to assume a textbook will provide the lesson and all you need to do is follow the steps presented. Saving time up front, unfortunately, does not lead to effective lessons later. I have seen teacher plans that look very much like this:

Reading: Inference p. 34-45
Math: Lesson 6 Rectangles and Squares
Social Studies: War of Independence

And as a beginning teacher, mine were similar. But it meant that I was often "shooting from the hip," during lessons—not a good feeling. I discovered pretty quickly that I needed to spend a lot more time on specifics to ensure that I was adequately prepared.

Obviously, there is not time to write out in detail every lesson that is presented during a week. But, particularly at the beginning of a teacher's career, a good amount of time does have to be devoted to planning. With experience, the process becomes easier and less information is required in the plan, provided the teacher has acquired sufficient experience to fill in the blanks and adjust lessons during presentations. Initially, however, **more** detail is needed—there's just no shortcut to learning how to plan and how to avoid problems that might arise in the course of a lesson. In this chapter, we take a look at lesson design, specifically lesson design that includes targets and formative assessment and sets students up for success.

An important caveat: when I say targets, I'm not talking about top down edicts from district administrators, requiring teachers to write common core standards in their lesson plans and creating more work for them. In reality, targets are not something you *have* to do; they are something to *help* you. They are very specific learning outcomes that help you plan and teach, and just as important, help students see **why** they are doing what is required in a lesson. Targets clarify what you are going for and make it easy to generate quick assessments that show the students, and you, how they are doing.

Lesson Design

Learning goals help students know what they're supposed to be learning, why it's important, and what their work will look like when they're done.[75]   —S. Brookhart & C. Moss

Good lesson design begins with targets. If we know the destination—the target—we can figure out how to get there, and we can check periodically along the way, using progress markers, to see if we are on track. An effective lesson, consists of four basic parts: identifying the target, reviewing needed procedures, using active engagement strategies during the lesson, and debriefing or assessing. Let's take each one in order and examine it more closely.

I. Developing Clear Targets & Progress Markers

Targets

In the first part of a lesson, present the target. As stated in the previous chapter, it should be written in student language, using explicit wording, and posted for all to see. Remember, targets begin with words such as:

- I know… (vocabulary, basic facts),

- I understand… (content knowledge) or

- I am able to… (a process).

Progress Markers

Once students know what they are supposed to learn, they need to know whether they are making progress. Sometimes kids, particularly struggling learners, do a lot of work, yet have little sense they are improving. This is where progress markers can be so helpful. Progress markers are simply criteria that students can use to see if they are reaching the target. Just like targets, they are written in very specific, student language, because students are the ones who will be using them. With progress markers, students can actually **see** results and take pride in the work ethic that made those results possible. Here are some examples of markers for the previous targets:

- I added 2-digit numbers and got the correct sum 4 out of 5 times.

- I am able to explain what I am doing using place value words.

- I wrote two reasons why European explorers came to the New World in clear language that made sense to my partner.

- I verified my reasons with information from a text.

- I made a drawing showing the life cycle of the butterfly.

- I wrote what was happening in each stage.

II. Reviewing Needed Procedures

Assuming students have been taught classroom procedures, review the expectations required for the lesson or task. For example, say to students:

- *Read the three expectations for our carpet procedure and choose one on which to focus.*

- *Whisper to your neighbor one expectation for our independent work.*

- *Remember, for partner work:*
    1. *Look like you're focused.*
    2. *Whisper only to your partner.*
    3. *Help each other.*

Later, you and your students can point to evidence of the community meeting these expectations. Doing so builds pride and reinforces the positive. Do a check-in after ten minutes or any time in the lesson when you want to keep the class focused on behaviors that help them be successful.

III. Outlining the Lesson

When you get to the lesson proper, anticipate as much as possible how it will go. Consider the challenges that might arise, key questions to ask, and the active participation strategies to include.

If you are using a textbook, read through the lesson, writing down possible questions, and note areas that might be challenging for students. Think through the activity sequence. Are there any steps missing? Are there steps that can be skipped? Will students need to spend more time on a particular step? Determine if there is unfamiliar vocabulary that should be addressed, and if math problems are part of the lesson—take the time to solve them!

If you are creating your own lesson, brainstorm the activities and sequence of activities that will help students meet the target(s). Consider the questions you might pose and the stumbling blocks that students could encounter. At the end of this chapter, I have included a lesson template to help you incorporate these considerations into your own lessons.

Active Participation Strategies

If a whole group lesson is presented, give students opportunities to process and think, as described in Chapters 15 and 17. Use active participation techniques such as think/pair/share, choral response, drawing, writing, etc. If a partner/small group activity will be used, what will you look for as you check for student engagement? How will you ensure there are opportunities for all students to share? If the activity is independent work, make sure there is a clear purpose to the assignment and that students are ready to do the work with a minimum of support. Be ready to adjust the lesson as you listen to student responses and watch kids work. If you hear or see students who are struggling with the target, consider continuing the whole group lesson, working in a small group with some students, or giving students more time to work with partners.

IV. Closure/Debriefing

At the end of a lesson, take a minute to debrief behavioral expectations and help students make that crucial connection between their behavior and their success/accomplishments. *Who was able to listen to their partner? How did that help you learn more? Who was able to stay working the whole time? How did that help you accomplish more?* The class can also celebrate learning or behavior that they noticed. As always, the focus is on what went well—that's what you want to reinforce.

This is also a good time to include formative assessment. For example, if the lesson's target involved differentiating between area and perimeter, give students a 3x5 card on which to complete a couple of problems. Give them a quadrilateral's dimensions and have them determine area and perimeter independently. This will quickly give you the information you need to plan next steps. More ideas for formative assessment will be presented in Chapter 23.

It's easy to jump right into a lesson activity and skip everything else, but don't do it. The amount of time you devote to presenting targets, reviewing behavioral expectations, including active participation, and debriefing afterward pays big dividends. It strengthens community, gets kids on board, keeps them involved, and helps you know where to go next. On the following page is a short template to help you pull together the four parts of an effective lesson as you do your own planning. Following this lesson format will push you to clarify your targets and behavioral expectations, formulate key questions, and make decisions about active participation and assessment. Initially, it takes time to plan this way, but soon it becomes second nature. Following the 2-page template (which can be duplicated back-to-back) are two sample lesson plans, using this format, that may prove helpful as you get started.

From My Experience: Larger Targets

While it is important to have specific, small targets, keep in mind larger, overarching targets as well. For example, an art target might be that students know how to make secondary colors from primary colors. You allow students to discover how to do this by mixing colors. At the same time, students are experiencing joy, appreciation for art, and being creative—meeting larger affective targets that enrich their school experience.

NOTES

Lesson Planning Template

Subject: _____

I. Target (choose one or more).

I know_____

I understand_____

I am able to_____

Progress Markers: *(How will we know progress is being made?)*

II.   Behavioral Expectation Review *(What procedures will be needed for this lesson?)*

III. Activity (*Outline steps, including possible questions and challenges*)

_____

_____

_____

_____

_____

_____

_____

_____

_____

I will provide opportunities (TURNS) for students to:

- ☐ Think, using wait time
- ☐ Share with a partner
- ☐ Repeat or use a student solution
- ☐ Echo or cloze read
- ☐ Write
- ☐ Respond chorally
- ☐ Use signals
- ☐ Use a small group protocol

IV. Closure (*Formative Assessment*)

Sample Lesson Plan #1

Subject: 2nd Grade Math

I. Target: *I am able to compare triangles and squares.*

Progress Marker: *I can use geometric vocabulary.*

II. Behavioral Expectation Review: *Partner Sharing*

Review the steps for sharing with a partner

III. Activity:

- *PS (partner sharing): Review attributes of triangles*
- *WG (whole group): Share & Record*
- *PS: Review attributes of rectangles*
- *WG: Share & Record*
- *WG: Notice similarities and differences.*
- *PS: Similarities and differences.*
- *WG: Share and Record*
- *(Add new triangles into the mix?)*

Possible Questions

- *Can we call squares rectangles?*
- *Can we call rectangles squares?*

Challenges

- *Students probably have learned the name of shapes without considering attributes and will have difficulty thinking about squares as also meeting the criteria for rectangles.*

I will provide opportunities (TURNS) for students to:

- ☐ *Think, using wait time.*
- ☐ *Share with a partner.*
- ☐ *Write.*
- ☐ *Use signals.*

IV. Closure/Debrief (Behavioral or Academic):

- *How many of you learned something new from your partner?*

- *Exit Card: Can we call rectangles squares? Why or why not?*

Sample Lesson Plan #2

Subject: 5th grade social studies: *War of Independence*

I. Target: *I can choose to be a loyalist, patriot, or neutral colonist and state reasons.* (Connect to persuasive writing attributes.)

Progress Marker: *I can state reasons for my choice that make sense to me and to my partner.*

II. Behavioral Expectation Review: *Whole Group Listening*

Review the steps for whole group listening, speakers stand and audience members turn

III. Activity:

- *Introduce Vocabulary: Loyalist, Patriot, Neutral*
- *Students partner read pp. 234-236, listening for attributes for each group: loyalist, patriot, or neutral.*
- *WG: Partnerships share the attributes they found with the whole group.*
- *Periodically have students partner share about other students' responses.*
- *PS: Brainstorm advantages and disadvantages for each group.*
- *WG share; record on T-charts.*

Possible Questions

- *What were the advantages of being a loyalist? patriot? neutral?*

- *What were the dangers of being a loyalist? patriot? neutral?*

Challenges
- *Students may have assumed that everyone was a patriot!*

I will provide opportunities (TURNS) for students to:

- ☐ *Read and share with a partner*
- ☐ *Restate or comment on another student's thinking*
- ☐ *Write*

IV. Closure/Debrief (Behavioral or Academic)

- *Did you change your thinking after listening to another student?*
- *Exit Card: Which group would you chose to belong to and why?*

Beginning a Lesson

When the Material is New for Students

Of course, the way you launch a lesson depends greatly on whether the learning target is new to students or they have been working on it for a bit. If the target is new, you should find out first what they already know. Start with a short pretest, something as simple as asking them to draw or write what they understand about a concept. It doesn't take much time and a quick trip around the room will tell you what you need to know. If the pre-test shows they have very little schema, you can launch right into the teaching point:

- *Our target today is to understand the characteristics of a quadrilateral.*

- *A quadrilateral is a two-dimensional shape with four sides. (Share examples and non-examples.)*

Right up front you are sharing the main idea of the lesson and priming students for what comes next.

When Students Have Some Schema

But if students already know something about the target, help them warm up their brains by activating prior knowledge: *Our target today is to understand the characteristics of a quadrilateral. Take some time to think. (Pause) Now share with your partner (or write in your math journal) what you understand so far.*

Creating a K-W-L chart with students can also give you an informal assessment about students' current schema. It is easy, however, to develop the chart with input from just a few kids. If you only call on students raising hands, the information will be less useful. Instead,

- give students time to think about what they know.

- let them first create their own KWL chart, listing what they know and want to learn.

- have students compare charts with partners, adding to their own chart.

- have each partnership share one thing they know and one thing they want to learn and record their responses on a class chart.

The last column, (L) is often forgotten after a lesson or unit has been completed. It is an important part of closure, however, to go back and revisit the accuracy of initial thinking and for students to realize how much they have learned.

Fishing Expeditions

Even routine questions we ask during the day can reinforce students' perceptions about themselves or the classroom community. For example, have you begun a lesson with a *Who knows...* question? It's a pretty common teacher strategy for starting a lesson, and I won't deny using it often as a rookie teacher. Here is an example:

Teacher: *Who knows what a quadrilateral is?*[bb]

Maria: *It is a shape.*

Teacher: *Yes.... but who can tell me more?*

Nia: *It has pointy things.*

Teacher: *And we call those pointy things...*

A few shout out: *Corners!*

Teacher: *Yes, that's right, but what else are they called?*

First of all, this is what I call a fishing expedition. You throw out the bait and hope students bite. Hands are up, and they seem engaged. Seems like a great way to begin a lesson, but is it? There are several reasons to steer clear of this overused technique. First of all, it doesn't give the teacher much information. You might find out what a few students know, but what about everyone else? Second, it takes up valuable teaching time and can lead off into tangents. Worst of all, it puts students in the business of trying to read your mind instead of doing some real thinking.

Certain phrases are also cues for student actions. The question, "*Who knows* what a quadrilateral is?" is a subtle signal that at least *one student must know,* and you have given them permission to shout out an answer. Other kids can sit back passively and decide they do not have to think at all. After that one student has shouted out the answer, the only thing that you have learned is that he or she already knew what the shape was. But what you really want students to do is to think. Not just a few, but all of your students. There are better ways to begin a lesson.

[bb] Research shows that the average elementary teacher may ask as many as 348 questions a day, whereas the students may not ask any." With all the practice we get, you'd think we'd be good at it.

Try instead beginning with the action you **really** want: "*Think* about this shape." "*Share* with a partner what you notice." "Take 15 seconds to *think* about what you know about quadrilaterals." The difference in wording is slight, but now you have dramatically increased the likelihood your kids will be engaged. The message is loud and clear—you expect all students to think and be engaged.

Planning Teacher Questions

Asking good questions is tough. We have so much schema in our teacher heads that it is hard to create a question that fits students' zones of proximal development. In fact, an obstacle for us is that it's nearly impossible to remember what it was like not knowing something. When planning, include possible questions of varying difficulty you can use during the lesson. That way you can avoid fishing expeditions and be purposeful about the questions you do ask. You can use strategies that engage all students and let them judge each other's answers for correctness. You can also use wait and second wait time. When questioning is strategic, it is an important step on the path to learning.

Teaching Students About Questioning

Let's spend a moment now thinking about students asking questions. Observing thousands of lessons, I have concluded that it is challenging for students to ask questions that move the discussion along, clarify a concept, or potentially add to schema. Why? Sometimes we just want to give students a chance to clarify basic information: *Does anyone have a question?* The intent is positive—we want to check for understanding during a lesson or before excusing students to begin work—and there is nothing wrong with that. But too often student questions are irrelevant or meant just to humor the class and get everyone off track. When a guest speaker, such as a fireman, is invited to a classroom, we remind kids, "Remember to think of questions. Do not tell stories." Without guidance, most kids don't know how to formulate relevant, meaningful questions. How can we *teach* them to do so?

First of all, decide if students have enough schema to even ask a question. Do they recognize when there are holes in their understanding? Do they realize that when they feel that sense of disequilibrium, asking questions can help them clear things up? A question indicates there is a gap between what a student knows and what he or she wants to know (learning target.) The gap must be small enough so that an answer to a question can bridge the two. Here are some ideas to help students learn to ask questions that will increase their level of understanding and promote deeper thinking for the whole class.

<u>Teach Students About Levels of Understanding.</u> Before asking good questions, students need to be cognizant of their own level of understanding. Here is an effective tool to help them decide: After a lesson, activity, or practice, prompt students to consider which of following statements pertains to them:

1: I understand thoroughly and want a challenge.

2: I understand and want more practice.

3: I do not understand yet and want more instruction.

They can hold up the number of fingers that indicates their level or write the number on their work. But this is important: **there is no judgment regarding the level.** It is a fluid number and just an indication of where a student is at that particular moment. Over time, your students will realize there is no shame in being a two or a three. It just means they haven't fully mastered a concept **yet**, and that's okay. If fact, if there is no disequilibrium, there is no real need to learn. Of course, we must guide students to recognize indicators or evidence of their level. We'll talk more about that in Chapter 24.

Once students understand their level, they are ready to think about real, meaningful questions, but they still need coaching on how to do it. Here are some steps you can use to guide them.

- <u>Start by listening to (and recording) the questions students ask.</u> What do you notice? Do their questions elicit one word answers or prompt others to deeper thinking? Are they focused on the subject or apt to go off on tangents? Find out what students notice about their questions.

- <u>Next keep track of the questions you ask them.</u> Do this for one subject each day and ask yourself if most of the questions are lower or higher level.

- <u>Analyze questions with students</u>. Teach them the difference between open and closed-ended questions and have them analyze the ones that appear in their texts.[cc] Which are easy to answer and which require more thinking? The goal here is to have students start to think about different levels of questions. They will begin to notice that easy questions often begin with "Who?" or "What?" Others are more challenging. Which questions require looking back at the text or story for supporting evidence?

- <u>Introduce students to Bloom's Taxonomy</u>. There are simple versions of the Taxonomy now with corresponding "question words" to help students analyze questions. With a little guidance from you they can begin determining the level of questions (from a text, or even you) using taxonomy vocabulary.

- <u>Give students a list of different questions</u>. After reading some text, have students determine which of a given list of questions helps them think harder or differently about the text. Which questions deepen their thinking? Which merely clarify basic information?

- <u>Have students begin to write their own questions</u> for reading (and later for other subjects), considering the level of thinking required to answer them. They can use a list of verbs from Bloom's Taxonomy to help them write questions at different levels. They can also compare their questions to the ones in the text.

Students will have a better idea of how to ask questions after they have explored in depth the purpose and vocabulary of good questions.

[cc] Close-ended questions can be answered by a simple "yes" or "no." Open-ended questions require more thinking and words.

Chapter 21 Key Points

Students' Roles

- ☐ Make sure you understand what you are trying to learn (the target). If you are not sure, ask.

- ☐ Understand how you will know when you meet the target.

- ☐ Look for the connection between activities and assignments you are doing and the target.

- ☐ Consider the behaviors that will help you learn the target.

- ☐ Learn to analyze different levels of questions.

- ☐ Think about the purpose of a question before asking it.

- ☐ At the end of the lesson, think about what you understand and what is still fuzzy.

Teachers' Roles

- ☐ Recognize that planning and assessing are your two most important tasks, once procedures have been taught.

- ☐ Spend the time needed to thoroughly plan lessons, including processing time and opportunities for active participation.

- ☐ Practice planning lessons with the four key elements. Plan the language to be used in lessons carefully, including key questions you will pose.

- ☐ Use different levels of questions—and teach students how to ask meaningful questions.

Hidden Steps: Targets

The issue: *My principal told me he asked my students what they were learning. Most were not able to tell him. And many said they were doing the work so they could go to recess. How can I get kids on board?*   —Second Grade Teacher

As discussed in Chapter 17, students see school as a place where they see friends and do a lot of work. But that work needs to be purposeful—to practice a strategy or skill in order to master a target. Begin with posting the target, making sure it uses language that students understand. Formative assessment will let students know how they are doing. Along with portfolios of work, they will be able to *see* the progress they are making and know that their "work" and effort has led to more understanding and success.

Here are the hidden steps that make this strategy work:

- Build community so that students know and care for each other.
- Post targets in student language.
- Discuss targets.
- Mention the target throughout the lesson.
- Use debriefing or formative assessment to help students determine their level of understanding.
- Help students recognize when they make progress and connect that to their hard work.

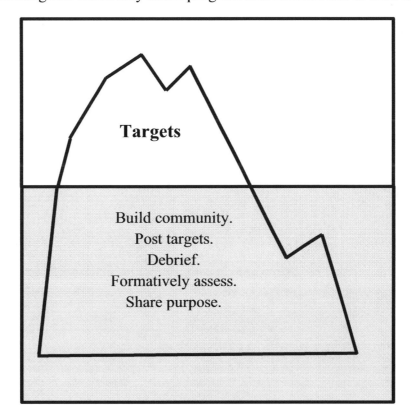

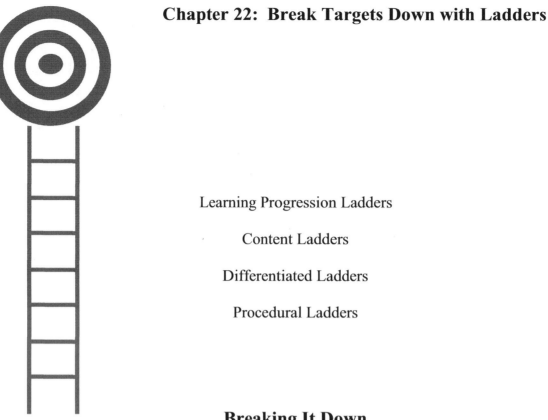

Chapter 22: Break Targets Down with Ladders

Learning Progression Ladders

Content Ladders

Differentiated Ladders

Procedural Ladders

Breaking It Down

In the course of a lesson, hundreds of large and small interactions occur. Our job is to take them all in, make judgments, and be ready to adjust our plans to meet the challenges that arise. Maybe we notice a few students who can't make sense of sums greater than ten, or some of our intermediate kids struggle with decimals. Some kids might have trouble managing time, or they can't seem to work with a partner. What do you do when issues pop up, as they inevitably do? Don't blame last year's teacher, lazy kids, or the ills of society. Take a step back, assess and analyze the situation. Try to find the point at which a student **is** successful, and then move him forward. Sometimes this requires breaking things down to what I call the "molecular" level. It's easy to make assumptions about what students should be able to do or understand. But if the schema isn't there, back up and rebuild the foundation. Consider the following examples, starting with a couple of common problems students face in math.

Academic Example: Math

Students often have "holes" in their mathematical understanding that interfere with their ability to learn something new. It is our job to uncover those holes and try to break concepts down into smaller bits they can grasp. For example, if an intermediate student has trouble reading and ordering decimals, back up and find out what he **does** know:

- Does he understand place value with whole numbers?
- Can he read and write simple decimals? Does he understand tenths, but not hundredths?
- Use visual representations; students may have developed holes because the leap to abstract notation was rushed while their understanding was still fragile. Using grids divided into ten, a hundred, or a thousand parts, students can "see" decimals. Play math games using cards with visual, not just numerical representations. Bring out the number line.

In the same way, if a primary student has trouble adding sums greater than ten, determine her level of number sense.

- Does she have a sense of numbers less than 10? (6 = 5+1, 4+2, 3+3)
- Is she able to "count on?" 9 + 6 = 9 +1+1+1+1+1+1
- Does she know her doubles? (6+6)
- Is she able to use a double to determine a neighbor? (6+7)

The big idea here is that you want to find the 'point of understanding' or success, and build from there.

Procedural Example: Getting Right to Work

Before helping individual students, scan the room to check who is working. Some students will benefit by having you stand discretely next to them as they get started. Debrief after a few minutes or at the end: *How many of you got right to work? How did that help you?* Getting right to work and staying focused is hard for some students, so expressly teach what it looks like and sounds like when everyone gets right to work. Break things down to the "molecular" steps:

1. Think about what you are going to do as you walk back to your seat without talking.

2. Sit down and take out the materials you think you will need.

3. Open up books or journals and find your spot.

4. Reread what you did the day before.

5. Continue thinking, and then begin. Take note of where you begin working.

6. If you get distracted, see how fast you can get back to work.

7. If you have 20 minutes to work, check how much you have finished after 10 minutes.

Example: Time Management

Managing time does not come naturally to some of us, adults and students alike. Show kids how to use time well by breaking assignments into smaller parts. For example, if there are 10 sentences to write, and you have given students 20 minutes, help them figure out that they should have completed 3 sentences after 6 minutes, 6 sentences after 12 minutes, etc. Students don't necessarily have a sense of time passing, so strategies like this are helpful. Another useful tool for time management is the **Time Timer©.**[76] It visually shows time passing and is great for concrete learners.

Intermediate students with multiple assignments or projects often find it challenging to keep things on track and to allocate their time successfully. Teach kids to list and prioritize their tasks. At the beginning of a work time, model how to choose the most pressing task and set a goal. When the period is over, have students evaluate how well they used their time. If students are writing, they can put a dot where they begin and end. This very concrete strategy helps them see how much they accomplished.

Example: Partner Work

When students have difficulty working with partners, they need explicit instruction and coaching. Teach them HOW to work with a partner and WHAT to say. Then model and practice. Give students key conversational strategies to initiate dialogue. For example:

- *Ask your partner, "Do you want to go first? Or which part do you want to do?"*

- *Actively listen to your partner. After she is done sharing, tell her what you heard.*

- *Give compliments: Thank your partner after completion of the task.*

Break it down. We often fail to realize that a task that is easy for us may not at all be easy for kids. Breaking it down gives them a chance to be successful, too.

Breaking Targets Down with Ladders

Target ladders can help teachers and students see the breakdown of concepts and skills. At the top of the ladder is the goal, and listed underneath, in ascending order, are the many smaller steps, or rungs, students must climb to reach that goal. Other terms associated with target ladders are *learning progressions* and *task analyses* (from the work of Madeline Hunter in *Elements of Instruction*). The idea is to break a concept down into its essential components. When you create a target ladder, you clearly see which elements students must understand before being able to complete a task, and you can ascertain the steps kids might be missing when they struggle. Let's take a look at how target ladders can be helpful in four crucial areas: understanding a learning progression, developing a unit, planning for differentiation, and addressing behavioral issues.

Learning Progression Ladders
Breaking Down Concepts or Skills

W. James Popham, in *Transformative Assessment*, defines a learning progression as *a sequenced set of sub-skills and bodies of enabling knowledge that students must master en route to mastering a more remote curricular target* (the "big" target).[77]

Popham outlines the steps needed to construct a learning progression ladder:

1. Choose the **standard** that students need to attain (the target):

   - Example: Second Grade: Determine the value of mixed collections of coins to $1.00.

2. Think of the **concepts and skills** students must comprehend and possess in order to reach that standard. You need to thoroughly understand the standard to be able to do this. For example, starting with the goal in the example above and working backwards:

   - I can figure out the value of a collection of coins to $1.00 (pennies, nickels, dimes, quarters).
   - I can add pennies, nickels, dimes, and quarters.
   - I can add pennies and nickels.
   - I can add coins of the same value (e.g., a collection of pennies or nickels).
   - I can count by 25s.

228

- I can tell the value of each coin.

- I can identify the names of the coins (penny, nickel, dime, quarter).

- I can count by 5s and 10s.

3. Decide which of those concepts and skills are **measurable** with formative or summative assessment.

4. **Sequence** the concepts and skills—and put them on the rungs of a ladder in ascending order of difficulty.

Standard: **I can figure out the value of a collection of coins to $1.00**
7. I can add pennies, nickels, dimes, and quarters.
6. I can add pennies and nickels (Starting with larger values.)
5. I can add coins of the same value (e.g., collection of pennies or nickels.)
4. I can count by 25s.
3. I can tell the value of each coin.
2. I can identify the names of the coins (penny, nickel, dime, quarter)
1. I can count by 5s and 10s.

With the learning progression ladder, students generally move from a lower rung of understanding to a higher rung in a sequential fashion.

Students' Perspectives: Targets can seem insurmountable to kids if their schema is weak. Figuring out the value of a collection of coins is harder for students who never count jars of change at home. For them, seeing that there are small steps they can learn on the way to the target, is reassuring. As students master each step, they can see they are making progress, and know they will be able to figure out the value of a collection of coins after a bit more practice.

Content Ladders and Unit Planning

Content ladders are very useful in planning units. Start with a question: *What do I want students to take away with them at the end of this unit?* In a unit on the American Revolution, for example, should they memorize the names of key people, dates, and battles? Or would you rather they understand the reasons for the conflict and the significance of the outcome? Students typically have little schema about this or indeed most historical topics. Unless you are clear on the intended learning outcomes, students can end up with misconceptions and bits and pieces of disconnected information.

Once you decide the learning outcome, brainstorm all the things kids need to do or understand to reach that target. In order for students to grasp the significance of the American Revolution, for example, they should to be able to:

8. Give two reasons why the Americans won the Revolutionary War. *(Analyze)*[dd]

7. Decide why the decision to pursue independence was a risk. *(Evaluate)*

6. Explain how acts of the British Parliament lead to the unification of the colonies. *(Analyze)*

5. Understand what a protest is and the different forms protests can take. *(Know, Comprehend, Analyze)*

4. List three events that antagonized colonists. *(Know, Comprehend)*

3. Understand why the French and Indian War was a factor leading to the Revolutionary War. *(Analyze)*

2. Understand what a revolution in government is. *(Comprehend)*

1. Understand the purpose of government. *(Comprehend)*

Students don't have to exactly climb this ladder in order—but the activities and assessments that you design should begin at the bottom rung and move up. That way, you can be sure you are building the foundation they need to reach the overall goal.

[dd] From Bloom's Taxonomy

Differentiated Ladders: Helping Students Reach Deeper Levels of Understanding

Here is another use for target ladders. When you want students to understand their level of comprehension and at the same time push them toward something deeper, try using differentiated ladders. These ladders have a basic level that all students are expected to meet, but they also include additional levels that kids can strive toward. Take the example of vocabulary acquisition. At a minimum, you might want students to know a new vocabulary word when they come across it in a book, but if they can also use the word in writing and conversation, they demonstrate much deeper understanding.

Vocabulary
4. I can use the word correctly in conversation.
3. I can use the word correctly in my own writing.
2. I can define the word in my own words.
1. I can understand the word when I read it in a book.

Once new vocabulary words are introduced, it is important to give students multiple opportunities to define and use them. They can partner share definitions, mime the words, create new sentences using the new vocabulary, etc. Each activity helps them move up the ladder. Along the way, have students determine their current level of understanding, and give them opportunities to share how they used their new words in writing or conversation. Here are two other teacher-developed differentiated ladders, illustrating how they can be used in other content areas:

Multiplication Facts
5. I can orally give answers for multiplication facts. (0-9)
4. I have strategies for the 6-9 facts.
3. I can orally give answers for facts 0 through 5.
2. I know that 3 x 5 = 5 x 3. (commutative property)
1. I have strategies for the 0-5 facts.

Reading Fluency	
5. I can read a page smoothly and with expression.	
4. I can read a page smoothly.	
3. I can read a page, stopping occasionally.	
2. I can read a page with only a few mistakes.	
1. I am working on reading a page fluently.	

Procedural Ladders

Target ladders are useful with procedures later in the year. They show students how to move beyond simply following a procedure to becoming more focused, independent learners. If your class is following a procedure independently and consistently, consider stretching students a bit by discussing how to expand on it, benefiting them and the community even more. For example, in the first section of the book, we discussed how to set clear expectations for partner learning:

Look like you are focused.

Whisper only to your partner.

Help each other.

Once students have mastered these expectations, you can help them move to higher levels of responsibility. Let them know that as they climb this ladder, they can increase the number of times their neurons fire and thereby increase their learning and achievement. A procedural ladder for partner work might look something like this:

Partner Learning	
5. I am able to use my partner's thinking to deepen my understanding.	
4. I am able to ask my partner questions when I do not understand.	
3. I try to understand what my partner is saying.	
2. I am able to give specific compliments to my partner.	
1. I can follow the procedure for partner learning.	

Here is another example, this time for small group learning. The procedure in this case is:

We have equal time to share.

I am courteous.

My actions keep the group on task.

And the small group learning ladder is:

Small Group Learning
6. All group members have an equal number of turns.
5. All group members share their thinking at least once.
4. I am able to ask questions of the group if I do not understand.
3. I try to understand what each group member is saying.
2. I am able to give group members specific compliments.
1. I can follow the procedure for small group learning.

Teaching and learning is a messy business, and it can be remarkably inefficient. Consider how often teachers spend time teaching concepts that some students already know and other kids are not ready for. Think how often students check out, believing that just being "familiar" with a concept (they have "heard" of it) is enough, not realizing how much more they could deepen their understanding with a little more work.[ee] Target ladders are tools that address both of those issues and more. You decide the purpose for a ladder. Then you go through a task analysis process that helps you:

- know how to sequence lessons.

- raise your awareness of requisite skills needed when using a lesson from an adopted curriculum.

- know if you need deeper content knowledge in order to create a ladder.

- understand the steps students might be missing when they have trouble learning or behaving.

With clear **targets,** students realize what they are supposed to learn—and teachers know what to focus on in a lesson. **Target ladders** help teachers plan key concepts for student understanding (content ladders), outline requisite skills or concepts students need in order to

---

[ee] Benedict Carey, in *How We Learn* describes the fluency illusion as "the belief that because facts or formulas or arguments are easy to remember right now, they'll remain that way tomorrow or the next day (p. 82).

master a larger target (learning progression ladders), provide steps students can take to deepen their understanding (differentiated ladders), and help students reach higher levels of responsibility (behavior ladders). With **formative assessment**, students get concrete evidence on their level of understanding, and teachers are able to design instruction around that evidence. These tools—targets, target ladders, and formative assessment—help us make the time kids spend in our classrooms really count. Without them, we are as good as teaching "blindfolded" —it wouldn't really matter which students were there!

The Student's Perspective

Clearly, target ladders are useful to teachers, but when you share them with students, you empower kids to take charge of their own learning and spur them to 'climb higher.' After completing a pre-test, students review their results and decide on which rung to place themselves. Each student has their own copy of the ladder, and they keep track of their progress during the unit. After a period of lessons, practice, and formative assessments, students put a different colored dot on their new rung on their ladder. Of course, you also keep a record of students' progress. These ladders are student-centered because kids are motivated to climb the ladder of understanding and now have decisions to make as to the work that they do:

- Are they ready for independent work? If so, provide a choice of activities, practice pages, and games for different rungs of the ladder. Each student knows their practice level—and the next level they want to reach. And this is crucial: Model how to make good decisions on their choice of activities.

- Should they be working with you in a small group? You can meet with groups of students who are on the same rung, providing instruction to help them climb to the next level.

- Which homework should they choose? Students can select the homework choice that would most help them move up the ladder.

Chapter 22 Key Points

Students' Roles

☐ Challenge yourself to reach higher levels of understanding and behavior.

☐ Understand your level of learning and the purpose of assignments or homework.

☐ Choose what you need to practice, based on formative assessment evidence.

☐ Track your progress on lesson target ladders.

Teachers' Roles

☐ Analyze targets and break them down into smaller steps.

☐ Teach students about the concept of ladders—that there are small steps to be taken on the climb toward mastery of a target.

☐ Help students determine their current placement on a target ladder and see what steps are next.

☐ Show them the small steps they will be taking as they move up a ladder.

☐ Show and discuss levels of understanding and behavior that can stretch students to achieve higher goals.

☐ Use formative assessment to provide evidence for ladder movement.

Target Ladders

NOTES

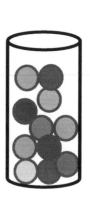

Chapter 23: Check Student Understanding:
Formative and Summative Assessment

However beautiful the strategy, you should occasionally look at the results.
—Winston Churchill

Formative Assessment is assessment *for* learning. It lets students and teachers know how they are doing and it is not graded. Teachers make future instructional decisions based on results, and students know where to focus their attention. Examples: Short quiz, rough draft essay, Venn diagram, quick write, exit card, written answers on white boards.

Summative Assessment is assessment *of* learning. It is graded. Examples: chapter or end of unit test, final draft essay, final presentation or speech, state assessment.

Students' Perspectives

Why do many students fear tests? They seem to learn early on that tests are scary events, don't they? Maybe there is a reason. I have heard teachers warn kids with statements such as the following:

- *You need to know this for the test.* (This is meant to be motivating?)

- *You are not listening. Let's have a quiz.* (Tests are punishments?)

- *Test on Friday!* (Threats will scare them into studying?)

None of these scenarios are likely to motivate students, and they can undermine the supportive community kids require to do their best work. Instead, students can be taught that formative assessments are ways to find out what they know, understand, or can do. *They are not judgments, and they are not graded!* Instead, they inform teachers *and* students about next steps and give evidence to determine levels of understanding. Summative assessments are celebrations of what has been learned over a longer period of time. Both formative and summative assessments, when we view them positively and take out the sting of judgment, help students connect effort to results and let them celebrate learning, progress, and changes in thinking.

The Research

As a rookie teacher, the idea of assessing before the end of the unit was not part of my modus operandi. It was "teach, test, and hope for the best," and I often relied on "cardiac assessment" to tell me whether or not students were understanding a concept. Cardiac assessment is that feeling *deep in your heart* whether kids are getting it, based on how smoothly the lesson goes, or on the answers of a few students. I didn't know back then that there was a better way—something that could give me the information about my students' evolving understanding when it really counted—in the thick of learning, long before final tests were given. With this kind of feedback, called **formative assessment**, I could receive timely updates on student understanding, updates that affected my instructional decisions, and my students could get vital feedback, helping them perform significantly better on academic tasks.

The importance of ongoing formative assessment for teachers and students is backed up by robust research. This research shows a stunning correlation between relevant feedback and student achievement.[78] In *Classroom Assessment for Student Learning*, the authors found that

> *The effect of assessment for learning on student achievement is some four to five times greater than the effect of reduced class size.... But the most intriguing result is that, while all students show achievement gains, **the largest gains accrue to the lowest achievers.**[79]*

This astonishing finding should change professional practice in every classroom in the country.

Formative assessment is a powerful tool because it does three crucial things: It provides data that informs teacher instructional decisions, it lets students know how they are doing, and it gives everyone the opportunity to recognize and celebrate the many small and large successes that occur every day. Susan Brookhart states, *From the student's point of view, formative assessment reads something like, "Here is how close you are to the knowledge or skills you are trying to develop, and here's what you need to do next."* [80] And I would add: *Look what you've achieved so far!*

Informing Teacher Instructional Decisions

Providing students with immediate, frequent, and relevant feedback about their performance...allows the teacher to make better instructional decisions, offers continual information relative to individual student performance and fosters authentic performance assessment.[81]   —M. Hardiman

Again, unlike summative assessment, formative assessments are FOR learning, not OF learning. Daily checks allow us to monitor student understanding and find out what students are getting or not getting in order to make future instructional decisions. By carefully listening to students, without judgment, and by frequently assessing them, we get a truer picture of their understanding and are more likely to uncover misunderstandings that arise. McTighe and Wiggins remind us that when designing lessons, *given the likelihood that learners will misunderstand key ideas and make performance errors (not necessarily signs of poor teaching or learning) the design must make sure that teachers as well as learners get the feedback they need to rethink, revise, and refine.*[82]

Formative Assessments: Informal

After you develop clear targets for a lesson or unit, create a menu of short informal formative assessment strategies to check understanding. These will give you a general idea as to how a lesson is progressing. Plug them into your lesson plan book so you don't forget or run out of time. The following is a list of possible assessments.[83] Some take a bit of planning, but others are quick and easy to implement. For example, you can have students:

- respond to questions with letter/word cards (A, B or True, False, or Yes, No, Maybe). They can keep a set of cards inside their desks or in a book pocket taped to the top for easy access.
- use signals (to agree or disagree) or fingers (to show a number answer).
- display red, yellow, or green cards to show their level of understanding. (This works particularly well during independent work times.) Alternatively, students can hold up one, two, or three fingers to indicate their understanding level.
- write and show responses on white boards.

Formative Assessments: Formal

Short assessments that kids complete independently will give you a truer picture as to how individual students are progressing. For example, they can

- complete pre-tests. This tells you what schema they are starting with and which concepts they are likely to need help understanding.[ff]

- solve problems before and after a lesson on 3x5 **exit cards**. Later you can sort the cards into two stacks: those who understand and can help others, and those who need extra support.

- Write responses to a prompt in journals.

- Whisper into your ear the answer to a question before lining up for recess.

- Sit down with you for a quick interview while other students work independently.

Regardless of which assessment is used, it is imperative that no judgment be attached. Whether students understand, don't understand, or are getting it but need more practice, this kind of formative assessment is simply an indication of their understanding so far.

Example:

A fifth-grade teacher used exit cards to collect information about her students' understanding of volume. 97% of the students could calculate the volume, but about half of them were confused about notating their answers, mixing up yards squared with yards cubed. As part of the next day's lesson, she showed drawings of rectangular prisms and rectangles with their volume or area calculated. She notated each answer with squared or cubic units—some correct and some incorrect. The students' task was to determine which volume/area units were correct—and why. The ensuing class discussion helped many students clarify their understanding. Without the formative assessment on 3x5 cards, she could easily have missed this gap in their understanding.

[ff] Testing—recitation, self-examination, pretesting, call it what you like—is an enormously powerful technique capable of much more than simply measuring knowledge. It vanquishes the fluency trap that causes so many of us to think that we're poor test takers (*How We Learn*, Benedict Carey).

Improving the Quality of Student Work:
Summative Assessment

Let's shift our focus now to summative assessment, the evaluations we do at the end of projects or units. When a culminating project is assigned, we often exhort students to do great work, but do they know what great work looks like? Don't assume they do. Help your students develop that vision with some of the following strategies:

- Provide concrete examples and criteria for student assignments. When kids see a science work sample, completed project, or final draft story, they begin to understand what high quality work looks like. I used to show kids examples of work at different levels and let them deduce which ones were higher quality and why.

- Make sure students know what you are looking for in terms of format. Break projects down into small steps and show examples all along the way. I often completed a project right along with my students to help them more clearly understand what to do.

- Develop specific criteria for grading students' final projects. As they are working, give kids feedback so they know how they are doing and give them opportunities to use that feedback soon after receiving it.

- Use the criteria from an official scoring guide or develop a rubric together. Here is one example:

Map Project: The Geography of the New England States

Trait	Unsatisfactory	Satisfactory	Exemplary
Map Accuracy	Some incorrect features	Has most of the important features	Has all the key mountains, lakes, and rivers
Map Completion	No Color	Colors show elevations	Also has a legend
Written Commentary	No Writing	Writes about most important features	Writes about how features impact people

In the primary grades, the rubric might consist of pictures or student examples of varying quality. Ask <u>students</u> to notice the differences and make a chart together, listing the characteristics of high quality work. Giving students a clear picture of quality work is like giving them a road map. They can see the path to success.

How Did Students Get from A to B?

It's exciting, isn't it, when students make sudden breakthroughs in their thinking? But as we know, most learning doesn't happen like that. It develops incrementally, with a few wrong turns and periods of disequilibrium along the way. In the end, the result is rewarding, but students can be surprisingly unaware of how they got there. One group of fifth graders I know was having difficulty identifying themes across literary texts. They experienced quite a bit of disequilibrium at the outset, but with time and persistence, they succeeded, amazing even their teacher with the conclusions they were able to draw and their ability to analyze themes. But how did they get from point A to point B? Those are questions their teacher wanted his students to answer. If they could see the process that led to their success, they would be more likely to persist when presented with difficult tasks in the future. So, together he and his class brainstormed a list of all the things they had done to improve their understanding of theme. Here's what they said:

- We read many texts and focused on comprehension.
- We reread texts when necessary.
- We had a purpose for each reading experience.
- We discussed the given topics and questions (trusting that that discussion would improve our comprehension.)
- We shared with partners and listened to feedback.
- We determined what our level of understanding was.

As the students compiled this list, they gained a clearer understanding of their learning process. I recommend some kind of debriefing for all students, even younger ones, when new learning occurs. In the beginning, you'll be doing the debriefing for them, but after a while, students will emulate you. Just don't skip the step—it's one more way to show kids that their work has purpose, and that hard work pays off.

Celebrations

Celebrating learning can be very motivating for students. From time to time, give kids the opportunity to compare current work with past efforts. For many, the growth and achievement they see will be a surprising revelation. When students see progress, their self-esteem rises and everyone can celebrate. In fact, the school day is full of opportunities to celebrate. Make your classroom a joyful place with some of the suggestions below:

- Provide an audience for student work:
  - Set up a mat for each student on a bulletin board (construction paper) where best work is displayed.
  - Each week, showcase a few students' work by giving them a whole bulletin board to fill.

- Have students choose an audience for a story they are working on. It could be a staff member, a parent, or a buddy. Then arrange for them to read the finished piece to that audience.

- Write students a celebratory note. It reinforces the things that did go well, and lifts your spirits, too, especially after a challenging day.

- End the day by having everyone talk about a success. Kids will leave the classroom proud of the many great things that occurred through the day.

- Send positive notes home or call parents. It might be the first positive feedback they have ever gotten about their child.

- Have students write about a recent success as part of morning work.

Of course, giving a simple high five at the moment of success is sometimes all you need!

Chapter 23 Key Points

Students' Roles

☐ Use your formative assessment results to determine levels of understanding and show what to work on next.

☐ Think about how your effort connects to your results.

☐ Learn what quality work looks like.

☐ Celebrate successes, large and small, along the way to mastering new learning.

Teachers' Roles

☐ Use formative assessments frequently.

☐ Use the results to help plan future lessons.

☐ Teach students the purpose of formative assessments.

☐ Develop criteria for summative assessments and show students what quality work looks like.

☐ Celebrate progress and achievement.

NOTES

Hidden Steps: Formative Assessment

The issue: *I want to give my kids some kind of assessment at the end of lessons. But it takes a lot of time to correct and grade. I just don't have that kind of time.* —Intermediate Teacher

Do not grade these formative assessments! Their purpose is to provide you with information for planning or revising the next day's lesson. They also give students a better idea of their own level of understanding. Decide when you need more assessment information to plan— you do not need to assess every subject every day.

If you want a general idea about levels of understanding, you can use informal methods— students can show answers with their fingers (1, 2, 3), put a thumbs up or sideways, write on a white board, etc. For more individual assessment, use exit tickets (3x5 cards). I once observed a teacher standing by the door collecting students' tickets which had solutions to two problems. She quickly sorted them into three piles which she could use to create small groups or differentiate practice the next day. Here are the important steps to assure success with formative assessment:

- Build community so that students know and care for each other.
- Let students know the purpose of formative assessment—and that it is not graded.
- Design **short** formative assessments to check for understanding (e.g., two math problems or one reading question.)
- Sort the assessments into three piles: understands, needs practice, needs assistance.

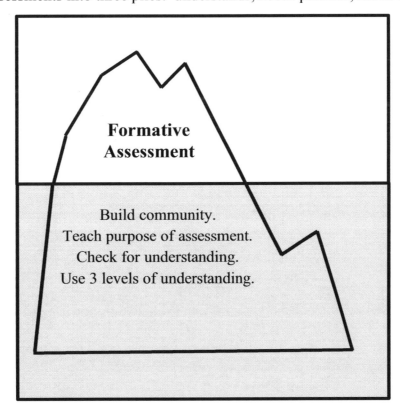

Formative
Assessment

Build community.
Teach purpose of assessment.
Check for understanding.
Use 3 levels of understanding.

Chapter 24: Determine Three Levels of Understanding

Notice when your thinking changes.
It is a sign of new learning.

How do you identify students who are not getting it? Even if you use active participation techniques, some kids are very good at hiding their lack of understanding. Worse yet, they become accustomed to not getting it—sometimes for years! This is why it is so important to create a community where it is OK to come out of hiding. And why formative assessment should be a daily part of your routine.

When formative assessment shows a majority of the class doesn't understand a new concept, it's an easy call—revisit and reteach. But very often, students have widely different levels of understanding. What do you do then? How can you harness the power of your classroom community to reach those students who need help or need to come out of hiding? Try some of the following strategies, and you will see.

Know Your Targets and Pre-Assess

Before you can identify students who are not getting it, you must know what "it" is. Once you determine the target, pre-assess your students. You will likely find that some understand the concept very well and are able to apply it right away. You can provide them with challenges or partner them up with those who are not quite getting it. If you notice that some students are lacking the necessary prerequisites to access the target, do some pre-work with this group, perhaps teaching the lesson ahead of time. When they participate in the lesson a second time, as part of the whole group, their engagement will increase dramatically and so will their confidence.

Evidence of Understanding: 1-2-3

Determining their true level of understanding is an important skill for students, so teach them to look for evidence that will help them decide. Show students how to rate their understanding by using 1, 2, or 3:

> 1: I understand thoroughly and want a challenge.
>
> 2: I understand and want more practice.
>
> 3: I do not understand yet and want more instruction.

Ask them, *what assessment evidence and feelings can help you determine how well you understand the target?* A chart such as the following can help them answer the question.

Evidence for Level of Understanding		
Level	Assessments	Feelings
Level 1	• Correctly solving problems consistently • Understanding and following the lesson • Able to help others understand	• Confident • Easy to stay engaged • Eager to share thinking • Want a challenge
Level 2	• Making some mistakes and knowing why • Able to follow the lesson	• Feeling OK about asking questions • Willing to share thinking • Able to stay engaged
Level 3	• Making mistakes and not knowing why • Not understanding or following the lesson	• Confused • Want to hide work • Disengaged • Nauseous

Formatively assess students by having them solve a couple of problems. Then give them the answers, asking them to rate their understanding by putting a 1, 2, or 3 on the assignment. By using formative assessment, you can place students in one of three groups for a couple of days, and address the needs of each.

Helping Students Determine Their Level of Understanding

Many of my students determine their level of understanding incorrectly. Those that are struggling say, "I am a 2." Some who seem to get the target say, "I am a 3." What is going on?   —Third Grade Teacher

In the beginning, students *will have* a difficult time determining their level of understanding. In math, for example, it's often easier for students who are confident mathematicians and are used to solving problems correctly to decide they are at the '1' level. For other students, it is more of a challenge. *Everyone wants to be a '1.' No one wants to be a 3—so it's better to say, "I am a 2."* Why? There is a simple explanation. Students have always had teachers (and other adults) evaluate their level of understanding for them. The teacher corrects papers and hands them back, decides if criteria from a rubric have been met, or tells students whether their answers are right or wrong. Students have not had enough opportunities to gather data or think about their feelings to know how to figure out their level of understanding.

Opportunities to Self-Check

In a classroom community where students feel free to voice misunderstandings, share mistakes, express disequilibrium, and feel supported by their peers, give them multiple opportunities to check their own work with answer sheets, check their work with a partner, or decide what rubric criteria have been met. These strategies must be taught, however. When students check their own work, they get immediate feedback and teachers reduce their paper load—and can spend more time planning. Saying to students, however, "Here are the answers. Check your own work" does not help them understand the benefits of self-check. There is a lot of "set up" work to do for this strategy to pay off. First, students must know the benefits for their brain. They get immediate feedback by

- finding out what they know, understand, or are able to do.
- getting feedback from a partner after self-checking.
- reviewing solution paths with a partner afterward.
- reworking problems and answers to questions.

Teach a protocol for self-checking by modeling and practicing the procedure together. For example, if answers are displayed or students have access to answer keys, they should:

1. compare each answer with theirs.

2. highlight disagreements.

3. go back and rework problems or think about what was right and wrong when they are finished.

4. discuss with a partner right and wrong answers.

Stress with students that self-checking helps *them* master a target. The teacher's role is to walk around the room, looking to see where students are having difficulty. This is valuable information to inform subsequent instruction.

Three Groups

Knowing your students' levels of understanding will help you decide on next steps as you plan lessons and assignments. You can divide them into groups based on these levels, scheduling uninterrupted time with struggling students, and giving everyone else work at an appropriate level. Each group works on a different assignment, and students in Group 1 or 2 may not ask you for help during this time. Here's how it works:

Group 1 is given a challenging task that relates to the target. These students work independently for a while, and then they can share in partnerships. (Check the end of this chapter for ideas.)

Group 2 practices the skill. Students work independently and correct their own papers using answer sheets placed around the room. They can also compare answers with each other. If help is needed, they can get assistance from a designated student from group 1 by putting up their Need Input Card. This is simply a brightly colored 3X5 card that is folded in half and propped up on the desk when help is needed.

Group 3 works with the teacher. You can either reteach the lesson or try a different strategy, often focusing on more concrete representations. When you are differentiating, you can meet with Group 3 only or divide the session and meet with two groups each day.

For example:

	1st Session (15-20 min.)	2nd Session (15-20 min.)
Day 1	Group 3	Group 1
Day 2	Group 3	Group 2

Teachers often omit working with Group 1, but these students benefit from the additional challenges you can provide. They need to stretch their mental muscles, too! The 1-2-3 strategy is a powerful teaching tool and is not limited to math. Consider using it whenever there is evidence of different levels of understanding among your students. This is what it's all about—teach, check for understanding, adjust—and repeat!!

1-2-3 Partnerships

When students see how important it is to know their level of understanding, and they have a good grasp on how to determine that level, they can begin to assist each other. A fellow educator, teaching math, had a system that worked well in his classroom. First, he taught his students how to determine their level of understanding. Then, after formatively assessing his students, and finding them on different levels, he demonstrated to kids how to find a partner that could help them. Students would put up 1, 2 or 3 fingers. Kids at the 1-level would look for classmates at a lower level. Ones and twos partnered with threes; but threes could not partner with another three. He also taught students how to help each other, with an important caveat: *helping a partner does not mean doing the problem for them.* And he gave them questions they could ask to find out where their partner's misunderstanding or confusion was. For example,

- *What do you understand so far?*
- *How much of the problem can you do?*
- *Is there a specific part of the problem that confused you?*

The teacher and his students found out that everyone loved helping each other move up a level.

Some worry that kids at the 1-level spend too much time helping others, instead of being challenged, a valid concern. First, it is important to realize that 1-2-3 partnerships are not used every day. They are used strategically when the need for differentiation is great. Second, students who explain math concepts to peers find that the experience deepens their own understanding—they often have "aha's" themselves! And the positive feelings generated from students helping each other helps transform and strengthen the learning community.

Thumbs Up

Once students have had lots of practice determining their levels of understanding, you can sometimes use an informal method to see how things are going. For example, after a few lessons addressing a math target, some students are getting it, a few are overwhelmed, and the rest are somewhere in between. Ask kids to show their level of understanding by putting a thumb up (*I could teach this!*), sideways (I need a bit more practice), or down (I'm lost.). No matter what signal students choose, it's OK! This is not a statement of how smart they are; it's an honest self- assessment of their own current understanding. For the next task, have students partner up according to need. Those who are lost look for a thumbs-up partner. In a positive learning community, kids who get it **want** to help kids who don't. You could also have the first two groups work together while you reteach students who are struggling.

Students' Perspectives

The strategies just described are useful for teachers, but they are equally important for empowering students. When kids are able to determine their own levels of understanding, they can:

- focus their efforts on moving up a level.
- celebrate the progress they make.
- help other students move up a level.

Formative assessment and levels of understanding also underscore for kids the real purpose of school—to understand concepts and skills, not just to complete activities. They see that assessment is a tool to help them, not something to fear. Using these strategies, the students and you will know at the end of a unit that they will be successful on their summative assessment, also. To underscore that fact, maybe you'll want to do what I did and label their final tests "A Celebration of My Hard Work!"

Levels of Understanding

Here is a special target ladder, one for you and your students, showing the steps to achieve a student-centered classroom, using targets and formative assessment. I hope it proves helpful as you strive to create a community of learners.

Target Ladder for the Teacher and Students: **Assessment and Planning**
11. **Students** and I have created a **new culture** in the classroom, where assessment is used to determine levels of understanding, so that we can adjust what we are doing.
10. **Students** know their current 'rung' placement on a target ladder.
9. I am able to create target ladders to show the learning progressions that lead to an essential outcome.
8. **Students** are able to select from differentiated independent activities that match their level of understanding.
7. **Students** with different levels of understanding are able to help each other.
6. I teach students how to determine their level of understanding of a skill or concept.
5. I use formative assessment to check for understanding of targets, collecting evidence which I use to adjust my current and future instructional activities.
4. I understand the research and reasons for using formative assessment. I am able to differentiate between formative and summative assessment.
3. I post **targets in student language** and make sure students understand target vocabulary.
2. I plan **targets** for each lesson.
1. I use **standards** when planning lessons.

Challenging Students

As you plan for differentiation, how do you keep the level 1 kids, engaged? In math class, there are interesting problems you or they can devise to get their brains working. For example, students could

1. create real life problems to solve that apply the skills or concepts learned.

    For example, a box of 100 new pencils was given to a group of 8 students. If they share equally, how many would each get?

2. trade papers with a partner and work to solve each other's problems.

3. use learned skills or concepts to solve problems with larger whole numbers or smaller, less familiar fractions, decimals, or percentages.

4. solve problems in unusual formats, such as:

Add:

$$2 \ \square \ 4$$
$$+ \ \square \ 3 \ 7$$
$$\overline{5 \ 4 \ 1}$$

Box Math

Students roll a die,[gg] determining a single digit to put in each box, trying to make the largest or smallest number they can.

For example:

$$\square \ \square \ \square \ , \ \square \ \square \ \square$$

Or:

$$\begin{array}{r} \square\ \square \\ \times\ \square\ \square \\ \hline \end{array}$$

[gg] Use a 20-sided die that has the digits 0-9 twice.

The Disequilibrium Notebook

Sometimes you hear students complaining, *"I'm bored. I already know this!"* They don't realize they can delve deeper into a topic and explore questions of interest to them beyond the curriculum. A Disequilibrium Notebook is a great way to address this issue. It nurtures students' curiosity and keeps learning interesting and relevant, especially for kids whose pretest shows they already have a wealth of knowledge on a given subject. Basically, a Disequilibrium Notebook is a place where students can jot down things they wonder about. For example, in one classroom students were studying the circulatory system, and some of them began to wonder what a heart attack was, or whether hearts of animals were similar to human hearts. A few decided to do some research on their own and share what they learned with the rest of the class. Some students depend on their teachers to keep them interested, but that puts all the responsibility on us. When students generate their own questions, they take that responsibility on for themselves and begin developing the kind of thinking and curiosity that we see in lifelong learners.

From My Experience: Pre-assessing

Before we began a unit on geography, I had students draw a map of our state and include any information they already knew— cities, mountains, bodies of water, and so on. At the end of the unit, I asked them to draw it again. When they compared the pre-map with the post-map, they were amazed at the difference! This was the perfect opportunity to talk about how that learning happened.

Chapter 24 Key Points

Students' Roles

☐ Use evidence to determine your level of understanding.

☐ Try to increase your understanding by focusing on assignments appropriate for your level.

☐ Help other students raise their levels of understanding.

☐ Celebrate new learning.

Teachers' Roles

☐ Teach students how to determine their level of understanding. Develop a rubric.

☐ Show them how they can use that level to focus on the things they need to learn next.

☐ Use levels of understanding to differentiate—dividing students into 3 groups with different tasks.

NOTES

Hidden Steps: Independent Work or Partner Work & Levels of Understanding

The issue: *I'm only one person. I just can't get around to all the students who need help.*
—Fourth Grade Teacher

Getting around to all the students has been problematic as long as I can remember. It took me a while before I realized there was one resource I would never run out of: students! By building a community of learners where everyone was supporting everyone else and rooting for each other, I essentially had a class full of "student teachers" who could pitch in whenever help was needed. When my kids taught each other, they reinforced their own understanding…or sometimes found out they didn't understand as well as they thought—a realization important for them to know. Use partner work for students who already understand or are getting there and just need more practice. Then, spend your time with kids who really need it. Set kids up for success first by showing them how to work together:

- Teach them that in partnerships, both students must have time to explain their solutions or answers.
- Give students sample questions to use when helping:
    - What do you understand so far?
    - Where do you get stuck?
    - Are there any words that you do not understand?

Steps:
- Build Community, so that students know and care for each other.
- Teach kids how to work with partners. (Just giving your partners the answer doesn't help!)
- Discuss with kids the value of mistakes and persistence.
- Every once in a while, use the 3 levels of understanding to give students challenge, practice, or more time with you.

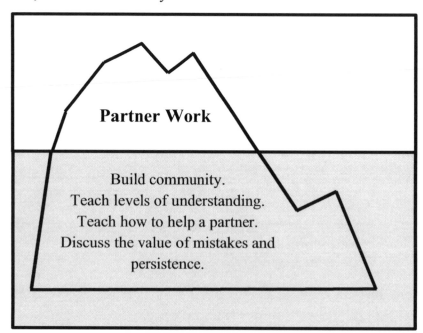

Chapter 25: Differentiate: Anticipate, Assess, and Plan

Before the school year even begins, we know there will be some students in our class who will struggle, some with limited English, and some who will breeze through work and claim they are bored. So why are we so surprised when it happens? We scramble to adjust as the lesson proceeds, our stress level rising, and the students in various stages of frustration. There is a better way: anticipate! Before a lesson even begins, plan how you will modify for kids who struggle and how you will challenge the hotshots. Decide which sheltered instruction techniques you will use for English language learners. In this chapter, we look at strategies that help you anticipate problems and incorporate differentiation into daily planning. Just as important, we discuss how students can learn to respect and support the different learning levels of their peers and help one another achieve and succeed.

Students' Perspectives

In most classrooms, students are used to seeing everyone in the class get the same assignments throughout the day. Those who struggle look around and see that most kids are finishing before them—and that can be really disheartening. They see that during reading time, students are divided into groups and have different books. They figure out early on who the good readers are and who, like them, are still reading the easy books or worse yet, only pretending to read. These scenarios, repeated year after year, are enough to discourage any student. That's why it is so important for kids to understand that we each have our own learning level and speed, depending on the subject or activity. In a supportive classroom community, these differences are respected, and students learn to have patience with themselves and others.

Carol Ann Tomlinson, in her book *The Differentiated Classroom,* suggests talking with students early and often about what is going on in the classroom—and the purposes of differentiation. Begin with activities that demonstrate differences in how everyone learns. A great way to start is to ask students to research when they first walked, talked, lost a tooth, and rode a bike.[84] When you use this data to create timelines, kids can clearly see the differences in development that reside in each of us. Then ask them whether teachers should consider these differences when creating lessons and assignments—or whether such information should be ignored?

Our students need to be reminded that in every area, whether it is academics, social ability, or coordination and athleticism, we each develop at our own rate. (This is a good time to revisit earlier discussions about brain development.) Just as it does not make sense that all children walk at exactly 12 months, it does not make sense that all students learn to read proficiently at the same age. What is important is that each student gets the instruction and assignments at a level that is right for them and that will move their learning forward. Everyone will be at different levels, and that's OK.

Harness the Power of the Community

As you create your learning community, help kids imagine everyone working together so that each person is successful. What would it be like if students cared about everyone's learning in a classroom, not just their own? Otherwise, as the more proficient students finish assignments, they might be feeling good about their accomplishments, but also thinking, a bit smugly: *I'm smart, and those guys aren't,* or *I'm done, and they're not.* How much better it would be if they adopted a broader point of view: *I want to challenge myself to think more, I want to help everyone to get this,* or *I want to hear other ideas, strategies, and solutions.* A more expansive perspective means the thinking doesn't stop when the assignment is finished. It also fosters respect for diverse thinking, and supports the learning of everyone. By explicitly teaching this way of reasoning to students, you set the stage for a collaborative classroom.

Anticipate

Anticipation begins with pre-assessment. If you don't pre-assess, you end up teaching things some students don't need and miss deficits that can keep others from succeeding. I recommend pre-assessing a couple of weeks before a unit begins in order to give yourself a chance to plan for differences. If you have created target ladders (See Chapter 22), you will quickly see which rungs most students should start on. And you will know which students need language support, extra time to complete tasks, or more time with manipulatives in the case of math. *Use* this knowledge as you plan. By anticipating kids' needs in your lesson plans, you increase the odds that **all** your students will be successful.

Plan

Most of my students have a very weak understanding of place value. But I don't have time to teach that. We have to cover 3-digit addition and subtraction. What should I do?

—Third Grade Teacher

The third-grade teacher quoted above has a dilemma every teacher faces: what to do when the curriculum demands one thing, but the class is not ready. In this case, without a strong understanding of place value, the students' subsequent work with the number system and operations will remain fragile. The choice is clear: when *most* students would benefit from a review of place value (using manipulatives), do so! Subsequent progress with whole number operations will be increased, and comprehension will be a good deal more solid. If *some* students would benefit, a few days of small group and independent work are in order. It is ineffective and inefficient to move on to the next target or standard without at least 80% of students meeting the target.

During the Lesson

I sometimes see a teacher sitting at his or her desk, correcting papers or checking a computer while the class is working. By doing so, they are missing out on a valuable opportunity. This is the time to listen to student responses, watch kids as they work, and ask questions. It is when you get a sense of how kids are doing—what they understand, and what is confusing to them. As you move through a lesson, move around the class as well, collecting informal assessment, perhaps with a checklist. With this information, along with formative assessment at the end of a lesson, you can confidently determine next steps. For example:

- If data shows that most students don't understand the target, additional whole group lessons are warranted.
- If most students do understand, you can plan a couple of small group (1-2-3) days. (See Chapter 24)
- If students in disequilibrium are working together, you can shift partnerships.

There is a certain level of confidence when you stand before your class, knowing that you have anticipated the needs of all your students and are prepared to give each the level of support or challenge they need.

Differentiation That Supports High Achievers

Some students need more of a challenge. What do you do when a student scores 100% on a pre-test? Challenging high climbers doesn't mean just pouring on more work. These students need the opportunity to use higher-level thinking skills, not just grind out more multiplication problems. (See the end of Chapter 24.)

Teach students to challenge themselves. *I'm done* is a signal that kids are seeing an assignment as isolated work to finish, not an opportunity to check and deepen their understanding. Instead, push students to come up with more questions, seek new resources, create their own problems, or assist others. (Remember the Disequilibrium Notebooks?)

Use progression and differentiated target ladders (Chapter 22): There are rungs on a learning progression ladder that you want everyone to master. But some kids are ready to climb higher, so take time to plan for them. If the target is that all students learn to calculate the mean, an extra rung might be added that challenges students to find a missing piece of data, given the mean. Or if you want all students to know how to represent probability with a fraction, an additional target might be to differentiate between theoretical and experimental probability.

Check the next grade level's targets. If students are working on the standard, *I can figure out the value of a collection of coins to $1.00,* add another rung from the next grade level: *Represent money amounts to $10.00 in dollars and cents, and apply to situations involving purchasing ability and making change.*

Use Bloom's Taxonomy (See Chapter 21): Typically, after reading a story, there are questions to answer from the teacher or the text for checking comprehension. Here is a different take: ask students which questions in the text are easy to answer and which require more thought. Then analyze why. Later, introduce Bloom's Taxonomy, and begin analyzing questions as to the level of thinking required. Do some words in the question itself indicate its level? Eventually, students can generate their own questions. They can identify the level and quiz each other. After a while, looking for challenges becomes an integral part of everyone's thinking. It enhances student learning and helps create a vibrant classroom community.

<u>Have students create their own math problems and assessments</u>—and trade with other students. (You can even use their work later with the rest of the class.)

<u>Add a project</u> to the choices for students: For example, kids could explore other money systems or bases, they could create their own illustrated vocabulary books, or they could write an original poem in the style of one they read.

Differentiation That Supports Struggling Students

In *Discipline with Dignity*, the authors state "educators do not have the luxury to choose which students to support and which to ignore."[85] As a teacher, I knew I did a pretty good job of teaching intrinsically motivated and well-behaved students. The challenge was not giving up on struggling students, treating them with dignity, and finding opportunities for celebration. Our mantra for all students needs to be, "Get better today than you were yesterday in whatever needs to be learned." Above all, students' work and behavior should be compared with their previous work and behavior, not someone else's.[86] In a race, only one person can be first—but everyone can finish. The same is true in the classroom. For struggling students that means:

- **Encouragement**: *You wrote two lines yesterday and today you wrote a whole paragraph!*

- **Anticipation:** Make sure you have taken all students' needs into account when planning a lesson—you know who is going to struggle. How will you adjust the lesson for them?

- **Pre-teaching**: Give some kids an introduction to material before it is taught to the whole class. Enlist the help of parents or aides if you don't have time. When kids are introduced to new vocabulary, math concepts, or other learning ahead of time, they are primed to learn and their confidence rises.

- **Practice:** On key targets, give more practice to students who need it. Repetition and practice are two effective methods to ensure that concepts and skills make it to long-term memory.

- **Less competition**: It's tough to continually get low scores on spelling or multiplication tests. Emphasize students being competitive with themselves—write one more word or read five more minutes today than yesterday.

- **More formative assessment**: For example, instead of giving a 20-word spelling pretest on Monday and post-test on Friday—give some students a shorter list and test more frequently. Enlist the help of classroom volunteers or assistants if you don't have time.

- **Choice**: Students can choose which problems to practice based on their level of understanding. This option requires kids to understand why practicing a certain set of problems is beneficial to them.

- **Dignity**: Consequences for misbehavior must maintain a student's dignity and be predictable and flexible. Discuss problems with students privately and help them come up with solutions. Each student gets what he or she needs to be successful and act in a more responsible way.

- **Celebration**: Celebrate every little bit of progress—with notes, phone calls, and praise that link effort to achievement.

Ladders and Struggling Students

A benefit of the target ladder concept is that you know every student is on the rung of some ladder. You will have kids who, based on the pre-test, are already at the top of the ladder. You may also have students who are not ready for the first rung or for whom the distance between rungs is too great. Take another look at the money learning/progression ladder first introduced in Chapter 22:

Standard: **I can figure out the value of a collection of coins to $1.00**
7. I can add pennies, nickels, dimes, and quarters.
6. I can add pennies and nickels. (Starting with larger values.)
5. I can add coins of the same value (e.g., collection of pennies or nickels.)
4. I can count by 25s.
3. I can tell the value of each coin.
2. I can identify the names of the coins (penny, nickel, dime, quarter)
1. I can count by 5s and 10s.

What if you have a student who is not yet able to count objects by ones (one-to-one correspondence)? We have a lot to teach and time is limited. Should we just move on and hope he will somehow move up the ladder on his own? Experience tells us this is unlikely to happen. It is our job to back up and think through what even lower rungs of the ladder are (e.g., check out the previous grade level's standards). What are smaller steps that can be added between rungs? Until this student is able to count by ones, counting by fives and tens is not going to happen. Create some tasks for this student to practice counting.

For example, drawing from a deck of number cards, the student counts out the number of objects indicated. This can be done with a parent, instructional assistant, peer, or at home. If we neglect to help this student develop the skills in order to eventually hop on a grade level ladder, he will continue to fail. If the rungs are too far apart for some students—they aren't able to leap with understanding from rung to rung—add some intermediary rungs, breaking down a concept or skill even further.

To anticipate and challenge, you need to know your students' needs. Then, as you become more familiar with the curriculum, you can think ahead when designing a week's lesson plans so that all students will be successful. I have found this quote to be inspirational, from *Discipline with Dignity:*

I will not give up on you.
I will not quit on you.
I will not lose control with you.
I will not be angry at you.
I will always be here no matter what.
Because I am a teacher and my job is to show you a better way.[87]

Equity

Currently, many school districts are providing professional development for teachers around the concept of equity—*giving students access to the resources they need to learn and thrive.*[88] It's an attempt to level the playing field, so all students have a chance to succeed. Regrettably, there are many classroom practices that disregard equity, and in most cases, teachers don't even realize they are doing so. Research based on TESA (Teacher Expectations and Student Achievement) is still being used for professional development sessions. TESA looked at teacher interactions with students and found the following very common inequities.[89] Teachers:

- were less likely to call on perceived low achievers.

- gave less wait time to girls and perceived low achievers than to perceived high achievers.

- consistently asked perceived low achievers lower level questions.

- gave perceived low achievers little or no feedback.

- were less likely to praise them, especially for their academic work.

- spent 25% less time listening to perceived low achievers than high achievers.

- treated many female and minority students discourteously.

Equality and Equity

If you implement the strategies in this book, you will not fall into these traps. Take a look at the charts on the next page to see how good classroom practices lead to greater equality and equity.

COMMUNITY		
Strategy/Practice	**Equality**	**Equity/Cultural Competency**
Team Building Activities	All students feel influential and included.	The benefits of diverse thinking can be drawn out with discussion.
Ice Breaker Activities	All students feel influential and included.	Students discover commonalities and celebrate differences.
Clear Classroom Procedures	Routines are the same for all.	Check to make sure procedures are clear to all students.
Teaching Procedures	Students know the benefits of classroom procedures for their own learning and that of others.	Students are given the amount of practice and teaching they need to learn procedures.
Re-teaching Procedures	Procedures are for all students.	Students receive needed instruction to understand procedures.
Positive Language	Students learn to use positive language with all students.	Students increase their understanding of how language can (unconsciously) reinforce stereotypes and decrease learning.

INSTRUCTION		
Strategy/Practice	**Equality**	**Equity/Cultural Competency**
Learning Targets	All students know what they are supposed to learn.	Targets can be broken down into smaller steps so that all make progress.
Language Targets	All students learn to communicate clearly and correctly.	Students receive targeted language assistance.
Success Criteria	All students know what success looks like.	All students will make progress and feel successful.
Breaking Targets Down (Target Ladders)	All students know the small steps that lead to mastery of the target.	Students who need smaller step are given them so they can be successful also.
Scaffolding	All students build their schema.	Students receive the help they need to build their schema.
Think Time	All students get think time.	Students need different amounts of 'retrieval time.'
Partner Share	All students get to share with a partner.	Students get the needed time to practice stating their thinking and getting feedback.
Group Protocols	All students get equal turns/time to share.	Diverse opinions are shared and respected.
Active Participation Strategies (Signs, signals, cards, and whiteboards)	All students participate.	Different ways of participating address different learning styles.

ASSESSMENT		
Strategy/Practice	**Equality**	**Equity/Cultural Competency**
Formative Assessment	All students find out how they are doing.	Individual needs can be addressed.
Debriefing or Closure of Lessons	All students get to think about how they did academically and behaviorally.	Previous information is often repeated to help students who need to hear it again.
Feedback	All students receive feedback.	Feedback can be increased or decreased as needed by the student.
Celebration of Success	All students celebrate success.	All students increase their competence and confidence by getting the support they need, based on assessment.

NOTES

Chapter 25 Key Points

Students' Roles

☐ Find out what your level of understanding is.

☐ Work hard to move up another rung on the target ladder.

☐ Understand that brains are developing at different rates and that classmates need different amounts of time and instruction, different activities, and different ways to show what they have learned.

Teachers' Roles

☐ Pre-assess.

☐ Anticipate, assess, plan.

☐ Use target ladders.

☐ Add rungs to ladders if students are not successfully moving up a ladder or need a challenge.

☐ Elicit help from other students, parents, and classroom aides if you have them, to maximize learning opportunities.

☐ Treat students with dignity and respect regardless of their race, gender, or ability.

Chapter 26: Transform a Community of Teachers

Persist. Stay on Message. Keep the vision of a student-centered classroom. It is the daily words and actions that add to or subtract from the feeling of community.   —G. Peterson

Teaching is hard work, and confronted with the heavy responsibility of educating students with widely diverse backgrounds and needs, it's easy to feel inadequate. You are only one person. What do you do when problems arise? Who do you talk to? When I was a rookie teacher, I didn't want to talk to anybody about all the difficulties and challenges that arose. It was safer to pretend everything was going great—or blame students when things went awry. And at first, I was not ready to doubt the vision of the classroom I had begun developing from the time I was 5 years old—you know, the one where all the students are interested in learning and they willingly do things because the teacher asks them to.

But you don't get better pretending all is well when it isn't. The best teachers have the courage to be vulnerable and start talking about difficulties. Most importantly, they separate their classroom practice from their own self-worth, and they problem solve instead of blaming kids or beating themselves up when things don't go well. It should be clear from the get-go: challenges in the classroom are a given. They **will** happen. The key is learning how to have honest conversations with colleagues, to examine the issues dispassionately, and problem solve, not blame, and complain.

I eventually did begin talking with fellow teachers, and their thinking led me to new perspectives and solutions. Slowly I realized that the only way for me to get better was to open up— discuss what was going well, admit what was not, and to analyze both with the help of my peers. Just as my students did their best in a supportive community of learners, I needed a supportive community of teachers in order to reach my potential!

Imagine having a cadre of peers who are implementing the same new strategy as you, discussing it, and fine tuning the rollout …working in a school where teachers feel safe to try new instructional practices, to brainstorm solutions together, and to risk failure…teachers actively participating in constructive discussions about students, formatively assessing new strategies, and sharing what is working and what isn't. That's the ideal, and teachers in such situations are fortunate indeed. In reality, not everyone in a school community is so willing and open, but don't let that stop you. Find the people who are, or make connections with teachers in other buildings. Even in less than ideal situations, a community can form and prosper.

Discuss what you are doing and noticing with a trusted colleague. As you gain more confidence, begin sharing with teachers at your grade level and invite the principal in to observe a lesson. Give your principal a list of behaviors to look for. Remember, you are now using a different lens, a student-centered lens, to look at what your students are doing and thinking, and your principal needs to use that lens, too. Eventually, as more and more teachers start trying out these strategies and having conversation, the whole school community will begin to transform.

When that happens, you and your fellow teachers can develop a progression of procedures and practices to be taught from grade to grade, insuring each level builds on the one preceding. School wide decisions such as these have the greatest impact on student success because year after year, they reinforce the habits and perspectives students need to become lifelong successful learners. Take a look at a possible progression of active participation strategies teachers could introduce, beginning in kindergarten.

Progression of Active Participation Strategies, K-5

Procedures developed in an earlier grade are in *italics*

Kindergarten
1st half: Think time; knees toward speaker
2nd half: Partner share

First Grade
Think time

Knees toward speaker

Partner share (A & B)

Students stand when sharing with whole group

Second Grade

Think time

Knees toward speaker

Partner share (A & B)

A share what B said; B shares what A said.

Students stand when sharing with whole group

Refer student responses back to partners

Dry erase boards

Third Grade

Think time

Knees toward speaker

Partner share (A & B)

A shares what B said; B shares what A said

Students stand when sharing with whole group

Refer student responses back to partners

Dry erase boards

Agree or disagree (& why)

Levels of understanding

Fourth Grade

Think time

Knees toward speaker

Partner share (A & B)

A shares what B said; B shares what A said

Students stand when sharing with whole group

Refer student responses back to partners

Dry erase boards

Agree or disagree (& why)

Levels of understanding

Self-partnering based on level of understanding

Table group protocols

Fifth Grade +

Think time

Knees toward speaker

Partner Share (A & B)

A shares what B said; B shares what A said

Students stand when sharing with whole group

Refer student responses back to partners

Dry erase boards

Agree or disagree (& why)

Levels of understanding

Self-partnering based on level of understanding

Table group protocols

Students lead discussions and question each other

Imagine starting the year with students already immersed in these active participation strategies? When the decision to implement strategies is school wide, teachers are building on lessons from the year before and not starting from scratch every September.

Just like in the classroom, when everyone in the school community is willing to offer "building materials" to the educational community, everyone benefits. In the same way, if some teachers are not willing or ready to risk this kind of openness, the community cannot reach its full potential. That's not something you can control. What you can do is respect where others are, continue to focus on your own practice, and start building a community of teachers who share your values. Little by little, you'll be changing the learning experience of your students for the better and positively influencing the whole school community.

Getting Started

All plans for educational reforms depend on the teacher for their proper realization. Unless carried out by personnel sincerely imbued with the philosophy animating the reforms and trained in the arts of effective teaching, they are doomed to failure.[90] — *Sidney Hook*

We all hear about public schools not doing well and not having enough money. But it doesn't cost anything to empower students. Remember, you can start in your own classroom with a few simple steps, like teaching your students to:

- stand when speaking to the whole group.
- turn their knees toward speakers.
- put their erasers away.
- think about ideas and answers without looking toward the teacher for confirmation.
- be aware of the purpose of the work they do.
- notice and recognize things their classmates are doing that support the community and learning.
- work independently, in partners, or in small groups.

With good observational skills, pay attention to even subtle differences in students' engagement, level of confidence, willingness to share fragile thinking, and their level of focus on what classmates are saying. Be relentless about developing your community of learners.

These steps and others outlined in this book can change the learning experience of students in dramatic ways. They can foster learning communities that support kids and help them develop the skills they need to be successful learners. Immerse your students in this culture of community, and you, too, will hear students saying, *What is the target for the lesson?*

- *How will I know if I meet the target?*
- *I'm learning……., so I am practicing.*
- *I need some time to process that information.*
- *Could I clarify my thinking with a partner?*
- *I cannot hear what Noelle is saying.*
- *I'm in disequilibrium.*
- *I am not sure, but I'd like to share my solution anyway.*
- *I need some more practice.*
- *I understand, and I want more challenge.*
- *Can I have some more think time?*

Appendices

Appendix A summarizes different strategies and roles for students in a diagram.

Appendix B presents brain research supporting the instructional framework presented in this book: building community, using active participation strategies, and planning using formative assessment.

Appendix C shows examples of target ladders for each part of the instructional framework.
1. Community
2. Instruction
3. Assessment & Planning

Appendix D has self-assessments for each part of the instructional framework. Teachers can administer the students assessments also—near the beginning of the school year and then later to assess progress.
1. Building Community
2. Developing and Monitoring Classroom Procedures
3. Engaging Instruction
4. Planning and Assessment

References

Bibliography

Appendix A: The Student-Centered Classroom

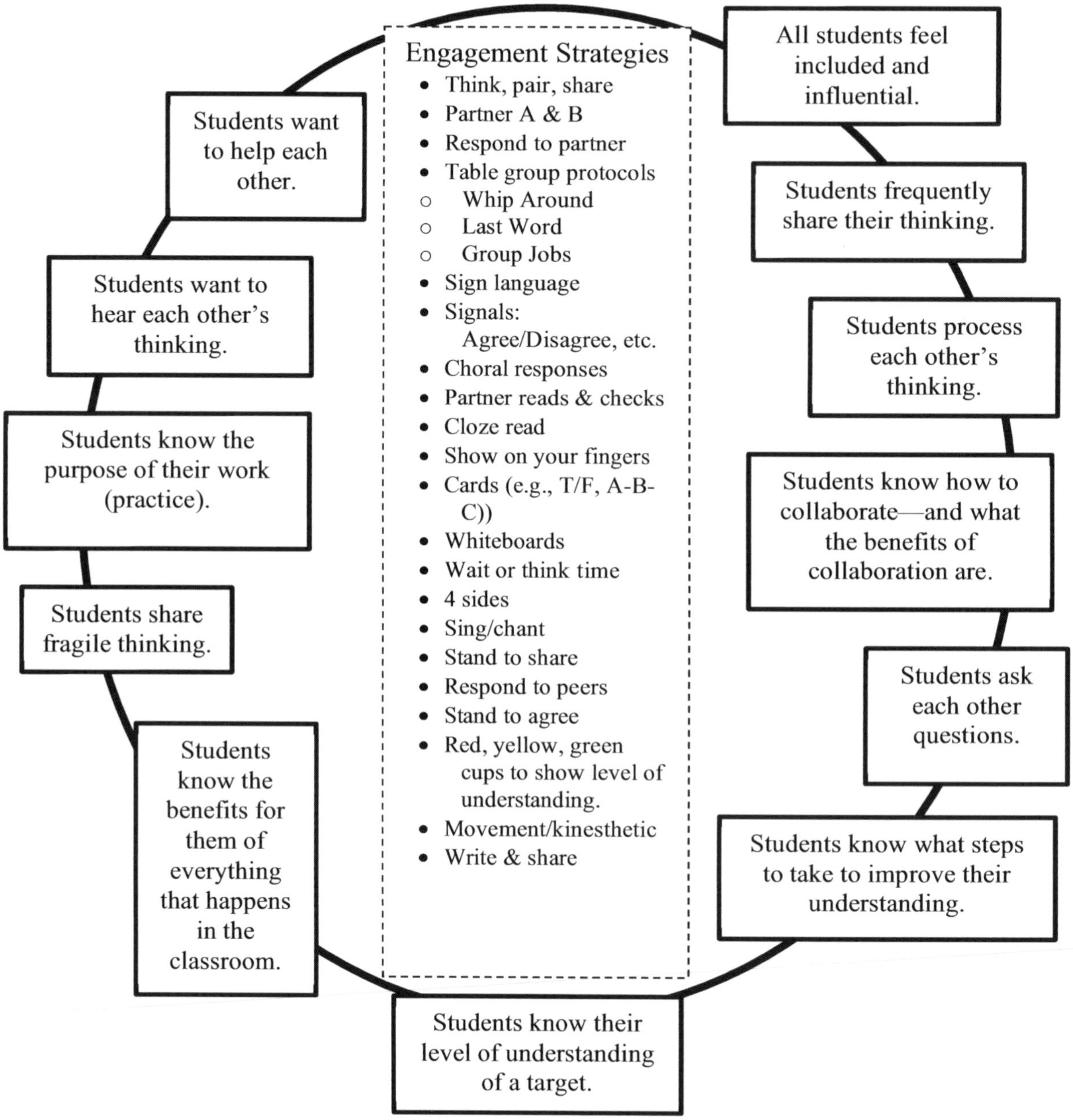
Engagement Strategies
• Think, pair, share
• Partner A & B
• Respond to partner
• Table group protocols
○ Whip Around
○ Last Word
○ Group Jobs
• Sign language
• Signals: Agree/Disagree, etc.
• Choral responses
• Partner reads & checks
• Cloze read
• Show on your fingers
• Cards (e.g., T/F, A-B-C))
• Whiteboards
• Wait or think time
• 4 sides
• Sing/chant
• Stand to share
• Respond to peers
• Stand to agree
• Red, yellow, green cups to show level of understanding.
• Movement/kinesthetic
• Write & share
All students feel included and influential.
Students frequently share their thinking.
Students process each other's thinking.
Students know how to collaborate—and what the benefits of collaboration are.
Students ask each other questions.
Students know what steps to take to improve their understanding.
Students know their level of understanding of a target.
Students know the benefits for them of everything that happens in the classroom.
Students share fragile thinking.
Students know the purpose of their work (practice).
Students want to hear each other's thinking.
Students want to help each other.

Appendix B: Brain Research

Brain research supporting community building, active participation, and formative assessment strategies is presented in the texts of these authors who have provided all educators with valuable insights and connections between teaching and neuroscience:

1. Mariale Hardiman, *Connecting Brain Research with Effective Teaching*
2. David Sousa, *How the Brain Learns*
3. Eric Jensen, *Teaching with the Brain in Mind*
4. Eric Jensen, *Teaching with Poverty in Mind*
5. Pedro Noguera and A. Wade Boykin, *Creating the Opportunity to Learn*

Here is some of that research.

Section 1: Community

Build relationships and teach procedures.

- Create community agreements: *Before students will turn their attention to cognitive learning, they must feel physically safe and emotionally secure.* (Sousa, p. 43)

- Use community-building activities: *It is impossible to separate emotions from learning.* Reduce stressful classroom environments and use positive emotional experiences to enhance learning. (Hardiman, p. 25)

- Use community-building activities and a morning meeting: Students need positive feelings toward their peers. Team building activities and morning meetings help them to get to know each other.

- Use the language of community and task/effort specific praise: Teacher-Student Relationship Quality indicated by positive, nurturing interactions vs. a feeling tone of negative exchanges *directly affects kindergarteners' levels of classroom participation.* (Boykin & Noguera, p. 73)

- Use positive language; keep discussions of negative behavior private: *Students don't care about how much you know until they know how much you care. Teacher-student relationships have a whopping 0.72 effect size when it comes to student achievement.* (Jensen #4, p. 23)

- Develop routines: Traditions and rituals reduce threat and stress. Traditions create a sense of shared values and agreement. (Jensen #3, p. 69)

- Use wait time, think, pair, and share or table share: *Teachers need to avoid such subtle stress-inducing tactics as calling on learners who have not volunteered.* (Hardiman, p. 31)

- Create an environment where mistakes are seen as opportunities for more learning: *Surprisingly, it doesn't matter to the brain whether it ever comes up with an answer. The neural growth happens because of the process, not the solution.* (Jensen #3, p. 36)

Section 2: Instructional Strategies

Actively Engage Students.

- Give students clear targets and activate prior knowledge: *The brain uses prior knowledge to categorize stimuli into concepts that are either familiar or novel and then combines these concepts to create new patterns of thinking and understanding. This also involves students creating learning goals: what they will know and do as a result of instruction.* (Hardiman, p. 23)

- Use wait or think time: *Calling on the first hands that go up signals the slower retrievers to stop the retrieval process. The rate of retrieval is independent of intelligence.* (Sousa, p. 108)

- Give students processing time: *The teacher can either have their learners' attention or they can be making meaning, but never both at the same time. The human brain is poor at nonstop attention. Working memory is active for preadolescents for about 5 to 10 minutes, for adolescents and adults for 10 to 20 minutes, after which the average person loses focus.* (Hardiman, p. 16)

- Use active participation strategies: *Neuroscience supports instruction involving the active engagement of students in the learning process rather than lessons promoting only passive learning. Active learning not only enhances educational outcomes but also results in chemical changes in the brain.* (Hardiman, p. 68)

- Give students multiple opportunities to share: *The brain itself is exquisitely designed to operate on feedback. When students talk to other students they get specific feedback on their ideas as well as behaviors.* (Jensen #3, p. 33)

  A student struggling to make sense of an idea may understand it better when a peer explains it. Peer teaching gives students the opportunity to use two of the highest order thinking skills—synthesis and evaluation.

- Give students opportunities to share with partners and practice: *The most important factor in determining how well we remember information is the degree to which we rehearse and repeat that information.* (Hardiman, p. 57)

- Develop sharing routines and provide feedback to students: *Helping students feel comfortable with sharing their ideas in class...and providing supportive and nonjudgmental (but rigorous) feedback are all associated with smaller achievement gaps in reading, writing, and math.* (Boykin & Noguera, p. 72

Section 3: Assessment and Planning

Plan based on formative assessment.

- Use formative assessment: *Providing students with immediate, frequent, and relevant feedback about their performance allows the teacher to make better instructional decisions.* (Hardiman, p. 75)

- Give students immediate feedback: *8 studies with correlation of .90+: students who received relevant feedback performed significantly better on achievement measures than students who did not receive the feedback.* (Hardiman, p. 76)

- Break concepts down into smaller pieces: *The brain does not process and store information as an integrated whole but rather through distinct components or modules.* (Hardiman, p. 68)

276

Target Ladder for Teacher and Students: **Community**

12. **Students** and I have created a **new culture** in the classroom where everything that happens and is said adds to the feeling of community. Students know that the community has a potential that can only be reached if every class member achieves—and if everyone feels included and influential.

11. **Students** know that success is their reward for working hard. They connect that success to efforts and then celebrate.

10. I model positive, concrete, reinforcing language every day. **Students** learn to use positive language with each other.

9. A continuum of responses is used to help students refocus on procedures. Discussions with students about negative behavior are private.

8. **Students** who need more practice with procedures receive additional teaching.

7. **Students** understand the reasons for classroom procedures and their benefits for them and their teacher. They are given time to learn and practice the procedures.

6. **Students** and I develop classroom procedures. We understand that they help us achieve our goals.

5. **Students** and I create classroom community agreements. We understand that they help us achieve our goal.

4. I give students opportunities to get to know each other, e.g., through morning meetings.

3. **Students** develop goals for the school year. They also write short-term goals for specific concepts and skills.

2. Community building activities have targets and are debriefed afterward.

1. I use community building activities in my classroom all year.

Target Ladder for Teacher and Students: **Instruction**

15. **Students** and I have created a **new culture** in the classroom where everyone is cognitively engaged.

14. **Students** make sure everyone in their small group has equal opportunities to respond— and that everyone understands the group's thinking.

13. I teach students small group protocols to use when they are discussing questions in a group.

12. I teach students evidence of engagement, and they know their level of engagement.

11. **Students** are given opportunities to respond to each other's ideas.

10. **Students** know how active participation helps their brains make connections and grow more dendrites.

9. **Students** are able to define engagement in their own words.

8. I teach students to stand when sharing to the whole group. Other students point their knees at the speaker and try to capture his or her ideas.

7. Students know the reasons for sharing with a partner. It is a verbal rehearsal for responding to the whole group, it helps them know their level of understanding, and they get feedback.

6. I teach students how to share with a partner.

5. I use a variety of whole group active participation strategies e.g., partner sharing, choral response, choral reading, cloze reading, white board responses, and non-verbal signs and signals.

4. **Students** know the purpose of processing time. They use such time to think about a response.

3. I limit teacher talk to 5-8 minutes at a time, giving students time to process.

2. I call on students randomly after giving them time to think.

1. I give students think time after asking a question. (Also, called wait time.)

Target Ladder for Teacher and Students:
Assessment and Planning

11. **Students** and I have created a **new culture** in the classroom where assessment is used to determine levels of understanding so that we can adjust what we are doing.

10. **Students** know their current 'rung' placement on a target ladder.

9. I am able to create target ladders to show the learning progressions that lead to an essential outcome.

8. **Students** are able to select from different independent activities that match their level of understanding.

7. **Students** with different levels of understanding are able to help each other.

6. **Students** know their level of understanding of a skill or concept.

5. I use formative assessment to check for understanding of targets, collecting evidence by which I adjust my current and future instructional activities.

4. I understand the research and reasons for using formative assessment. I am able to define formative assessment and differentiate between assessment of and for learning.

3. I post **targets in student language** and make sure students understand target vocabulary.

2. I plan **targets** for each lesson.

1. I use **standards** when planning lessons.

Appendix D-1

Self-Assessments

For Teachers: Building Community

1: *I understand and could teach these strategies.*

2: *I need more practice and observational feedback.*

3: *I do not understand these strategies and would like to know more.*

0: *I do not use these strategies.*

___I use community building activities all year.

___Community Building activities have purpose and targets. (Ice breakers or Team builders)

___Students have opportunities to get to know each other.

___ I teach students about their brains.

___ I use positive reinforcing language.

___ I guide students to connect success and effort.

___We celebrate our successes.

For Students: Building Community

1. *All of the time*

2: *Some of the time*

3: *I am still working on it*

____ I participate in community building activities.

___I know the benefits of community building activities for our community.

___I use positive language with my teacher and peers.

___I know how to grow more dendrites!

___I understand that my efforts lead to my success.

___I understand that everyone benefits if everyone succeeds.

Appendix D-2

For Teachers: Developing and Monitoring Classroom Procedures

1: *I understand and could teach these strategies.*

2: *I need more practice and observational feedback.*

3: *I do not understand these strategies and would like to know more.*

0: *I do not use these strategies.*

____I have developed 2-4 step procedures for key behaviors in my classroom.

____I have procedures for:

- ☐ Morning routine
- ☐ Dismissal routine
- ☐ Whole group lessons
- ☐ Partner sharing
- ☐ Independent work
- ☐ Walking in line
- ☐ Small group work/stations
- ☐ Other: _____

____ I (or students) review needed behaviors before a lesson begins.

____ I give students time to reflect on how well they followed procedures after a lesson.

____I vigilantly notice and positively reinforce students who are following procedures (without using names).

____I have identified students who consistently follow each procedure.

____I provide private lessons for students who need practice following a procedure.

For Students: Following Procedures

1. *All of the time*

2: *Some of the time*

3: *I am still working on it*

____I understand and follow our classroom procedures consistently.

____I know the benefits of each procedure for me.

____I think about the needed procedure before a lesson.

____I reflect on how well I followed a procedure after a lesson.

____I can compliment students who I notice following procedures.

Appendix D-3

For Teachers: Engaging Instruction

1: *I understand and could teach these strategies.*

2: *I need more practice and observational feedback.*

3: *I do not understand these strategies and would like to know more.*

0: *I do not use these strategies.*

____ I give students think time after asking a question.

____ I call on students randomly after giving them time to think.

____ I do not rely on students raising their hands to call on responders.

____ I use a variety of whole group active participation strategies:

      ☐ Think time.

      ☐ Partner share

      ☐ White board responses

      ☐ Stand/sit

      ☐ Non-verbal signs and signals

      ☐ Choral response

      ☐ Other:

____ I teach students how to use the active participation strategies and their benefits.

____ I teach my students how to determine their levels of engagement in learning.

For Students: Engaged in Learning

1. *All of the time*

2: *Some of the time*

3: *I am still working on it*

____ I use think time to develop a response.

____ I use opportunities my teacher gives me to engage.

____ I share with my partner.

____ I try to capture my partner's thinking.

____ I listen to speakers (turn my knees) and stand when sharing with the whole group.

Appendix D-4

For Teachers: Assessment and Planning

1: *I understand and could teach these strategies.*
2: *I need more practice and observational feedback.*
3: *I do not understand these strategies and would like to know more.*
0: *I do not use these strategies.*

___ I know how to use standards when planning lesson.

___ I plan targets that can be assessed for each lesson and share them with students.

___ I formatively assess students on a regular basis.

___ I teach students how to determine their levels of understanding.

___ I use formative assessment results to plan and differentiate.

___ I teach my students the purposes of summative and formative assessment.

___ I teach students how to use formative assessment to determine their areas of focus.

For Students: Assessment

1. *All of the time*

2: *Some of the time*

3: *I am still working on* it

____ I know the target(s) for a lesson.

____ I know the purpose for formative assessment.

____ I know the purpose for summative assessment.

____ I can determine my level of understanding for a target.

____ I work harder to understand targets that are challenging for me.

References

Chapter 1: STAND UP! Empower Students

[1]Jensen, E. (2013). *Engaging students with poverty in mind.* Alexandria, VA: ASCD. p. 74.

Chapter 2: Students' Roles

[2]Eleanor Roosevelt, quoted in, Blankstein A. & Noguera, P. (2015). *Excellence through equity.* CA: Corwin. p. 5.

[3]Jensen, E. (2011) *Engaging students with poverty in mind.* Alexandria, VA: ASCD. p. 26.

Chapter 3: Teacher's Roles

[4]See Fisher, D., Frey, N., & Rothenberg, C. *Content area conversations.* (2008). Virginia: ASCD. See chapter 5 for an in-depth discussion of accountable talk and responsibilities of the listener.

[5]Strange, J. & Hindman, J. (2005). Hiring the Best Teachers. *Educational Leadership, 60*(8),48- 52.

[6]Teacher Quality and Student Achievement: Research Review from *Center for Public Education* (November 2005). Retrieved from http://www.centerforpubliceducation.org/

[7]Rand Corporation. (2012) *Teachers matter: Understanding teachers' impact on student achievement.* (2012). Retrieved from http://www.rand.org/pubs/corporate_pubs/CP693z1-2012-09.html

[8]Boykin, A. W. & Noguera, P. (2011). *Creating the opportunity to learn.* Alexandria, VA: ASCD. p. 174

[9]Thompson, J., Windschitl, M. & Braaten, M. (2013). Developing a theory of ambitious early-career teacher practice. *American Educational Research Journal, 50*(3), 574-615.

[10]Pollock, J. (2007). *Improving student learning one teacher at a time.* Alexandria, VA: ASCD. p. 17.

[11] Lortie, D.C. (1975*). Schoolteacher: A sociological study.* Chicago, IL: University of Chicago Press

[12]Petrilli, M. (2013). *Hell yes, we want instructional change.* Thomas B. Fordham Institute. Retrieved from https://edexcellence.net

Chapter 4: Develop a Community of Learners

[13]Kohn, A. (1996). *Beyond discipline: From compliance to community.* Alexandria, VA: ASCD. p. 101.

[14]Gibbs, J. (1987). *Tribes.* Cloverdale, CA: CenterSource Systems.

[15] Lee, K. (2015). *Your five-year-old child: Emotional Development.* Retrieved from: https://www.verywell.com/the-emotional-development-of-a-5-year-old-620713

[16]Gibbs, J. (1987). *Tribes.* Cloverdale, CA: CenterSource Systems

[17] See http://www.songsforteaching.com/chantsraps.htm

[18] Randerson, J. (2012, February 28). How many neurons make a human brain? *The Guardian.* (According to Dr. Suzana Herculano-Houzel). Retrieved from https://www.theguardian.com/science/blog/2012/feb/28/how-many-neurons-human-brain

Chapter 5: Teach Students About Their Brains

[19] https://www.quora.com/How-do-dendrites-grow

[20] Hardiman, M. (2003). *Connecting brain research with effective teaching: The brain-targeted teaching model.* MD: Rowman & Littlefield Education. p. 13.

[21] Willis, Judy. (2009). How to teach students about the brain. *Educational Leadership, 67*(4).

[22] Carey, Benedict (2015). *The surprising truth about how we learn and why it happens.* NY: Random House.

[23]Carey, Benedict (2015). *The surprising truth about how we learn and why it happens.* NY: Random House.

[24] Bucko R. (1998, November.) Toward a Brain Compatible Elementary School. *Educational Leadership, 2*(3).

[25] Ricci, M. C. (2013). *Mindsets in the classroom.* IL: Sourcebooks. p. 11.

Chapter 6: Write Goals and Community Agreements

[26] Sasson, D. (2010). *Effective goal setting for students.* Retrieved from: http://teaching.monster.com/benefits/articles/9440-effective-goal-setting-for-students

[27] Boykin, A. W. & Noguera, P. (2011). *Creating the opportunity to learn.* Alexandria, VA: ASCD. p. 55.

[28] Atance, C. & Meltzoff, A. (2005). My future self: Young children's ability to anticipate and explain future states. *Cognitive Development, 20*(3), pp. 341-361.

[29] Denton, P. and Kriete, R. (2000). *The First six weeks of school.* ME: Center for Responsive Schools.

Chapter 7: Create Procedural Agreements

[30] Whitaker, T. (2011). *What great teachers do differently.* KY: Taylor & Francis. p. 17.

Chapter 8: Debrief Procedures: Connect to Learning

[31] Dweck, C. (2007). *Mindset.* NY: Random House. pp. 71-74.

Chapter 9: Step Back and Observe

[32] Force, N. (2010). Humor, neuroplasticity, and the power to change your mind. *Psych Central.* Retrieved on November 28, 2017, from https://psychcentral.com/blog/archives/2010/10/20/humor-neuroplasticity-and-the-power-to-change-your-mind/

[33] Jensen, E. (2013). *Engaging students with poverty in mind.* Alexandria, VA: ASCD. p. 29: Embrace clarity. Use fewer words; Replace *I need your eyes up front* with *Eyes up front please. You'll need to know this later.* Effect size of 0.75).

Chapter 10: Use Language to Build Community

[34] Davis, S. (2007). *Schools where everyone belong.* Research Pr Pub: https://openlibrary.org

[35] Denton, P. (2013). *The power of our words* (Turners Falls, MA: Northeast Foundation for Children. p.106.

[36] Denton, P. (2013). *The power of our words.* Turners Falls, MA: Northeast Foundation for Children. p. 96.

[37] Dweck, C. (2007). *Mindset.* NY: Random House Publishing Group.

[38] For more on effective praise, an excellent resource is Denton, P. (2013). *The power of our words* (Turners Falls, MA: Northeast Foundation for Children.

[39] Kohn, A. (2006). *Beyond discipline: From compliance to community.* VA: ASCD. p. 99.

Chapter 11: Respond to Misbehavior with Kind Intent

[40] Fay, J. (1998). *Love & logic.* CO: Love & Logic Institute.

Chapter 12: Analyze Common Challenges

[41] Boykin, A. W. & Noguera, P. (2011). *Creating the opportunity to learn.* VA: ASCD. p. 92.

[42] Kohl, A. (2005). Unconditional teaching. *Educational Leadership, 63*(1), 20-24.

[43] Jensen, E. (2013). *Engaging students with poverty in mind.* VA: ASCD.

[44] Kohn, A. (2006). *Beyond discipline: From compliance to community.* VA: ASCD. p. 103

[45] Cohen, E. & Lotan, R. (2014). *Designing groupwork.* VT: Teachers College Press.

[46] Tugend, A. (2012). Praise is Fleeting, but Brickbats We Recall. *The New York Times.* Retrieved from: http://www.nytimes.com/2012/03/24/your-money/why-people-remember-negative-events-more-than-positive-ones.html

[47] Mather, N., & Goldstein, S. (2001). *Learning disabilities and challenging behaviors: A Guide to Intervention and Classroom Management.* Baltimore, MD: Paul H. Brookes. pp. 96-117.

Chapter 14: The Tired Trifecta

[48] Kahn, S. (2012). Retrieved from http://ideas.time.com/2012/10/02/why-lectures-are-ineffective.

[49] Hardiman, M. (2003). *Connecting brain research with effective teaching.* Washington, D.C.: Rowman & Littlefield. p. 16.

[50] Hardiman, M. (2003). *Connecting brain research with effective teaching.* Washington, D.C.: Rowman & Littlefield. p. 16.

[51] Hardiman, M. (2003). *Connecting brain research with effective teaching.* Washington, D.C.: Rowman & Littlefield. p. 68.

Chapter 15: Engage Students

[52] Jensen, E. (2013*). Engaging students with poverty in mind.* VA: ASCD. p. 40.

[53] Hattie, J. (2012). *Visible learning for teachers.* United Kingdom: Taylor & Francis.

[54] City, E. (2014, November). Talking to learn. *Educational Leadership, Vol. 72* (3), 10-16.

[55] Roake, J. (2013, August). Planning for processing time yields deeper learning. *Education Update, 55*(8).

[56] Hattie, J. (2012). *Visible learning for teachers.* United Kingdom: Taylor & Francis. p. 115.

Chapter 16: Listen and Capture Thinking

[57] Reinhart, S. C. (2000, April). Never say anything a kid can say*! Mathematics Teaching in the Middle School, 5*(8).

[58] Stahl, R.J. (1990). *Using think-time behaviors to promote students' information processing, Learning and On-Task Participation.* Tempe, AZ: University of Arizona.

[59] For an exhaustive list of active participation techniques see: Himmele, Persida & Himmele. William. (2011). *Total participation techniques: Making every student an active learner.* VA: ASCD.

[60] Hattie, J. (2012). *Visible learning for teachers.* United Kingdom: Taylor & Francis. p. 72.

[61] Curwin, R., Mendler, A. & Mendler, B. (2008). *Discipline with dignity.* VA: ASCD. p. 208.

Chapter 18: Guide Students Toward Independence

[62] Tough, P. (2012*). How children succeed.* Alexandria, Virginia: ASCD. p. 98.

[63] Retrieved from KIPP Public Charter Schools: www.kipp.org/Riverdale Country School: www.riverdale.edu/

[64] Tough, P. (2012) *How children succeed.* Alexandria, VA: ASCD. p. 98.

[65] Fisher, D. and Frey N. (2008, November) Releasing responsibility. *Educational Leadership*, (3), 36.

[66] Fisher, D. and Frey N. (2008, November) Releasing responsibility. *Educational Leadership*, *66*(3), 37.

[67] Hattie, J. (2008). *Visible learning for teachers: maximizing impact on learning.* U.K.: Taylor and Francis

[68] Hattie, J. (2008). *Visible learning for teachers: maximizing impact on learning.* U.K.: Taylor and Francis

Chapter 19: Deepen Thinking with Partnerships and Small Groups

[69] *Critical Friends Group* provides multiple protocols and training. Harmony Education Center Indiana. Retrieved from https://www.nsrfharmony.org

[70] Cohen, E. (1994). *Designing groupwork.* NY: Teachers College Press.

Chapter 20: Give Purpose to Student Work

[71] *Critical Friends Group* provides multiple protocols and training. Harmony Education Center Indiana. https://www.nsrfharmony.org

[72] Green, E. (2015). *Building a better teacher: How teaching works (and how to teach it to everyone).* NY: WW Norton. p. 245.

Chapter 21: Design Lessons with Four Components

[73] Stigler, J. and Hiebert, J. (1997, September). Understanding and improving classroom mathematics instruction. *Phi Delta Kappan, 79*(1)*,*20.

[74] Wiggins, G. (2013, December 5). *Mandating the daily posting of objectives and other dumb ideas.* Retrieved https://grantwiggins.wordpress.com/2013/12/05/mandaing-the-daily-posting-of-objectives-and-other-dumb-ideas/

[75] Brookhart, S. and Moss, C. (2014, October) Learning targets on parade. *Educational Leadership*. pp.18-33.

Chapter 22:   Break Targets Down with Ladders

[76] http://www.timetimer.com

[77] Pophan, W. J. (2008). *Transformative assessment.* Alexandria, VA: ASCD. p. 24.

Chapter 23: Check Student Understanding: Formative and Summative Assessment

[78] Marzano, R. (2007). *The art and science of teaching* VA: ASCD, p. 12.

[79] Arter, J. A., Chappuis, J., and Stiggins, R. J. (2011). *Classroom assessment for student learning.* NY: Pearson, p. 37.

[80] Brookhart, S. (2007, December). Feedback that fits. *Educational Leadership, 65* (4), 54-59.

[81] Hardiman, M. (2003). *Connecting brain research with effective teaching.* Washington, D.C.: Rowman & Littlefield Publishers. pp. 75-76.

[82] McTighe, J. and Wiggins G. P. (2005). *Understanding by design.* Virginia: ASCD, 192.

[83] See Himmele, P. & Himmele, W. *Total participation techniques* (2011) for an exhaustive list of strategies and explanations.

Chapter 25: Differentiate: Anticipate, Assess, and Plan

[84] Tomlinson, C.A. (1999) *The differentiated classroom.* VA: ACSD.

[85] Curwin, R., Mendler, A., Mendler, B. (2008). *Discipline with dignity.* Alexandria, VA: ASCD. p. 30.

[86] Curwin, R., Mendler, A., Mendler, B. (2008). *Discipline with dignity.* Alexandria, VA: ASCD p. 178

[87] Curwin, Mendler, A., Mendler, B. (2008). *Discipline with dignity.* Alexandria, VA: ASCD p. 133

[88] Safir, S. (2016). *Equity vs. equality: 6 steps toward equity* retrieved from https://www.edutopia.org/blog/equity-vs.-equality-shane-safir

[89] Good, T. (1981). Teacher expectations and student perceptions: A decade of research. *Educational Leadership, 38*(5), 415.

[90] Hook, S. (1963). *Education for modern man.* NY: Alfred Knopf. From Chapter 10.

Bibliography: Key Books

Boykin, A. W. & Noguera, P. (2011). *Creating the opportunity to learn.* Alexandria, VA: ASCD.

Carey, Benedict (2015). *The surprising truth about how we learn and why it happens.* NY: Random House.

Cohen, E. & Lotan, R. (2014). *Designing groupwork.* VT: Teachers College Press.

Denton, P. and Kriete, R. (2000). *The First six weeks of school.* ME: Center for Responsive Schools.

Denton, P. (2013). *The power of our words* (Turners Falls, MA: Northeast Foundation for Children. p.106.

Dweck, C. (2007). *Mindset.* NY: Random House. pp. 71-74.

Gibbs, J. (1987). *Tribes.* Cloverdale, CA: CenterSource Systems.

Green, Elizabeth. (2015). *How to build a better teacher.* NY: W. W. Norton & Company.

Hardiman, M. (2003). *Connecting brain research with effective teaching: The brain-targeted teaching model.* MD: Rowman & Littlefield Education.

Hattie, J. (2012). *Visible learning for teachers.* United Kingdom: Taylor & Francis.

Himmele, P. & Himmele, W. (2011). *Total participation techniques.* Alexandria, VA: ACSD.

Jensen, E. (2013). *Engaging students with poverty in mind.* Alexandria, VA: ASCD

Kohn, A. (1996). *Beyond discipline: From compliance to community.* Alexandria, VA: ASCD.

Pollock, J. (2007). *Improving student learning one teacher at a time.* Alexandria, VA: ASCD.

Pophan, W. J. (2008). *Transformative assessment.* Alexandria, VA: ASCD.

Tough, P. (2012). *How children succeed.* Alexandria, VA: ASCD.

Made in the USA
San Bernardino, CA
09 November 2018